Gathered Remains:
Essays on Wildness, Domestication, Community, and Resistance

Kevin Tucker

Anti-copyright @ 2018, Kevin Tucker

Art courtesy of
MAZATL
http://www.graficamazatl.com/

ISBN: 978-0-9972017-6-5

Black and Green Press
PO Box 402
Salem, MO 65560

kevintucker.org
blackandgreenpress.org

Printed in Canada on recycled paper.

Gathered Remains

The natural world around me—the forest or desert or sea—is, like my genes, more permanent than I.

- Paul Shepard, *Man in the Landscape.*
1967

For Mica, Dyani, Yank, and the world more permanent than I.

Contents

viii. Preface: John Zerzan
x. Introduction

Part One: The Consequences of Domestication

1. Gathered Remains
36. I am Complicit
40. The Suffocating Void: Domestication and Pathological Distraction
65. Hooked on a Feeling: The Loss of Community and the Rise of Addiction
153. Society Without Strangers: Conflict Resolution, Domestication and Systemic Violence
232. To Speak of Wildness
255. Subjects Object! Thoughts on Symbolic Thought

Part Two: The Ecology of Resistance

267. Do Humans Deserve to Survive?
274. Ecology of a Bubble
294. Means and Ends: The Coming Nomadism and the Struggle for Community
303. The End is a Good Start: Activism in the Age of Collapse
308. Social Media, Revolt, and Civilization: an Interview with *It's Going Down*

Preface:
John Zerzan

Much has gone down since Kevin's earlier collection, *For Wildness and Anarchy*, appeared in 2010. Amongst radicals not much has been added, however, that inspires or that deepens critique.

Egoism and nihilism, having contributed little or nothing, seem to have faded after an embarrassing infatuation of some with murderous psychopaths. Lowest-common-denominator leftist and liberal populism has been on offer, co-existing with decidedly postmodern elements, which favor a cynical relativism on the part of at least a few self-described anti-authoritarians.

But a radical, if often inchoate energy exists, flaring into prominence on a regular basis. Standing Rock pipeline resistance grew in 2016-2017, until snuffed out—most importantly by tribal governance. Summer 2017 saw three days of anti-G20 fighting in Hamburg, that required ever more pig reinforcements from across Germany, and the Olympia Commune blockade against fracking stood out in late fall 2017.

The Olympia blockade featured a strong and articulate anti-civilization component. I see this slowly growing in general, as deeper doubts spread through society at large. A significant anti-technological feeling, for instance, now animates many novels and films.

Kevin was the editor and publisher of *Species Traitor* and a key contributor to *Green Anarchy* magazine (2000-2008). He initiated *Black and Green Review* in 2015 and is essential among five editors, first among equals. *BAGR* is a flagship anarcho-primitivist project

Preface: John Zerzan

and would not exist without Kevin, I think it is safe to say.

The essays of *Gathered Remains* form a coherent whole, in the best traditions of the likes of Paul Shepard and Fredy Perlman. They explore wildness, community and resistance and are grounded in the realities of struggles past and present. They inform what faces us today, the depth that our blows against it must achieve.

His work is a rare example of the deeply from-the-heart, and of first-rate scholarship. His wide-ranging essays are tops in both categories. Kevin Tucker is unrelenting and uncompromising. His writings are stand-out, must-read offerings, all the more so in these days of crisis. I'm honored to be his friend.

Introduction

> ...the fact remains that all captive-held wildlife, who by definition are denied normative social interactions and the expanse of natural habitats, live lives of profound deprivation. No interconnecting burrows, toys, or patched-together assemblage of conspecifics can make up for what they have lost or never had—freedom, agency, and the chance to live a life on their own terms with their loved friends and family.
>
> -GA Bradshaw, *Carnivore Minds*

Each of us was born wild.

You, me, your friends, and your enemies: every one of us. If you're reading this book, you've been subjected to the process of domestication. The process that turns each of us—born to take part in wild, nomadic communities of hunter-gatherers—and breaks us into our roles as consumers, workers, and conscripts: fodder for the world of civilization.

Here, we are captives.

Captives saturated with a sense of entitlement to the specifics of our cage-free ranges. We yearn for wholeness, we settle for installments. Some by choice, some by force: always by design. We are sold a sense of individuality to prove that we are unique, special. As though being defined by our choices as a consumer gives us freedom. As if allegiance to abstract constructs and ideologies gives us community.

Our world, the world catered by programmers and domesticators; politicians, priests, and bosses, is built upon tearing apart our needs as social animals—community, sustenance, ground-

True!

ing—and selling their supplementary forms back piecemeal. We are meant to buy it and to perpetually come back for more.

For the most part, we do. Because within each of us is that want. That sense of loss. Our need for a sense of place, in an ecological and psychological sense, pulses beneath the surface.

The reality that civilization has created threatens all life on this planet. It has taken life that will not come back. Every day, lives are on the brink of not coming back. It has created waste that, for all intents and purposes, won't go away.

Yet, for whatever reason, we are still here. Captive and sedate though we may be, there is a piece of us that knows something is wrong. Something huge is missing. Something worse is unfolding.

Most likely, that feeling is why you are holding this book now. I can relate, that feeling is what got me started down this path. That feeling is a burning rage: a refusal to accept a life of passive captivity. It is a surge of life resisting the world-eating growth of an increasingly mechanical apparatus.

It reminds us that we are still alive. And it keeps us tied to the world that never forgot.

Sedate, broken, wounded; if you're still breathing, at least a part of your wild self hasn't stopped fighting yet.

It is that part that I am speaking to. That is my target audience. The arguments, the research, the endless digging: all of that is to explain that aching burn in our guts to our brains. It's hard to listen to because we've been taught to ignore it. Since birth we are trained to see the world as a dead place. We deny our instincts, our gut reactions, even most of our senses.

We silence ourselves. We become complacent: we become complicit.

The more we understand about that process—where it comes from, what it's costs are—the better our odds are at breaking it. To un-domesticate, to re-wild: to tear apart the cracks in the veneer of domestication and to embrace the wild. Suppressed, enslaved, and under assault though they may be, those wild communities are still there. Struggling. Resisting. Existing.

Domestication has never been a choice, we were born into it by chance.

When we recognize what has been done and what is being

done to this world, when we stop seeing ourselves as separate from it, then we will say the same about resistance.

The contents of this book were written in a relatively short period, the oldest piece being from 2013, but this work has been building for a long time. This is built upon over two decades of research, with early drafts of 'Hooked on a Feeling' going back to 2004.

What connects these pieces is a particular thread, which goes back to a shift in perspective. My own movement within the world of anarchism to anarcho-primitivism was a want to understand where the roots of social power lie. The more apparent that it became that domestication was the root, there was grounding, a baseline.

Though civilization is built and maintained through historical time, domestication isn't an event; it's an ongoing process. The egalitarian, rooted world of the nomadic hunter-gatherer is never truly that far from any of us. For lack of a better term, wildness is a current that runs through all living things. The world I sought to find exists in historic and anthropological terms, but its reality is still here with us. It surrounds us. Our history is a chronicle of the ways civilization has tried to suppress and eliminate it. That history is living and we are living it.

The lingering question I had was why indigenous resistance was infinitely more successful than revolutions. The answer was simple: it's one thing to have ideals and ideologies; it's another to have community, to embrace the wild. Simple though that realization may be, it took decades to really understand what I had already felt.

At its base, the search for the origins of civilization requires a clearer picture of the world that civilization must continually attempt to undermine. It means looking at the wild world on its own terms rather than glorified or glamorized visions of it. To really grasp how and why domestication works demands a clearer vision of life without it.

Patterns emerge. Amplified by technology, scaled by growth: civilization is best understood as maintenance rather than innovation. Structures and infrastructure arise as escalations of shamans turned priests and big men turned chiefs. We carry the mythos

Introduction

and bravado of the colonizer, the indignation of the victor, but hubris hasn't protected civilizations in the past from collapsing under their own excesses.

As our world burns and climate destabilizes, prompting endless resource wars, political turmoil, and waves of climate refugees, we will quickly learn that we are truly no different. It is my intent to undermine domestication by showing how we are still wild.

'Gathered Remains' is the most direct take on this. 'Hooked on a Feeling' and 'Society Without Strangers,' two essays that make up most of this book, are complimentary in understanding the form and function of wild communities and how the needs we have as social animals are supplanted once domestication enters.

Both essays and 'To Speak of Wildness' emphasize that the beauty of our wild, anarchistic egalitarian baseline doesn't require religious and moral visions of purity. Far from it. Brutal things happen in an unquestionably wild world. That would only detract from idealized, voyeuristic views of the wild as an ideal. A version more akin to wilderness and religious fantasy: yet another part of ourselves to shed. The lion may sleep alongside the lamb (more aptly, antelope), but it benefits both the lion and the lamb that a lion eats a lamb from time to time.

'The Suffocating Void' is the exception to the rule here. That essay arose because the terms that Lewis Mumford and Jacques Ellul used to speak about technology needed an update. The Interface Revolution that resulted in cell phones for half of the worlds' adult population, along with fiber optic cables and wireless internet access in areas that had not previously had electricity, is the fastest technological change in the history of humanity. It also represents a largely unchecked and unrecognized shift in the nature of civilization.

When I started *Black and Green Review* in 2014, it became quickly apparent that this change needed to be addressed. It also reflected an exceptionally significant move from Progress, as the idealized justification for civilization, to Progress as a constant flow of information. People stopped caring about grand schemes and the future of development when they lived it vicariously through phones and other "integrated" devices.

The second part of the book, 'The Ecology of Resistance,' deals more directly with the current and unfolding modernized threats to the world of wildness, our world. 'Ecology of a Bubble' in particular.

It is not my intent to create blueprints for a future world. I have no want to offer a package of thoughts and notions to foster cannon fodder for ideals. It is my goal to pick up the pieces of our fragmented world and to expose the means by which it was shattered.

I'm more interested in showing that civilization has blueprints. And schematics. At their heart is the means by which the domestication process is maintained. The more we begin to feel, the more we become rooted, and the more we embrace the wild and build real community: the more likely we are to do something about that.

As a process, domestication may not have been a singular historical event.

But rest assured, it does have a starting point.

And it will have an end.

I've had a lot of help in editing and developing these arguments and their resulting essays, most of which appeared in *Black and Green Review*. For their dilligence, thank you to all past, present, and future *BAGR* editors. Any errors or grammatical mistakes are ultimately my own.

Eternal thanks to John Zerzan, who pestered me relentlessly at the times when I shut up and graciously did his best coping when he probably wished I would have. Four Legged Human never let me off easy, always pushing and, I would hope, to great affect. Lilia Letsch has been invaluable in all matters related to this book, its contents, its completion, and pretty much everything else too. Evan Cestari lent a heavy hand in editing and helping focus the ideas. There is no better source for fatherly encouragement and disappointment than Cliff Hayes. Without the prompting and direction of Natasha Alvarez, it's hard to say any of this would exist.

The closing piece is an interview with *It's Going Down*, who I've also written columns for. Thank you to Doug Gilbert and the other IGD folks. 'The End is a Good Start' was published in *Earth First! Journal* and had a hand from their editorial collective. The

Introduction

amazing artist Mazatl was gracious enough to let me use his art and it's a far more complete book for it.

In no particular order, the following people have offered inspiration, support, critical feedback, and/or pushed me in my processes (intentionally or not): Jared Ondovchik, Sloth, Joel Cimarron, Delia Turner, Lorraine Perlman, Will and Lyndee Garnett, Gay Bradshaw, Nora Gedgaudas, Steve Barcus, Andrew Badenoch, and to countless others that I'm inevitably not thinking of: sorry, my bad.

There will always be a place in my heart for the wild soundtrack of my late night writing sessions: coyotes, whippoorwills, spring peepers and tree frogs, numerous owls, cautious opossums and raccoons, the comically incautious armadillos, beaver tail splashes, hunting river otters, the sound of moths flying into my light, and a chorus of insects.

I'm forever indebted to Yank, who has never missed a chance to prod in the right direction, even if it didn't look that way at the time. Some of us just refuse to be tamed more than others and I'm thankful for being pushed out of my comfort zone. She's the source of my best ideas and most of my world-changing realizations.

Above all else, this goes out to my daughters, Mica and Dyani, whose wild spirits inspire and inform everything for me. May they never be taken from you. I have seen the world I want you to live in, and I will fight for it.

Part One:
The Consequences of Domestication

Gathered Remains

Out there walking round, looking out for food,
A rootstalk, a birdcall, a seed that you can crack
Plucking, digging, snaring, snagging,
Somehow getting by.
No good out there on dusty slopes of scree—
Carry some—look for some.
Go for a hungry dream.
Deer bone, Dall sheep,
Bones hunger home.
Out there somewhere
A shrine for the old bones,
The dust of the old bones,
Old songs and tales.
What we ate—who ate what—
How we all prevailed.
　　　　　-Gary Snyder, 'Old Bones: For Paul Shepard'[1]

The story of our lives is written in fragments.

Each of us carries the lineage of millions of years of evolution within us. Our past, even prior to anything resembling our contemporary human form, shapes how we see the world. How we interact with it. How we interact with each other.

The story we are told, the narrative driven into our lives, is that this lineage is a process. That we are the outcome of evolution: not just the most current rendition of it. That thought grants pride and privilege. It has allowed us to draw maps and then to shift the lines according to geopolitical interests. To wage wars. To conquer and colonize other parts of the world and their inhabitants.

That narrative fractures a living world into pieces.

At its core, it dispossesses us so that we can displace and destroy the world that created us. It is a veneer that we place over a confusing and contradictory situation where we are still present in the place where we once thrived, but connected to it only as an ideal or through mediation. That is, if we show any cognizance of it at all.

It is a heavily catered vision. One that must compete with living in a hyper-technological and inter-connected globalized society. Each of us is a bastard of history: an amalgam of colonizer and colonized, dispossessor and dispossessed. Every one of us a fragment of the world civilization has created, comprised of the shattered remains of living worlds.

That is true for me just as much as it is true for you.

And just as much as it was true for Ken Saro-Wiwa.

I never met Ken Saro-Wiwa, but the intersections of our lives and, subsequently, the end of his life begin at the gas pump.

Civilization creates a situation where our reach as individuals is amplified exponentially. Any time we take part in the technological hubris we surround ourselves in, there is a string stretched throughout time and place. The fabric of that thread is shattered lives and decimated ecosystems. Tragedy on a local scale supported by international powers. Every point in our lives can be anchored back hundreds to thousands of years.

Ken was born in 1941, a member of the Ogoni people in Nigeria. The Ogoni live in what is known as Ogoniland in the Niger Delta. This is a region, like all others, that is shaped by history. Ken was born in Bori, a small town near the coast: an area that had been a part of the indigenous Ibani kingdom as far back as 1000 AD. The Ibani were a tribe of the maritime-agrarian Ijaw peoples who had built an elaborate inland society and used their tributary port access to strong-arm regional control.[2]

Europeans would eventually know the resulting city-state, Okolo-Ama, as the Kingdom of Bonny.[3] But prior to the Europeans, the slaves captured by the Ibani were sold to Muslim slave traders into Egypt and the Mediterranean.[4]

Fast forward to the close of the nineteenth century; Bonny becomes a protectorate of Britain.[5] As the slave trade wanes, the use of slaves for procuring coal rises. In 1912, a British mercenary, Frederick Lugard, founded the city of Port Harcourt: new management for an old kingdom.[6] By 1916, the capital of Nigeria, Lagos, looked like a European city, but only for the white population. Now governor, Lugard claimed that the colonized "neither appreciates nor desires clean water, sanitation or good roads and streets."[7]

Pull on any of these strings and the fragments continue to pile up.

This is just a glimpse of the stage set when, in 1956, Royal Dutch Shell strikes oil in Nigeria. Long-standing tensions continue to rise and culminate in a civil war that left somewhere between five hundred thousand to two million Nigerians dead. Most of those deaths were caused by starvation.[8]

Ken is now a teenager.

This background didn't need another natural resource thrown into it, but that is exactly what it got. The deployment went as most would expect: horribly. And horribly violent.

Statistics from the Nigerian Department of Petroleum Resources "indicate that between 1976 and 1996 a total of 4,835 incidents resulted in the spillage of at least 2,446,322 barrels (102.7 million U.S. gallons), of which an estimated 1,896,930 barrels (79.7 million U.S. gallons; 77 percent) were lost to the environment."[9] Presumably less shocking, even though oil accounts for 90% of Nigeria's exports, 80% of those funds go straight to one percent of the population. Between Nigeria's independence, in 1960, and 2012, $400 billion dollars are considered "stolen or misspent."[10]

The Ogoni people were left on the frontline of an oil extraction frontier. Pipeline blowouts became common. The water undrinkable. Fishing became impossible. The fields infertile. Ogoni and Iko peoples demanded that Shell clean up their homes in 1970, 1980, 1987, and again in 1990. They were met with force. Corporate heads spoke from atop the high horse of the economy to their shareholders: everything is fine.

Everything was not.

In 1990, Ken, now an accomplished television writer and playwright, becomes central in the formation of the Movement for the Safety of the Ogoni People (MOSOP). MOSOP is a council of elders and chiefs seeking the protection of Ogoniland and the Ogoni people from Shell and other oil companies. Thirty-three years of oil extraction had decimated the land.

In Ken's words: "All one sees and feels around is death. Environmental degradation has been a lethal weapon in the war against the indigenous Ogoni people."[11] His words weren't hyperbole. At the end of October 1990, there was a massive protest outside of a Shell facility, just east of Port Harcourt. Shell requested the Mobile Police Force to assist and 80 unarmed demonstrators were killed, hundreds of homes destroyed.[12]

This happened again and again.

The Ogoni spoke up. Shell and its militarized agents killed and suppressed. Ken was detained and released. Elders and chiefs were killed. Rinse, wash, repeat. One of the chief embezzlers of Nigeria's oil wealth, Sani Abacha, seized power in 1993. He vowed to crack down on any resistance to his revenue streams and whatever ecological hell they might entail.[13]

Just after New Years 1993, disturbances of oil production were declared treason. MOSOP continued its protests. Arrests, legal battles: releases, seizures, and mass killings. Oil flows, money siphoned off, the situation continues to worsen.

Across the world, in the United States, all of us are unknowingly fueling this conflict every time we pump gas at the station.

Round and round we go.

In 1994, Ken and the "Ogoni Nine" are locked up over the false murder charges of four Ogoni chiefs. This time, it's for good. Before they were hung on November 10, 1995, Ken spoke these words in his final statement:

> *The Company has, indeed, ducked this particular trial, but its day will surely come and the lessons learnt here may prove useful to it for there is no doubt in my mind that the ecological war that the Company has waged in the Delta will be called to question sooner than later and the crimes of that war be duly punished. The crime of the Company's dirty wars against the Ogoni people will also be*

punished.[14]

Ken was 54 years old.

Bones Hunger Home: The Power of Narratives

> *History does not belong only to its narrators, professional or amateur. While some of us debate what history is or was, others take it in their own hands.*
> — Michel Rolph-Trouillot, *Silencing the Past*[15]

It's now been 23 years since Ken's statement and execution.

Not only has Shell's day not come, it most likely won't. There will be no truth and reconciliation with Shell, no justice for Ken even with a posthumous Nobel Peace Prize for his efforts.

Intersected though our lives may be, the civilized world is absolutely dependent upon oil. So it will cling to and propagate any mythos that keeps us going to the gas pumps and bury any evidence of what it takes to get that oil across the world, into your gas tank, then back into our atmosphere where we all have to live with its consequences once again.

The pieces are there, but unable to see them, we are ill equipped to put them together. We are unable to understand a world that is infinitely closer to our reach than it was ever meant to be.

At the time of Ken's death, I was aware of who he was. I was aware of the Ogoni and Shell's role in the most contemporarily orchestrated variant of Gold Coast exploitation. I had read about him and his execution only because it was information I had sought out. It wasn't in the news. It most certainly wasn't at the gas station.

I would cross paths not with Ken, but with MOSOP and hundreds of Ogoni refugees. They literally wound up in the same city as me for reasons that show the interwoven world of a global civilization as both large and small. The Ogoni I met had escaped Nigeria, their home. It was stay and fight with a price on their heads or leave.

They left. That is, those that remained left.

Of all places, they chose St. Louis, Missouri. Along with civilization's stick, the Ogoni got a glimpse of its carrot of choice: sugar. C&H sugar to be exact. C&H was headquartered in St. Louis, as evidenced by the address listed on the packaging that the Ogoni were familiar with.

Oil came from Ogoniland and, when they lived there, they couldn't avoid the stuff even though they tried. Pipelines crisscrossed the towns and villages. They would burst or rupture regularly. The local police were Shell's paramilitary. If you wanted oil, and the Ogoni certainly didn't, it was everywhere. It stands to reason that if sugar came from a company in St. Louis, it would be everywhere there as well. Needless to say, it wasn't.

More fragments, more strings.

Here was a crash course in the strange world of global economics. While there were sugar refineries in St. Louis, none of it was grown anywhere remotely close.

Sugar cane was first domesticated in Papua New Guinea.[16] The Muslim slave traders, whom the Ibani kingdoms had bartered with, subjected slaves to a Mediterranean sugar cane industry. In 1000 AD, few Europeans had any experience with sugar cane. But as industrial methods of extracting sucrose—a form of sugar—from sugar cane arose, so too did the plantations. In England, sugar became a treat of the nobility by 1650. Come 1800, it had arisen to a costly necessity for all the English. By 1900, sugar supplied one-fifth of the calories in the English diet.[17] Not to be outdone, studies in 2012 found that Americans were each eating an average of 130 pounds of it *annually*.[18]

Columbus carried sugar cane to the New World on his second voyage in 1493. And in 1516, the Spanish colony of Santo Domingo had started shipping sugar back.[19]

The sugar plantations were a major player in the Atlantic slave trade. Slavers were very specific about sugar production, arguing that only Africans were suitable slaves for working the cane fields. George Whitfield, a Calvinistic Methodist slaver of the eighteenth century, stated plainly that cane "cannot be cultivated without negroes" due to the extreme heat and exhaustion.[20] There's some comfort knowing he's dead, but clearly death didn't come early enough for him.

And where did many of those enslaved Africans come from?

The Niger Delta—which would come to be known as the "Slave Coast" for some time—provided many, if not most. After the Mediterranean slave trade began to die down, the native kingdom of Benin was selling pepper and slaves to the Portuguese, ultimately becoming the first Slave Coast power to obtain their own firearms.

The guns furthered the Benin expansion eastward beyond Bonny—just south of Bori, where Ken was born—becoming a major source of slaves for the Atlantic trade by the seventeenth century.[21] Old Calabar, a port region towards the east end of the Niger Delta, exported an estimated 250,000 slaves between 1650 and 1841 alone.[22] From Africa, slaves were sent to work plantations in the tropics, namely South America and the Caribbean.

While no Ogoni were reportedly brought into the slave trade, the impacts were unavoidable.[23] Slaves became the wealth to barter in a world where sugar would become exponentially important both as a tool of trade and as a source of enslavement. The carrot and the stick: forever bound together. Sugar and oil: my world and the world of the Ogoni intersected once more.

I spent years demonstrating with MOSOP.

A number of the men behind it were to be killed by the military junta General Abacha led. They had run to the hills when the Ogoni Nine were locked up, plotting their own exile while their families prepared to leave the very place they had fought and died for. Having faced military puppet tribunals and trigger-happy agents of Shell, no amount of confrontation was going to rattle them.

I've seen them smile calmly while racist, white suburbanites tried to run them down with their cars or provoke fights. I've never had their restraint nor personally understood it, but by comparison, it's most likely a drop in the bucket for what they had experienced. These were people who literally had their lives on the line, had lost friends and family at the hands of an oil company. Here they were, being confronted by people who wished death upon them solely for continuing to exist. More than that, they were a reminder of the price tag that doesn't show up at the pump.

Even there, this is just a piece of it.

And this is just one tiny fraction of one story. It's hardly just Shell and it's most definitely not just the Gold Coast of Africa, even if the history there should be enough to undermine every myth of civilization.

The reaction coming from drivers angry that someone dared to rain reality on their charade is the anger of having their comforts confronted. And it is an uncomfortable feeling: having the sanctuary of the Self we're sold violated by reminders that none of us are an island nor isolated.

Our lives are complicated by an exploitative network that expands well beyond our vision and grasp. None of us are ever freed from the consequences that come with civilization. We just relish in the false sense of security we are afforded.

The ability of not having to confront that reality is a privilege, not earned, but given. It carries no true sense of safety, but it offers the delusion that we have choices and that we can reap the rewards if we're willing to play along. Those of us in the First World aren't, after all, the Ogoni. Even though the cops were always on guard to defend the helpless Shell stations we demonstrated outside of, they weren't militarized.

And they weren't wearing Shell badges.

So what's the point? What's the point of this story or of any other like it? What is the point of pulling the strings when we feel we don't have to?

Even amongst radicals (often especially), these are the kinds of questions that this bit of history might be met with. That we can even ask the question is enough justification for why we should dig deeper. It boils down to this: not only are narratives important, but history is living. Nothing that has happened is simply done and over with. Things morph, politics, economics, religion; these core institutions might change face, but they never change their form and function.

It is the epitome of modernity's apathy that we can disassociate our lives from the consequences of our role within civilization's perpetuation. This isn't a one-sided issue, even though it's clearly more heavy-handed on the side of post-consumer societies where there's a ludicrous amount of stuff and, even when broke, there's still a lot of options for debt. To be honest about where that comes from and where we are headed seems like a good place to start.

Going beyond angry, racist suburbanites, you can look directly at the military-corporate institutions in Nigeria, to the coal barons and slave brokers before them, and to the slave-owning agrarian kingdoms before them and see that narratives matter. The very prospect that the divine rights of kings, capitalists, and priests may be rendered void and useless by the presence of free, egalitarian or, even, more ecologically sane societies is absolutely important.

The existence of power relies upon physical infrastructure, but it's demand for obedience and subservience is what keeps it running. All these fragments, all these pieces and remains of a world without political and economic power, not only undermine those narratives, but they indicate weaknesses.

Even with just a brief glimpse, it is easy to see that oil, like all extracted energies, is a glaring example of that.

And beneath that surface of petro-politics and conflicts, at every single step, there is another piece of this world, more intact, more diverse, more alive. This world is living. Our world is alive. Clearly, it struggles with what we've thrown at it, but it doesn't give up.

It doesn't create philosophical or moral principles to stop its functions. It has no mind: it has no Self. Our world is a network of integrated, ecological networks and feedback loops. The more we come to know, the more we realize how little we understand about these connections. It's a habit we learned well from resource-bartering slave traders, forager-killing farmers, forest-decimating organic palm plantation owners, from those wielding bibles and swords or those yielding credit default swaps and structural adjustment policies.

Our reality stands upon scar tissue: scorched earth covered in Astroturf. Wounds inflicted in layers. What isn't dead or enslaved is buried in plain sight. Struggling, but not dead.

Yet.

And, if you're reading this, neither are you.

This is why we dig.

The World As It Is

> *To know the name on the door is to know nothing. Knowledge*

begins on the other side of the threshold.
  - Fredy Perlman, *Against His-Story, Against Leviathan*[24]

As an anarcho-primitivist, I want to see civilization undone. Completely. Buried in its ruins. That is the fate ensured as storehouses, fields, and diverted waterways led to the mathematically impossible equation of infinite growth on a finite planet.

Every step intensifies, but all victories for civilization are temporary.

As those fragments surround us, we don't have to pull many strings to arrive at the conclusion that civilization and domestication haven't done much for us, as individuals and as societies, most definitely not as living beings. Digging isn't necessary to get to that outcome. Subjective experience is a good point of departure. If you find yourself digging, ostensibly subjective experience got you started.

Subjective experience, however, is not enough.

My connection to Ken was objective, not subjective. Subjective came later, long after civilization had dominated the Gold Coast, significantly after the trade of humans turned to the reality of coal extraction and then, subsequently, oil. The impact of my life hit Ken long before a noose ended it.

That was a conclusion that all of our intertwined lives ensured.

The reality we live in is far more muddled than the reality our minds and bodies were shaped in. As nomads, our realm of understanding spreads fairly wide. As foragers, that realm expands above the tree line and beneath the soil. As hunters, it moves into the will and intents of other species. We quickly unfold into our surroundings. So when I say that our consciousness defaults bioregionally, even that lacks any real discernable boundary.

Our ancestors—and relatives who still struggle to maintain their wild communities against the intrusion of civilization—lived without concepts of history. Or future. Time existed on a continuum. Numbers were for accounting a surplus they didn't need. Calendars were for agrarian schedules they had no use for. Without technology, they weren't likely to bring about ecological or social change to radically upend what millions of years of adaptation and resilience bred.

Past, present, and future lived in one place. And without contradiction.

The foragers may have never known about the lives thousands of miles away from them, but there was no necessity to do so. Curiosity withstanding: myths certainly sufficed. Not being able to negatively impact their existence, they didn't have to philosophize about morality and consequence. There was no need to justify action or inaction.

For us, we are left with the baggage that civilization carries.

There is no biological or ecological precedent that explains my relationship to Ken and the people of Ogoniland. That is a historical situation. A purely civilized predicament.

In the want to undo the domestication process, the world of the immersed hunter-gatherer is closer to me than Ken was. It calls. For anthropologist Stanley Diamond, that primal urge is "consonant with fundamental human needs, the fulfillment of which (although in different form) is a precondition for our survival."[25] It manifests itself organically in the way our eyes move and the way that our bodies want to run; down to the way that our ears absorb information and that technology overwhelms our reaction to it.

We may consider ourselves the beneficiaries of thousands of years of civilized progression, but our minds are pacing just the same as the captives in zoos and farms.

While the means to walk away from domestication are easily at our disposal, literally in the case of our legs, to unearth them we have to remove the concrete poured over them. Even then, we're only more likely to see the concrete pen that we live in. Walking away isn't liberation. Even where it is possible, it remains illegal. I don't believe the law merits respect, but, like all of civilization, we aren't simply going to will it away. And the reason why anti-economic subsistence is illegal brings us right back to why hunter-gatherers were buried in the first place: the narratives underlying domestication were never strong enough on their own.

I'm not speaking historically here.

This is a situation that the Bushmen, nomadic hunter-gatherers of the Kalahari, now face.

The Bushmen were forced into the crosshairs of civilization

on numerous occasions. In 1652, following the enthusiastic prospects reported by formerly shipwrecked Dutch slavers, the Dutch United East India Company built a fort in what would become the Cape Colony of South Africa.[26] This was an area occupied by the Bushmen's pastoral neighbors, the Khoikhoi, after being pushed further south by the agrarian Bantu empires in the third century AD.

Genocide follows colonizers. Neither count was an exception.

The Company inevitably expanded. Between 1703 and 1780, the white population had grown tenfold in the region, encroaching with gusto into the lands of the Bushmen. They did what colonizers do best: systematically exterminate any living thing. By the 1770s, the Bushmen were forced to resist the colonizers. They began killing the expanding pastoralists' cattle and sheep, being met, in turn, with genocidal force. Commandos had killed 503 Bushmen by the end of 1774, further enslaving 241 others.

The Bushmen continued to fight back, but the colonizers had the numbers and technology to decimate:

According to official records, between 1786 and 1795, Bushmen killed 276 herdsmen and captured 19,000 cattle and 84,000 sheep; the commandos, for their part, killed 2,480 Bushmen and captured 654 others. With official permission, Bushmen children were indentured on white farms.[27]

The Bushmen, often considered over-romanticized and idealized for their degree of sheer egalitarianism, prevalent for years after violent confrontations and incursions, rightfully deserve credit where it is due. That the egalitarianism implicit in their nomadic hunter-gatherer lives could overcome such history isn't just exemplary of their demeanor, but of the resiliency of the wild, anarchistic human spirit.

And tested it most certainly was.

Towards the end of the nineteenth century, the modernizing, technological precision that Germans would celebrate with the Holocaust was being field tested in Namibia, the western expanse of the timeless land of the Bushmen. Beyond them lay the lands that the pastoral Herero took up residency in during the seventeenth century. Then the ambitions of German colonialists had outgrown the outposts that they had established in 1882.

In 1903, the German General Lothar von Trotha was leading those commands. Not to muddy his intents, Trotha was clear on the matter: "I wipe out rebellious tribes with streams of blood and streams of money."[28] Here the arms that came to define World War I, such as the Gatling gun, were used to decimate entire villages.[29] Entire societies. Entire cultures. The slave trade was largely gone: this was extermination.

Genocide.

By 1905, all Herero land was formally expropriated. By 1907, the same was true for nearly all Nama lands. In 1912, the Germans erected a statue memorializing the dead colonizers in Windhoek, at what was formerly a concentration camp for the remaining Herero. The German governor, Theodor Seitz, declared at it's unveiling that: "The venerable colonial soldier that looks out over the land from here announces to the world that we are the masters of this place, now and for ever."[30]

A hundred years later, I would like to state that forever is a bold statement in a timeless land. German control was lost after World War I. Ceded to British-South African forces, we know full well that the new management weren't particularly kinder.

Keep pulling the strings…

The Herero that survived the Germans did so by flooding the Kalahari, the land filled with the Bushmen, whom they called *Ovakuruha*, the First People.[31]

And the Herero feared them.

Like all agrarian and pastoral societies, the Herero viewed the Bushmen as wild. In the words of a Ju/'hoansi living at Nyae Nyae, "To them it is nothing to take our land and our blood."[32]

Like the Dutch before them, the Herero colonized the Kalahari. Fearing, as all farmers do, that wild predators would decimate their cattle and sheep, they left poisoned carcasses to eradicate them. As with the Dutch, they decimated the ecology wherein the Bushmen existed. The cycles of oppression and repression continue to flow downhill. Colonized becoming colonizer.

The Bushmen survived, once again, but colonization continued to modernize.

By the mid-twentieth century, that included forced settlements, missionary and corporate incursions, and increased military presence. The impact was immediate.[33] A partial response was the creation of the Central Kalahari Game Reserve in 1961. It was a move not unlike the creation of reservations for indigenous communities in the wake of globalizing colonizers across the earth.

True to form, the state determined that the allure of the Bushmen was a sufficient stand in for the actual presence of living subsistence hunters in the region they had occupied for upwards of hundreds of thousands of years, if not more. Their story was better off as history than reality. The narrative could remain nostalgic without shaking the bravado of the conquerors.

In the mid-1990s, the tourism industry forced the remaining Bushmen out. Hunting was possible by permit only.

Overnight, the Bushmen became poachers for doing what they had always done. Twenty years of legal battles later, even after rights are partially given back in writing, the beatings and arrests of subsistence hunters goes on undeterred.[34] Children raised in settlements require permits to enter their ancestral lands.

Who are buying the permits? Wealthy First World trophy hunters.[35] Not unlike the background in the Nigerian Delta, where Ken was born and lived, Botswana doesn't make its money from tourism. Three quarters of the nation's exports are diamonds.[36] DeBeers has a notoriously bad history in this regard. But while the Bushmen continue their fight to subsistence hunt on lands touted in their visage, just this year, a Russian-British diamond firm was given six new prospecting licenses.[37]

Like Nigeria, the pillage certainly doesn't end there. Just over the last decade, the government of Botswana began issuing permits to use hydraulic fracturing, or fracking, for natural gas. Not one to miss an opportunity to pillage, of the two firms to chomp at the bit on that include Debswana, a joint venture between the Botswana government and DeBeers.[38]

The continued existence of an iconic society of hunter-gatherers, one of the oldest in the world, even in the second largest wild reserve in the world, is simply too much for civilization to bear. Mining diamonds and devastating the land for natural gas are seemingly compatible with the tourism the Kalahari has to offer. If you have the money, you can even get in on the hunt. If you don't, you face beating and imprisonment.

These laws were put in the books intently. And universally.

We play along with civilization because we believe we have the choice. We choose not to see ourselves as conscripts of civilization. If you want to step out of line, then coercion looks different. Privilege, in this world, is measured in how long you can escape capture and persecution. Effectively speaking, that's only as long as you remain a loner skirting the edges of the wilderness at best. Try to rebuild community and things will look vastly different. Genocidal.

In Ken's case, you don't even need that extreme. The agrarian civilization of the Ogoni people couldn't even stand a chance against the oil industry.

Freedom, the much-vaulted pride of civilization's intellectual development, is just another commodity. If you make enough money to afford it, you've already been bought. And no amount of Kalahari big-ticket trophy hunts will change that.

This is just another incidence of subjective versus objective experience. In this case, the subjective experience is based off of what you might get away with. And for a number of us, quite frankly, that can be pretty extensive. Plenty of people have gone off, in true lone wolf manner, and existed without civilization until they died.

Most often, that's exactly where that subjective experience ended.

Based on that alone, we miss the big picture. We miss the tie that binds us as captives. We miss the links between our lives and the slaves working in shanty diamond mines, the conscripts of warlords that organize and facilitate them, or the lives of indigenous societies with burst oil pipelines on their native lands and paramilitaries set in place to defend them.

The narrative of civilization is that you are important. The reality of civilization is that you are anything but. Workers, consumers, producers, farmers, or whatever title we get stuck with: we serve the bottom line. Otherwise our bodies become the foundation of our fairy tales about freedom. We can tell ourselves any story about our own experiences, but this is what they are, all with varying degrees of severity.

This is the world as it is: as we have inherited it.

This is the world that civilization has created.

Alive and bearing scars. Struggling, yet existing. Damaged, but not gone.

Strung together fragments of history, though we may be, our strings remain.

A Shrine for Old Bones: Unraveling History

> *Anthropology, abstractly conceived as the study of man, is actually the study of men in crisis by men in crisis.*
> - Stanley Diamond, *In Search of the Primitive*.[39]

In pulling on these strings, we do have tools at our disposal.

And they are far from perfect.

By 1938, both Nigeria and the Kalahari were British protectorates.[40] The export of palm oil from Nigeria was increasing alongside the rise in plantations of cocoa—brought from the Amazon River basin in the 1870s.[41] In the same year, we have *Kristallnacht* in Germany and Adolf Hitler named "Man of the Year" by *Time Magazine*.

And in Port Austin, Michigan, Napoleon Chagnon is born.

Chagnon is an anthropologist. Like the other colonizers mentioned already, he's no less a piece of shit. In 1968, as the world was undergoing an era of revolution of thought and praxis, unweaving the narratives of civilization in some places and strengthening the resolve of an industrializing, globalizing world with socialist vigor in others, Chagnon was making headlines for other reasons. Carrying on the narrative-building legacy of civilizers before him, Chagnon unleashed his contribution to their cause, the ethnography *Yanomamö: The Fierce People*.[42] A book that was and still is a standard in university classrooms worldwide.

The Yanomamö are a tribe of horticulturalists living in the Amazon, on the border of what would become Venezuela and Brazil. The history here is unsurprisingly, yet awfully, familiar.

Between 1630 and 1720, slave-hunting conquistadors decimated indigenous societies all along the Amazon River.[43] In the

1800s, Westerners finally found an industrial application for the rubber sap that Christopher Columbus had brought back from the New World. The industrialists couldn't be satiated. The carnage unleashed during the Amazonian Rubber Boom (the first from 1879-1912, and the second from 1942-1945),[44] in the words of anthropologist Wade Davis, "were like nothing that had been seen since the first days of the Spanish Conquest."[45]

Using the lightweight and easily maneuverable planes innovated by the Second World War, missionaries got another wind as the forbearers of colonization, clearing the path for a new wave of industrialists and civilizers to tighten their grasp on the Amazon.[46] Before Chagnon showed up in the mid-1960s, New Tribes Missions, the Society of Jesus, and the Silesians' had already been out to conquer souls for nearly a decade and a half. The "savages," once saved, could make perfectly good workers: salvation through wage slavery. Perhaps even more telling, the existence of steel tools and other manufactured goods had already invaded the Amazon for some time, "frequently even beyond the memory of the oldest informants."[47]

The stage was set. The routine was underway.

The process of colonization doesn't demand the physical presence of the colonizers. Their technologies, their vices, their grains and alcohols, and, most commonly, their diseases, can do a lot of the legwork for them. Virtually everywhere that Westerners have gone, the tide of contact was cast far beyond their actual movements. In what became the United States, the demand for fur and the introduction of trade goods—most notably, guns—led to the complete decimation of entire tribes, hundreds of miles beyond the outposts of white colonizers.[48]

You could see it in Papua New Guinea.[49] You could see it in New Zealand.[50] You could see it further down the Amazon River as it crept into what were once parts of the Incan empire and those who resisted it, the Jivaro.[51]

And you most definitely saw it among the Yanomamö.

The Yanomamo, like all slash-and-burn horticulturalists, had warfare.[52] Unlike nomadic hunter-gatherers, settled or even temporarily settled societies both lose the natural contraceptives that a nomadic life brings and the lack of property or group (tribal) identity that band societies maintain. Outside of the intrusions of farmers and colonizers, for the hunter-gatherer there is nothing to protect and no one to protect it from.[53]

On a certain level, warfare amongst horticulturalists is a leveling mechanism. It keeps expanding populations in check through a preference for male children (higher rates of female infanticide) and deaths from battlefield and raiding deaths. Preferable or not, it does have a certain degree of ecological and social function. Being social animals, we don't talk in terms of function, we talk in stories.

Social tension is better explained through myth. The more people, the larger the community, the more of a central role myth plays. If neighbors start dying because of ecological pressures, it makes more sense to our storied minds to blame people. Namely, other people.

For the Yanomamö, those other people are witches.

As the diseases of Europeans spread throughout the Amazon, so did their guns and machetes. The Yanomamö responded how they typically had: through warfare.[54] Only this time, there would be no level of ecological correction. No balance of carrying capacity to be found. The wound greater, the threat more severe, and the technology seemingly endless, by the time Chagnon had come to the banks of the Orinoco River, an area already threatened by numerous colonial intrusions, he found what he had expected to find in the Yanomamö: a pristine society, far from civilization, engaged in a Hobbesian battle to the death.

Beyond being an anthropologist, Chagnon is a sociobiologist. The imprint of sociobiologists spans across all of the sciences. It reaches back to the dawn of the Enlightenment, going back to Descartes insisting that the howls of tortured dogs were mechanical in nature rather than emotion, something reserved for humans. Hobbes, ever the philosopher, had given words to the ideology of the farmer: our nature is Nature, one that is fighting tooth-in-claw for survival and victory.

Just like the unflinching pastoralists poisoning lions and killing Bushmen without thought. Like the Shell paramilitaries shooting down protestors demanding clean water: we kill to know we're alive.

Chagnon was another figurehead carrying forth the narrative of consumable freedoms: you are nothing without us. We, the domesticators, keep you, the domesticated, safe. Play along. Play dead. Roll over.

More myths for a captive audience.

The reality was genocide.

Chagnon went into the Amazon with his mentor, James Neel. Their research was funded and backed by the Atomic Energy Commission. Their goal: to study the impact of disease and contamination on a "pure population." Not only did Chagnon celebrate the warfare unfolding before him, but he directly contributed to it as he and his party literally injected their presence into the veins of this unfolding trauma.[55]

When his ethnography came out, it was the force to combat the increasing radicalization spreading throughout the social sciences and throughout society at large. The waters were already murky, but this is the narrative colonizers-turned-programmers wanted: the fear of our own savage nature.

Some radicals responded by owning it: removing the contexts of post-contact war, the particulars of horticultural subsistence and life that made war even possible. Ultimately flipping the script that Chagnon was the latest author of. Anthropologist Jacques Lizot, living amongst the Yanomamö himself, was a staunch advocate for this decimated culture, but defiantly refused to accept that history might have created and amplified their proclivity for war.[56]

Pierre Clastres, friend of Lizot, anthropologist, and anarchist, went even further on this claim: "Should war cease, the heart of primitive society will cease to beat. War is its foundation, the very life of its being."[57] Clastres wasn't wrong in showing how the "stateless" societies of non-hierarchical horticulturalist societies were anarchist in nature. Not just "pre-state" societies, but societies actively *against* the state: their refusal of power was cognizant and intentional.[58] Yet it tellingly only occurred in societies where social power was made possible by a surplus in gardens or in storehouses.

Clastres and Lizot, among many other anthropologists, saw what was happening among the Yanomamö. Clastres saw the influx of Western tools, Lizot saw the decimation at the hands of the missionaries, but neither would see the picture fleshed out decades later by anthropologist R Brian Ferguson, among others: how recently the Yanomamö had settled, potentially how recent horticulture was for them, and the sheer extent of impact that the dual infusion of Western goods and sickness had upon them.[59]

Had Clastres not been tragically struck down by a car accident, I suspect he might have been more open than Lizot on the matter, but we'll never know.

Ultimately, it doesn't matter. The reality that we exist in is complex. The history is deep. This unending chain of fragments, of genocide and colonization, stands directly in the face of communities that had found their place within their ecology, their spaces.

In light of the level of complexity at the crossroads of our history and our present, a shallow and superficial analysis would lead us to believe that we can't trust anything. That the tools we are given are the master's tools. That using them is simply strengthening their narratives and that the only option ahead is to try to make up our own stories: to try and break out as loners on the edge, perhaps collected in temporary autonomous zones and communes or within the cavern of the Self. That we could just outlast civilization and hope to find our "true" selves in the process.

That is a fantasy, an escape.

Our reality is complicated. It is not only painful: it is actively causing pain. It might be more than our bioregional minds are capable of accepting, but this is the world that we inhabit, the one where each of us carries the weight of civilization alongside the lineage of egalitarian hunter-gatherers and the lineages of the farmers and industrialists that hunted, killed, and caged them.

History, for nomadic hunter-gatherers and small-scale horticulturalists, exists on a spectrum: it exists in places. Past, present, and future meld into each other. The same is true for us, but we have added in layers of misery, pain, suppression and realization. We stopped seeing the flow. We see in moments, in historic time. Lamenting the submission to living within historical times, ecologist Paul Shepard points to the aspects of life that elude us: "Lacking a sense of the spiritual presence of plants and animals of non-living matter, we do not feel our ancestors watching or their lives pressing on our own as did prehistoric peoples."[60]

At a certain point, trying to find an escape to start anew is a luxury that we can't afford. That is an escape that we arguably didn't deserve in the first place even if it was possible.

We don't need perfect tools; we just need a clearer understanding of their pitfalls. We need a clearer sense of what we're up against.

This isn't an escape. This is an ending.

Anthropology, the study of human cultures, has had many critics. Some of the loudest voices have come from anthropologists themselves.

There is no question that anthropology arose from the colonial encounter. That is a reality that has plagued some anthropologists from the start. Fortunately, many of them acted on it.

This, however, was not always the case, but anthropology certainly has had a lot of shaping from its more radical elements. Among the founders of anthropology, A.R. Radcliffe-Brown was an anarchist in his younger days.

Likewise, the founders of anarchist theory were shaped largely by anthropology. Peter Kropotkin's groundbreaking *Mutual Aid* (published in 1902) was nearly equal parts anthropology, history, and ecology. Early anarchist thinker Elisée Reclus' older brother was an anthropologist.[61] Amongst contemporaries, we have Brian Morris, Harold Barclay, and, until his death, Pierre Clastres. Nearly all of them were heavily influenced as well by Marx and Engels, both reliant upon anthropology. While I have no stomach for the degrees of communist and socialist civilizations they advocate or advocated, hindsight is far clearer.

The Marxists largely responsible for overturning anthropology, in particular, and the social sciences, in general, in the 1960s, owed more to the ultra-left defense of what they considered "primitive communism" amongst nomadic hunter-gatherers. Arguably, a number of them had more in common with anarcho-primitivists than Marx or even Kropotkin. That included some heavy hitters amongst anthropology, namely Richard B Lee, Marvin Harris, Andrew Vayda, Marshall Sahlins, Stanley Diamond, Roy Rappaport, and Eric Wolf.[62]

Under any reading, all of those anthropologists upended the narratives of civilization by looking at egalitarian societies without blinders. In varying degrees, they all questioned civilization itself. Anthropology, in the words of George Marcus and Michael Fischer, could be "a form of cultural critique for ourselves."[63] Our narratives needed to be challenged. And if our history was perceived as a one-way street, complete with global and nearly universal stages of development, the continued existence and struggle for indigenous ways of living against forces of genocide and colonization could unravel them. Marcus and Fischer elaborate:

> *One gains a thorough understanding of human subjects who exist buried as abstractions in the language of systems analysis. Without ethnography, one can only imagine what is happening to real social actors caught up in the complex macroprocesses.*[64]

For Eric Wolf, ethnography, the practice of listening and understanding, was itself a confrontation of the narratives we carry with us:

> *The anthropologist's hut provides no neutral ground, constitutes no privileged sanctuary. He and his tribal interpreter meet in a real world, tense with exploitation and the exercise of power. They cannot hide from each other; there is no hiding place. Determining one another, each asserts for the other his humanity and human possibilities. The field experience is, then, a political experience; it demands that the anthropologist expose the forces that imprison him and that he seek to expose the forces that imprison the native.*[65]

Anthropology could be a tool to undermine and expose repression and oppression.

And it is a tool that a number of anthropologists wielded as a weapon. Harris decried industrialism as a bubble.[66] Rappaport pointed to our present reality where "the 'interests' of machines that even powerful men serve are ultimately dominant" and loudly proclaimed that civilization itself is "maladaptive."[67] Diamond and Colin Turnbull were attacked for their "primitivism."[68]

Though these positions became predominant among anthropologists—who, at the same time, were heavily incorporating anti-patriarchal and pro-ecological underpinnings—this is definitely not where the field began.

Two of the founding fathers of ethnography, the practice of embedding within a culture or society to holistically understand them, Bronislaw Malinowski and E.E. Evans-Pritchard, typify the murkiness of the waters these later anthropologists would be rejecting.

Evans-Pritchard was a British anthropologist who cut his teeth working with the Azande, an agrarian society of North Central Africa in what is now the Congo and Sudan. His work caught the eye of the British military, then currently involved in a failing effort to conquer and settle the Nuer, pastoralists along the Nile Valley in what is now Sudan and Ethiopia. Evans-Pritchard was reluctant, having connected on a deeper level and interest with the Azande, but would eventually turn his attention to the Nuer.

Evans-Pritchard played the part of the professional. In doing so, he characterized what anthropologist Wendy James would brand the "reluctant imperialist." And she was dead on. Evans-Pritchard tried to follow the credo set forward by Raymond Firth, that the "greatest need of the social sciences today is for more refined methodology, as objective and dispassionate as possible."[69] True to Firth, Evans-Pritchard took funding from the military and the colonial government and wrote for military journals.

But, as Wolf would indicate, objectivity is easier on paper than on the ground.

Given the context under which Evans-Pritchard entered the world of the Nuer, it is not surprising that it took him far longer to develop any kind of personal rapport with them. By the time he had, his objectivity was wavering. He questioned the morality of colonial rule privately, but sought to humanize his subjects and hoping to appeal to the humanity of colonial administrators.[70]

At best, this was hopeless naivety.

In reality, it was complicity in ethnocide: the subjugation of an insurgent indigenous community to life under colonial rule. He had his sentiments and defaulted on optimism on the battlefield of conquest where the narratives of civilization itself were being tried.

For the Nuer, Evans-Pritchard's internal debate meant little to nothing. The attempts to humanize them in the eyes of colonial administrators failed. They were neither embedded nor engaged with the Nuer, nor did they intend to be. They were administrators handling insurgents. Enter settlements, enter missionaries, enter the entire weight of the civilized world crushing down on a pastoral society in the forms of both militaries and paramilitaries, civil wars, sporadic drippings of cash, and, of course, the influx of guns.

There was no smooth transition, just another iteration of the colonial experience. It was a bloody affair, leaving corpses and culture in its wake.[71]

This is a strong argument for Stanley Diamond's measured take on the history of anthropology versus its reality and potential:

> *Of course anthropologists are spiritual double agents. That is, they are marginal to the commercial-industrial society that created them, but they eagerly explore the areas opened up to them by colonialism. Anthropology is an academic discipline, but it also implies revolt, a search for human possibilities.*[72]

Malinowski's entrance to ethnography was vastly different. He got the opportunity to live among horticulturalists in Papua New Guinea, but then had his funds and chances taken away at the outset of World War I. He sat out the duration of the war living amongst the Trobrianders of Melanesia.

Malinowski wasn't reliant upon, or answering to, colonial administrators like Evans-Pritchard was. He was becoming enmeshed, having his objectivity thrown out in the process. Unlike Evans-Pritchard, who quietly bespoke the morality of colonization, Malinowski increasingly became critical of the colonial encounter, never quite the revolutionary on the matter, but outspoken.

He crossed the lines of objectivity and argued that documenting and recording wasn't sufficient, even if it's the bulk of an ethnographer's written work.[73] The role of the anthropologist wasn't just to quantify a society, but to understand and advocate on their behalf:

> *The Native still needs help. The anthropologist who is unable to perceive this, unable to register the tragic errors committed at times with the best intentions, at times under the stress of dire*

necessity, remains an antiquarian covered with academic dust and in a fool's paradise[74]

Did Malinowski go far enough? No. But it makes sense of the zeal of Lizot and Clastres to defend, beyond reason, something like the warfare of the Yanomamö in the face of Chagnon's celebration of their genocide: the proverbial dirt on their would-be graves.

What becomes clearer through this is that the baggage we carry as civilized people gets no free pass. There is no place, definitely no academic discipline, where some kind of clarity is implicit or can be attained without question.

What is clear is the need to dig, to exhume the corpses civilization has attempted to bury, to unearth the parts of ourselves enchained to the domestication process. That process will always take work. And skepticism. It can be easy to look at the history of anthropology, and even many of its contemporary practices, and write it off completely.[75] But the problem is that we can do so only by objectifying anthropology as an entity, as an object that can potentially be rejected.

I will split no hairs in saying that the "study of humans" has no place in the world of the nomadic hunter-gatherers: within the ancestral genome that each of us is born to embody. But while our minds and bodies weren't prepared for the world of civilization, this is where we exist.

Our elders are gone. Our world is being killed. The tools that we have, the very tools used to decimate indigenous and wild populations across space and time, may be imperfect, but they are what we have.

And we shouldn't be afraid to use them against themselves.

Fredy Perlman's *Against His-Story, Against Leviathan* is a blazing indictment of civilization and its use of history as the tales of conquerors.[76] It is also history and anthropology told in a way that speaks to the oral traditions of non-literate societies: places where stories still have meaning instead of just social power.

For Paul Shepard, history "is the great de-nativizing process."[77] The process of historization removes us from where we are. It separates us, as individuals, from that flow between past and future into an isolated present. A place where we can act without responsibility and reproach: without obligation.

Yet this doesn't keep him from arguing that "the prehistoric unconscious forms a better basis for the creation of a new history."[78] This is about methods, frameworks, and narratives: not constructing ideologies built around every single piece of information that we are presented with or having to interpret everything through a single lens. So long as we are stuck in the world of civilization, we have no safe space, no area to reflect a moralistic platform to stand upon without contradiction.

If we want to find a way out, then it is one thing to use the tools we have and another to simply become them.

Such is the case with post-modern revisionists within history and anthropology. If our intent was simply to construct a perfect theory of existence, they might have use. Seeing that I want to exist on a living planet where wild populations may soon thrive again, perfect theory is just a compilation of pretty words I couldn't care less about.

I strongly sympathize with the historian Michel-Rolph Trouillot's condemnation of post-modernism that "allows us to claim no roots." Speaking of its proponents, "I wonder why they have convictions, if indeed they have any."[79] And I sympathize equally with Stanley Diamond who stated, "Relativism is the bad faith of the conqueror, who has become secure enough to become a tourist."[80]

I identify with Marvin Harris' cultural materialism: equal parts historical materialism and cultural ecology. The aim of which is "to account for the origin, maintenance, and change of the global inventory of socio-cultural differences and similarities."[81] Cultural materialism is about identifying patterns, eliminating and identifying variables:

> *At the heart of the cultural materialist theoretical corpus is a set of theories dealing with the origin of the principal varieties of pre-state societies, the origin of sexism, classes, castes, and the state, and the origin of the principal varieties of state level systems. By 'origin' I do not mean the unique concatenation of historical events leading to the first appearance of a particular thought or practice in a particular geographical spot, but to the nomothetic*

process giving rise to a type *of institution under a set of recurrent conditions.*[82]

Many flinch at the concept of human nature. History has shown times when it became weaponized, but when looking at the patterns of civilization, the kinds of myths told by domesticators from farmers to marketers and priests to bishops and kings to presidents all take the same form. They strike at the same needs that each of us, as a social animal, born a nomadic hunter-gatherer, would find within the wild communities of forager life.

Such definitive narratives can and do play into the hands of those with power. As I seek to undermine and destroy the systems that enable social power to arise, I can't say I'm too concerned about the potential trappings its critics might fear. Like Shepard and Perlman, I feel confident in owning it.

As Perlman put it, to speak of human nature:

> *grates on the nerves of those who, in R. Vaneigem's words, carry cadavers in their mouths. It makes the armor visible. Say 'the state of nature' and you'll see the cadavers peer out.*
> *Insist that 'freedom' and 'the state of nature' are synonyms, and the cadavers will try to bite you. The tame, the domesticated, try to monopolize the word freedom; they'd like to apply it to their own condition. They apply the word 'wild' to the free. But it is another public secret that the tame, the domesticated, occasionally become wild but are never free so long as they remain in their pens.*[83]

We can understand what we have lost by eliminating variables. Removed from the naivety of the revolutionary that thinks we can recreate the world, understanding the patterns a historical world has created reminds us that the sacredness of individuality—and the perceived isolation that it grants—have offered us nothing concrete. That is, outside of concrete itself.

To undermine the narratives of civilization, we have to be willing to turn on ourselves. In digging up our roots among the fragments and strings that civilization has made of our world, there is a baseline there: a world that exists, that struggles, and is full of wild beings and communities that have and will outlast civilization.

The historic world seeks to bury them and place us within its dust.

It buried Ken. It buried Bushmen, Herero, and Nama bodies. It buried the Yanomamö and then danced upon the grave. *We* buried them.

But despite everything, the Ogoni, Bushmen, Herero, Nama, and Yanomamö still exist.

And so do we.

My point here and elsewhere is to show the links through time and place, to find the strings that go far and wide, deep and infinitely projected in space, and to pull them together. We don't exist in isolation even if our entire experience of the world as post-industrial consumers is set up exactly to give us that impression.

That means we take.

We take the tools available to us and we dig. We use them against the system. We expose the lies in its narratives and the weaknesses in its armor. The continued prevalence of civilization requires obedience. Those who have faced its guns, diseases, and decimation on the periphery have always stood against it. They still do. These strings are our link not only to understanding and finding them, but in pulling back the reigns of an overgrown and hemorrhaging leviathan.

This leviathan takes the form of Shell's paramilitary. It takes the form of DeBeers. It takes the form of slave traders, rubber barons, palm plantation owners, oil prospectors, and missionaries.

And it takes the form of Napoleon Chagnon.

Marshall Sahlins, the anthropologist behind the narrative barn-razing *Stone Age Economics*, speaks of the ferocity of the legends Chagnon left in the Amazon: "Representations of him grew more monstrous in proportion to the scale of the struggles he provoked, and even his trade goods were poisoned with the memories of death." The goods he left behind are viewed as black magic, "the products of a factory of xawara wakeshi, the deadly smoke of disease."[84]

The charges against Chagnon, once exposed, were presented to the American Anthropological Association. Upon their investigations, they claimed that Chagnon had not violated their charters and protocols overtly enough to merit exclusion. In protest, Sahlins resigned from their board.

The problem isn't anthropology: it is civilization. These tools can be used on all sides.

The dust of old bones, the blood of new wounds: it all lies before us.

Those strings, these fragments of time and place, all lead to one place.

The Dust of Old Bones in a Fool's Paradise

> *To change social life for the better, one must begin with the knowledge of why it usually changes for the worst.*
> - Marvin Harris, *Cannibals and Kings*[85]

The stories of civilization, the piecing together of fragments of a fractured world, are not my story, yet my role within it is inescapable.

The story of Ken's life is seemingly local. We never met, yet our lives crossed in profound and endemic ways. The Bushmen are among the oldest living societies on earth, having occupied one relative region for hundreds of thousands of years, most likely far more, living largely as they had until being relatively recently thrust into historic time. The Yanomamö came together from exiled hunter-gatherer and horticultural societies having escaped the intrusions of civilizations, both native and Western.

We all end up within the same system. Facing the same dying civilization. Watching it attempt to consume every last piece of our world to sustain itself for a fraction of historical time. A mere speck of biological time.

I am a fragment of a globalized world. I am the progeny of victims and victors, oppressors and oppressed. My parents were white, but their parents were not. The only universal amongst all my relatives is that they all came from and subsequently suppressed hunter-gatherers first, then each other later.

My blood is both conflict and resolution.

To unearth the hunter-gatherer lineage that links my nomadic forager-scavenger body and mind, there's a lot of baggage. Its exhumation wouldn't be necessary if I wasn't the awkward historical amalgam resulting in my own First World, American, white male standing.

A hundred years ago, it would have been vastly different. Seventy years ago, I could have faced extermination at the hands of Nazis. Two hundred years ago, some of my ancestors may have owned slaves. Two thousand years ago, some of my ancestors were slaves.

Yet every single one of us was born, psychologically and physiologically, a hunter-gatherer.

The circles link throughout time and place.

My grandfather managed to escape the Holocaust. A pogrom built upon the modernizing expansions of Germans into the Kalahari.

On the frontlines of the Herero concentration camps was Dr. Eugen Fischer, a German eugenicist who picked up the bodies of executed Herero men, women, and children to experiment upon. To build and test theories that ultimately culminated in his magnum opus, *Principles of Human Heredity and Race Hygiene* in 1921. A book discovered a mere two years later by a man imprisoned for a failed coup in Landsberg Prison in Germany. One Adolf Hitler.[86]

The book fed into Hitler's Final Solution. It gave his Third Reich more traction. Turning one genocide into the ideological basis for another. Turning the fear of lost identity into a weapon of conquerors.

Round and round we go.

Officially speaking, Shell pulled out of Ogoni land in 1993. With one caveat: "Ogoni land continues to serve as a transit route for pipelines transporting both [Shell] and third-party oil production from other areas." From the mouths of Ogoni people I had spoken with and stared at with wonder as they smiled at racist, white suburbanites, the pipelines *were* a major issue.

Shell could legally wash their hands of what was to come. They've gone even further now, continuing to claim that Ken was responsible for the murder of Ogoni elders, that his execution was the result of presumably fair trials. Meanwhile, they are calling for reconciliation with the Ogoni: an asinine attempt to find someone willing to take a payout.

To bury it.

To put it deeper into the bloodied grounds of Ogoni land, where the oil should have never been extracted.

I've spoken of the power of narratives. Words mean a lot. Framing means a lot. Context, all of it.

So when you find the above information on the website of Shell Nigeria, it's infuriating. But when you realize that it's under the sustainability subsection, blood boils.[87]

History is a lie we tell ourselves.

A lie that we are told.

Our narratives, our perceptions of our own world: this is how we remain complicit, how we keep working, buying, signing online, and just going with the flow. From the shattered version of the world that we embody, the allure of escaping into the suffocating void of the technosphere, a place where we can be as special and as unique as marketers tell us we are, can be apparent.

But it offers nothing. It is a blinder. It keeps us from picking up the pieces of our lives, our past, our present, and our future. From seeing the terrifying world we inhabit.

And, most importantly, it keeps us from pulling on the strings enough to see that it is fully within our power and reach to cut the cords that fuel the entirety of it.

Endnotes

1. Gary Snyder, 'The Old Bones: For Paul Shepard.' In Max Oelschlaeger (ed), *The Company of Others*. Durango, CO: Kivaki Press, 1995. Pg 7.
2. Eric Wolf, *Europe and the People Without History*. Berkeley: University of California Press, 1997 [1982]. Pgs 215-218
3. http://www.worldstatesmen.org/Nigeria_native.html#Okolo-Ama
4. Hugh Thomas, *The Slave Trade*. New York: Touchstone, 1999. Pgs 43-44.
5. https://en.wikipedia.org/wiki/Kingdom_of_Bonny
6. https://en.wikipedia.org/wiki/Port_Harcourt
7. Frederick Lugard, quoted in Clive Ponting, *A Green History of the World*. New York: Penguin, 1991. Pg 357.
8. Tom Burgis, *The Looting Machine*. New York: Public Affairs, 2015. Pg 69.
9. Human Rights Watch, *The Price of Oil*. 1999. Online at: https://www.hrw.org/reports/1999/nigeria/Nigew991-05.htm#P526_156650
10. Tobi Soniyi, 'Nigeria: U.S.$400 Billion of Oil Revenue Stolen, Says Ezekwesili.' *This Day*, August 29, 2012. Online at http://allafrica.com/stories/201208290453.html
11. Rob Nixon, 'Pipe Dreams: Ken Saro-Wiwa, Environmental Justice, and Micro-Minority Rights.' *Black Renaissance*, 1:1. Fall 1996.
12. Human Rights Watch, 1999.
13. Burgis, 2015. Pg 195.
14. https://en.wikisource.org/wiki/Trial_Speech_of_Ken_Saro-Wiwa
15. Michel-Rolph Trouillot, *Silencing the Past: Power and the Production of History*. Boston: Beacon, 1995. Pg 153.
16. Sidney Mintz, *Sweetness and Power*. New York: Penguin, 1987. Pg 19.
17. Ibid. Pgs 5-6.
18. Alice Walton, How Much Sugar Are Americans Eating? *Forbes*, August 30, 2012. https://www.forbes.com/sites/alicegwalton/2012/08/30/how-much-sugar-are-americans-eating-infographic/#59c9eac84ee7
19. Mintz, 1987. Pgs 32-33.
20. Quoted in Hugh Thomas, *The Slave Trade*. New York: Touchstone, 1997. Pg 136.
21. Wolf, 1997. Pg 215.
22. Ibid. Pg 218.
23. MOSOP, 'Highlight on Ogoni Kingdom.' http://www.chr.up.ac.za/chr_old/indigenous/documents/Nigeria/ILO/High%20light%20of%20Great%20Ogoni%20Kingdom%20from%20the%20official%20website%20of%20MOSOP.htm
24. Fredy Perlman, *Against His-Story, Against Leviathan*. Detroit: Black and Red Press, 1983. Pg 11.
25. Stanley Diamond, *In Search of the Primitive*. New Brunswick, NJ: Transaction, 1987 [1974]. Pg 207.
26. Martin Meredith, *The Fortunes of Africa*. London: Simon & Schuster, 2014.

Pg 130.
27. Ibid. Pgs 136-137.
28. Cited in James Suzman, *Affluence Without Abundance: The Disappearing World of the Bushmen*. New York: Bloomsbury, 2017. Pg 199.
29. Mark Cocker, *Rivers of Blood, Rivers of Gold*. New York: Grove, 1998.
30. Meredith, 2014. Pg 486.
31. Suzman, 2017. Pg 198.
32. Ibid. Pg 203.
33. For more on this, see my essays 'Hooked on a Feeling' in *Black and Green Review* no 3 and 'Society Without Strangers' in *Black and Green Review* no 4, as well as Suzman, 2017.
34. Survival International, 'Twentieth Anniversary of Eviction from Kalahari Highlights Bushmen Plight.' May 8, 2017. https://www.survivalinternational.org/news/11690
35. Survival International, 'Botswana's hunting ban: Bushmen starve, trophy hunters carry on.' March 31, 2014. https://www.survivalinternational.org/news/10112
36. Burgis, 2015. Pg 226. Ironically, Burgis notes that the residents of Botswana have fared decently (by Africa's standards) from the diamond trade, a dubious claim, as he mentions a mere fourteen pages earlier (212) that Botswana was among the top ten of nations that had failed to turn national revenue into improved quality of life for its citizens.
37. The Diamond Loupe, 'Botswana Diamonds & ALROSA JV Awarded Six New Prospecting Licenses.' April 25, 2017. https://www.thediamondloupe.com/articles/2017-04-25/botswana-diamonds-alrosa-jv-awarded-six-new-prospecting-licenses
38. The Guardian, 'Botswana faces questions over licenses for fracking companies in Kalahari.' November 17, 2013. https://www.theguardian.com/environment/2013/nov/18/botswana-accusations-fracking-kalahari
39. Stanley Diamond, *In Search of the Primitive*. New Brunswick, NJ: Transaction, 1987 [1974]. Pg 93.
40. David Thomas and Paul Shaw, *The Kalahari Environment*. Cambridge: Cambridge UP, 1991. Pg 16.
41. Susan Martin, *Palm Oil and Protest*. Cambridge: Cambridge UP, 1988. Pg 123. And 'Cocoa Production in Nigeria,' Wikipedia. https://en.wikipedia.org/wiki/Cocoa_production_in_Nigeria
42. Napoleon Chagnon, *Yanomamö: The Fierce People*. New York: Holt, Reinhart, and Winston, 1968.
43. John Hemming, *Red Gold: The Conquest of the Brazilian Indians*, Cambridge, MA: Harvard University Press, 1978.
44. Michael Edward Stanfield, *Red Rubber, Bleeding Trees*. Albuquerque, N.M.: University of New Mexico Press, 1998. Meanwhile, a similar trajectory was taking place in Africa's Congo. There are a lot of great books on the matter, but among the best is Adam Hochschild, *King Leopold's Ghost*. New York: Houghton Mifflin, 1999.
45. Wade Davis, *One River*. New York: Simon & Schuster, 1997. Opt cit.
46. Gerard Colby and Charlotte Dennett, *Thy Will be Done*. New York: Harper

Collins, 1996.
47. R Brian Ferguson, 'Blood of the Leviathan.' *American* Ethnologist, Vol 17, No 2, May 1990. Pg 244.
48. Francis Jennings, *The Ambiguous Iroquois Confederacy*. New York: WW Norton, 1984.
49. Paul Shankman, 'Culture Contact, Cultural Ecology, and Dani Warfare.' *Man*, New Series, Vol 26, No 2, June 1991.
50. Andrew Vayda, *Maori Warfare*. Wellington, New Zealand: Polynesian Society, 1960. Andrew Vayda, *War in Ecological Perspective*. New York: Plenum Press, 1976.
51. Daniel Steel, 'Trade Goods and Jivaro Warfare.' *Ethnohistory*, Vol 46 No 4, Autumn 1999.
52. Andrew Vayda, 'Expansion and Warfare among Swidden Agriculturalists.' *American Anthropologist*, New Series, Vol. 63, No. 2, April, 1961.
53. For more on this, see my essay 'Society Without Strangers.' *Black and Green Review* no 4, 2016.
54. R Brian Ferguson, 'A Savage Encounter' in Ferguson and Whitehead (eds), *War in the Tribal Zone*. Santa Fe, NM: SARS Press, 1992 and R Brian Ferguson, *Yanomami Warfare*. Santa Fe, NM: SARS Press, 1995.
55. Patrick Tierney, *Darkness in El Dorado*. New York: WW Nortion, 2000.
56. Jacques Lizot, 'Population, Resources and Warfare Among the Yanomami.' *Man*, New Series, Vol 12, No 3/4. December 1977.
57. Pierre Clastres, *Archeology of Violence*. New York: Semiotext(e), 1994. Pg 164.
58. Pierre Clastres, *Society Against the State*. New York: Zone, 1989.
59. See Ferguson, 1992 & 1995.
60. Paul Shepard, *Coming Home to the Pleistocene*. Washington DC: Island Press, 1998. Pg 12.
61. Brian Morris, *Anthropology, Ecology, and Anarchism*. Oakland, CA: PM Press, 2014. Pg 58.
62. I have distinguished elsewhere and will elaborate further in time on the matter of "primitive communism," a catch-all term where communism and communalism could almost be considered interchangeable. Communism means communal ownership of the means of production, but considering that immediate-return hunter-gatherers had methods of procurement without production (a lack of surplus); there was nothing to own. Hence my use of the term "primal anarchy" which applies to many societies widely considered "primitive communism."

It is also telling to me that Stanley Diamond's almost confusing allegiance to communism over anarchism had to do with his conflation of anarchism with the more libertarian-leaning sects of individualist anarchism, as typified by Max Stirner. If that were the be all, end all of anarchism, it would definitely make more sense.
63. George E Marcus and Michael MJ Fischer, *Anthropology as Cultural Critique: An Experimental Moment in the Human Sciences* (Second Edition). Chicago: University of Chicago Press, 1999. Pg 1.
64. Ibid, pg 82.
65. Eric Wolf, Introduction to Diamond 1987. Pg xii.
66. Marvin Harris, *Cannibals and Kings*. New York: Vintage, 1978.

67. Roy Rappaport, 'Maladaptation in Social Systems' in J Friedman and MJ Rowlands, *The Evolution of Social* Systems. Pittsburgh: University of Pittsburgh, 1978. Pgs 63 and 66.
68. For Turnbull, this was the primary "negative" review of his book, *The Human Cycle* (New York: Simon & Schuster, 1983). For Diamond, it was an even more prevalent theme as his 1987 book *In Search of the Primitive* makes clear. It was such a central point that the first volume of an anthology in his honor is titled, *Civilization in Crisis: Anthropological Perspectives*, and the second is subtitled, *A Critique of Civilization*. Both edited by Christine Ward Gailey (Gainesville: University Press of Florida, 1992).
69. Cited in Wendy James, 'The Anthropologist as Reluctant Imperialist' in Talal Asad (ed), *Anthropology and the Colonial Encounter*. Amherst, NY: Humanity Books, 1973. The whole collection is really excellent.
70. Douglas H. Johnson, 'Evans-Pritchard, the Nuer, and the Sudan Political Service.' *African Affairs*, Vol. 81, No. 323. April 1982.
71. Sharon Hutchinson, *Nuer Dilemmas*. Berkeley: University of California Press, 1996.
72. Diamond, 1987. Pg 89.
73. Oddly enough, the meticulous nature of recording information and stories is what makes ethnography as useful of a record as many explorers or historians accounts: they come down to data. Even when R Brian Ferguson was deflating the lies of Chagnon, he was able to use the data Chagnon had presented against him.
74. Cited in James, 1973. Pg 66.
75. It is worth noting that I stopped pursuing my own graduate studies in anthropology precisely because I had no interest in taking part in the colonial remnants that field work could find itself in: having to work with missionaries, being granted permissions from governments, dispensing medications and bribes. I think there are ways around it, but at the time found no clear path ahead on it.
76. Perlman, 1983.
77. Shepard, 1998. Pg 12.
78. Ibid. Pg 17.
79. Trouillot, 1995. Pg xviii.
80. Diamond, 1987. Pg 110.
81. Marvin Harris, *Cultural Materialism*. New York: Vintage, 1980. Pg 27.
82. Ibid. Pg 78.
83. Perlman, 1983. Pg 7.
84. Marshall Sahlins, Jungle Fever: review of *Darkness in El Dorado*. *The Washington Post*, BOOK WORLD; Pg. X01, December 10, 2000
85. Harris, 1978. Pg xiv.
86. Suzman, 2017. Pg 200.
87. Shell Nigeria, 'The Ogoni Issue' accessed online at http://www.shell.com.ng/sustainability/environment/ogon-issue.html

I am Complicit

I am complicit.

Genocide. Ecocide. Suicide. All of it.

I want to believe that I am not, but I can't fool myself anymore. We are all complicit in the destruction of this earth, our home, and all of its inhabitants.

And it makes me sick.

It makes my soul cry, it makes my stomach turn, it shoots pain through my spine, it makes my brain melt, it makes my hands shake and twitch, and it kills me that I can't do anything about it.

As I type these words, mountain tops are demolished to get easier access to coal, that composited decay of millions of years of life, a time capsule for an unwritten history, which feeds the grid. Ground water in the area I call home is being filled with hydrofracking chemicals to squeeze a little more life out of the earth to keep the power on. Nuclear power plants surround this area and they are ticking time bombs for the future of life. Rivers all around me are increasingly being filled with the toxic sludge of crude from tar sands.

Every bit of this sickens me to the core and yet I remain complicit.

We are sold a myth when we are born into this world.

The fairytale of Progress is that everything will not only get better, but that it is better. We are told that we are living longer and healthier than our "caveman" ancestors. We told that we are improving the lives of those in the third world through development programs. We are told that our quality of life is improving. We are told that we have access to more and better food than anyone in history. We are told that we have more access to information which gives us more freedom.

We are told that if we don't like it, then we can "love it or leave it."

But we can't.

In the midst of a globalized, technologically-rooted, finite resource-dependent, ideologically bound, and profit addicted modernity, the largely touted peak of civilization, there is no door. There is no core. There is no periphery. We are all stuck in this mess. It is only those that are the most complicit in the omnicide involved in flicking on a light switch that are told that it is our choice to stay.

We are trapped. All of us.

The remaining hunter-gatherers and horticulturalists are sitting on the front lines, while their cultural traditions which date back tens and sometimes hundreds of thousands of years are deemed illegal (poaching, trespassing), immoral (in the words of the missionaries, you must first become "lost" so that you can be "saved"), and impossible (mining, drilling, logging, and ranching). On the edges of expansion, any question you have about lifestyle choices can be directed towards the military, armed ranchers, miners, and loggers, or "revolutionary" groups that litter their homes.

All evidence to the truth about Progress swept under the rug.

In the Middle East, those questions look like birth defects from residuals of depleted Uranium. Beneath the Arab Spring lie unattainable food costs. In China, you have nets built around factories to prevent suicides and screens projecting sunrise and sunsets since you can't see them through the smog. Throughout Latin America you have displaced villages and toxin spewing factories demolishing forests. Throughout the affluent nations, you have chronic debt, depression, and people buried under their possessions and gadgets as real world connections wither.

You have a world overrun by resource wars, power grabs, ponzi schemes, crushed egos, isolation and separation induced anxiety and depression, suppressed populations, and unthinkable wealth. But you have no middle ground. You have no escape.

The myth of Progress, the world that civilization has created, needs a door. It needs to give the myth of the way out, because it needs to authenticate the feeling of choice, the myth of freedom. The eternal trick of the domesticators is that you are in this because you want to be. The reality of the domesticated world is that you are in this because you have to be.

That is what makes each and every one of us complicit.

It doesn't matter if you recycle. It doesn't matter if you buy local products. It doesn't matter if you dumpster dive and squat. Lessening your contributions to the economy does not end your complicity. Living on the edges of society does not end your complicity. Rebuilding community doesn't end your complicity. Rewilding doesn't end your complicity. As important as these steps are for our future, we can not buy into the delusion that we have a choice.

Civilization is killing this planet, our home. It always has. It always will. The only difference is scale. And with the disjoined and fragmented modernity that we are in, you can't click a button, turn a switch, or anything without effecting our own fate.

And that is our sickening reality.

It keeps me up at night. It haunts my soul. It has taken loved ones. It wears the body. It withers the mind. It makes me shake in anger and it makes me shake in fear.

We are all born as hunter-gatherers. Every one of us. It is who we have evolved to be.

The process of domestication cannot kill this part of us, but it can manipulate our fears, desires, hopes, and needs. But our souls know that something is wrong. Something is missing. But I can't mourn for our innate being, our wildness, the wildness that encompasses all life. I can't mourn it because it is not dead.

It can not die.

It will not die.

It is suppressed. Lying dormant in those of us who are complicit in it's suppression without knowing it. Being held back by fences, guards, miners, loggers, and missionaries for those on the front lines. It is being held back by laws and prisons and people who worship at the throne of economics.

Reconnecting with that wildness is within our reach, but it carries the impossible responsibility of expanding our Stone Age minds beyond the world of the forest, fields, beaches, and deserts, and recognizing the consequences of a globalized technocracy. Our reach has outgrown our comprehension. The domesticators know this and they have and will continue to use it against us.

I refuse to embrace my complicity, but I can no longer deny it.

I am Complicit

Part of my journey back into wildness means taking responsibility and acknowledging that consequence supersedes intention.

Running away isn't an option.

Putting my head in the dirt isn't an option.

Civilization needs to die so that the earth, our home, and all of it's inhabitants can live.

I will mourn the tragic losses that happen every second that the grid is intact. I am complicit in their destruction because, like all of us, I was born in a time of unthinkable destruction and into the culture that is squeezing every drop of life from this earth.

I am complicit, but I will not accept defeat.

I am complicit in the destruction caused by civilization by my birth and it sickens me. I am complicit in the destruction of civilization because it is what I must do.

I want to walk out that door. I want to pull the plug. I want to flip the switch. But those things are all a lie. We are all complicit and we are all stuck. We do not have an option to leave, but we do have a choice to accept responsibility for our actions and a choice to act on them.

I will mourn.

I will struggle.

I will fight.

I seek the guidance of the wildness that surrounds me.

I will find place from the wildness within me.

For my children. For my family. For my home. For those who have lost everything.

The Suffocating Void:
Domestication and Pathological Distraction

> *It would be imprudent to deny, or even to play down, the profound change which the advent of 'fluid modernity' has brought to the human condition. The remoteness and unreachability of systemic structure, coupled with the unstructured, fluid state of the immediate setting of life-politics, change that condition in a radical way and call for a rethinking of old concepts that used to frame its narratives. Like zombies, such concepts are today simultaneously dead and alive.*
> – Zygmunt Bauman[1]

Something has changed. Radically. And for the worst.

It is tellingly difficult to describe something without a name. And that something has quickly crept into our minds and psyche. We call it "social media" or the "social network," but those words normalize what is a revolutionary change in our relationship to technology. We're not talking here about a mere platform of technology, we're talking about a mindset, a constantly flowing stream of information whereby a refusal to participate renders the human, now reduced to the status of a "user," obsolete.

There has been a distinct turn away from the internet being relegated to a computer and it is now not only with us at all times, but always on, always moving, always watching. The internet has moved from a form of communication to the increasingly predominant one. So much so that the United Nations has declared internet access a human right.[2] As fiber optic cables are buried in plain sight, Wifi signals permeate our world.

Your muscles twitch. You believe it's your phone in your pocket, but you're holding it in your hand.[3] You didn't notice you were even checking it. Our immersion into the world of the machine is most notable in how little attention we pay to it.

We expect it and we are expected by it.

This is the suffocating void, the demanding emptiness of Modernity, the obtuse compliance with the domestication process as rendered in binary by programmers.

We need to stop.

Stop our movements, still our minds, silence our devices and for a moment, even just one moment, just be present. It's not easy. It's not easy to get there and it's not easy to stay there. The air is thick, it is difficult to breathe and even harder to get your bearings. It is overwhelming. The weight of our stuff, our drama, our baggage comes crashing in. In our world, stagnancy is the equivalent of death.

We are stuck in constant movement. We become the flood, the rushing waters, a conversation with no beginning, no end, and no content. To our nomadic hunter-gatherer minds, there's an inkling of familiarity. Our bodies want to move, to flow and respond. But this is not the movement of bodies within a rooted world: it is a trap. We are stuck within the eye of a tornado, so we try to move with it, but it never stops and it never ends. And when you attempt to stop and assess the situation, the true horror of our reality, the crushing impact of what the sociologist Zygmunt Bauman has aptly labeled "Liquid Modernity" will overcome you.

It will annihilate you.

Our ancestors, our shared lineage that formed our bodies and minds, were driven by movement. Within our crisis, the pathetic reflection of that primal urge is not movement, but restlessness. We are moving, but we are going nowhere. Shuffling to avoid stagnancy. Moving lifelessly to avoid death.

This is not an accident.

Nothing in our reality really is any more. We are a herd of

individuals vying for attention in a sea of selfies, tweets and yelps. The ecologist Paul Shepard long ago pointed out how domestication stunts development,[4] but technology derails it. Increasingly unable to find or define ourselves outside of the machine, we move further inwards. And the programmers pull the strings. We learn to express ourselves through the machine and, in doing so, we become one.

Our distraction keeps us from seeing the monumental change taking place: the immersion into a constantly connected, but never grounded social network. We are, so to speak, "always on." Smart phones, tablets, screens everywhere we look, wireless signals pervading nearly all spaces, check ins, GPS and monitoring equipment constantly reassuring the world that we are here and we are consuming this manufactured reality.

Within decades, we went from being sold the mythos and myths of Progress to rendering the narrative null through immersion. We no longer need to dream of a glorious Future, we are here. Progress is no longer spoken of, but expected and systemic.

Like the Agricultural Revolution, Industrial Revolution, and the Green Revolution before it, the Interface Revolution propels civilization beyond the boundaries and limitations of earlier systems. The firewalls of Jericho have been breached. Progress innovated, the processes integrated.

For the programmers, this is no small feat. This is the dream of every domesticator: people lining up and fighting for the latest technology, fighting for a place in line, paying top dollar for devices with built in tracking and data mining software and willing to remain in debt to sustain the terms of our bondage. Never mind that the world is suffocating under piles of waste, choking down makeshift mines for rare and difficult to extract metals, while workers are forced to sign anti-suicide clauses, villages are displaced, and sustained low budget warfare are both form and function; the expectation isn't just that all of this will be ignored, but that you, the consumer, will be back for more next year. Or sooner.

And when things are really moving along, not only are the consequences of technology (both internal and external) ignored, they are accepted and justified.

If the architects of Uruk had the foresight, they would have been seething with jealousy over the control and obedience this technocratic dystopia holds.

But in their place we have the ever-present bloated smiles of Bill Gates, Steve Jobs, and Mark Zuckerberg encoded into the machines we carry. The smiles of billionaires who built their impossibly massive fortunes on our desecrated earth: buried, literally, in a sea of intentionally outdated and short-lived devices. Devices filled with metals mined by the dispossessed under the directives of warlords. Devices built by the displaced and disempowered. Devices awash in toxic residue that dilute into groundwater, streams, rivers, and contaminate oceans.

Devices that whiten the blood stained teeth of programmers, of billionaires: of domesticators.

And their smiles are injected into every aspect of our lives.

The Flesh Machine

> *With this new 'megatechnics' the dominant minority will create a uniform, all-enveloping, super-planetary structure, designed for automatic operation. Instead of functioning actively as an autonomous personality, man [sic] will become a passive, purposeless, machine-conditioned animal whose proper functions, as technicians now interpret man's [sic] role, will either be fed into the machine or strictly limited and controlled for the benefit of de-personalized, collective organizations.*
>
> -Lewis Mumford[5]

Lewis Mumford long ago made the observation that the first components of the "Megamachine," the infusion of technology and society, were made of flesh and blood. It has long been the dream of the technocrats to make the flesh the last. While Mumford was talking about the coordinated efforts it took to build monuments and to clear and plow fields in the Mesolithic era, the programmers of our time just want to remove the clunkiness and messiness of their apparatus from our view.

This was the vision of Progress that we had been sold.

The Future would be better. The Machine would deliver us

from drudgery. Its "apparent purpose," as stated by former advertising executive turned neo-Luddite, Jerry Mander, "is to eliminate human ailments and human unhappiness..., to expand the human potential, and to create a world of abundance for human enjoyment." Meanwhile driving in the "unstated purpose" to "fulfill the inherent drive of technological society to feed its own evolutionary cravings, to expand its domination of the both Earth and space, and to complete the utter conversion of nature into commodity form."[6]

For many of us, the failures of Progress are no surprise. This is a mythos as distraction: your sacrifice now will benefit you later. It is not only a religious imperative, it is the origin of religious thought only to be readapted as seen fit through time. A cosmological delayed return economy.[7]

And within Modernity, that adaptation grew into and through the allure of new technology.

Change comes into the picture.

Marshall McLuhan spotted it with the printing press, Jerry Mander spotted it in the television, when Mumford saw the thread, he saw strong hints at the potential of the computer, but he seemingly would have hoped it could have not gotten to the point where we are now: change is expected, integration is constant. Speed itself, as John Zerzan aptly notes,[8] has become a virtue.

We have suddenly found ourselves at a strange impasse where narratives have collided. The need for the sales pitch of Progress has been surpassed by the want for the new. We aren't questioning the expectation that we are always available, "always on," we are lining up for the newest devices to further those intrusions.

Fighting *for* them.

Getting to this point didn't happen over night, but even within the history of technology, it all happened with unthinkable speed. The mobile phone took a remarkably fast slide from toy of the ultra-rich to nearly universal acceptance. By 2013, 91% of the adult population in the US owned at least one.[9]

The unprecedented nature of this has led two industry proponents to applaud the near universal acceptance of mobile phones as the most quickly adopted consumer technology in the history of the world. Gloating in their sickening book, *Networked*, authors Lee Rainie and Barry Wellman state: "the Mobile Revolution has allowed [Information and Community Technologies] to become body appendages allowing people to access friends and information at will, wherever they go." The key is being "always accessible," but, in true form, they see "the possibility of a continued presence and pervasive awareness of others in the network"[10] positively.

The architects of civilization have long understood that the power of the domestication process lies in its ability to be internalized. The mythos of Progress requires daily affirmation. The programmers, however, realized that affirmation could become integrated.

They just needed to eliminate any distance between a given technology and the user. Lo and behold, a trip into a recently built suburb or even newly gentrified city will show that the eyesore of power lines have been rid from sight. We go wireless so we no longer see the machine as separate. Unsightly and inconvenient wiring goes to routers in corners and under furniture. Corporations sponsor "Wifi Hot Spots" to customers. We remove the wiring from sight to internalize its function.

And this has sadly been effective. Very effective.

What you see when you step into public places are faces illuminated by backlit devices. Groups of teens walking together and each lost in their own virtual presence. 1.3 million car accidents in the US during 2011 were caused by drivers distracted with their cell phones.[11] You will see people constantly swiping their screens to look for updates, feeds, messages, or just blindly glancing out of habit at their phones, most seemingly with no recognition of what they are doing.

The conclusion of the Megamachine, the necessary step to furthering the goals of Progress, was to eliminate barriers. To make it so we treat phones as an appendage, while the Programmers dream of making them one.

To make us complicit.

To make us comply without even noticing it.

I have long held that the genius of civilizers is falsely attributed to manufacturing needs. Simply put, they aren't that smart and we aren't that gullible.

What it does come down to is an understanding of what a human being needs. We are social animals. In our minds and bodies, even when lost in some ridiculous App on an iPhone, we are trying to reconcile the world of the hunter-gatherer with the path that Modernity has set us on. For the most part, our emotional and mental free fall is held in place so long as our inertia is matched by social rebounding.

Community is etched in our Stone Age soul. We don't just want others; we need them.

And herein lies the tragedy.

This is our animality being torn from us, repackaged and then sold back to us. We want movement, we want connectivity, we want contact, and, in the absence of the physical, the electric options are literally inescapable waves penetrating our minds and bodies.

This is how Progress was sold to us and this is why we buy into this Void. Amongst 7 billion people and counting, in a sea of unending electric synapse and stimuli: we are lost, alone, and confused.

While it may be utterly unrecognizable, the mound builders of Mesopotamia and the high-tech sweatshop worker serve the same function: to become the apparatus so that we may consume it.

And that downward spiral is driven by our consumption.

The Zuckerburg Galaxy

> *There is a huge need and a huge opportunity to get everyone in the world connected, to give everyone a voice and to help transform society for the future. The scale of the technology and infrastructure that must be built is unprecedented, and we believe this is the most important problem we can focus on.*
>
> – Mark Zuckerberg[12]

Facebook didn't invent social media, but it has become iconic in its acceptance and usage. While often being joked about as a scourge, near the end of 2014 more than 1.35 billion people logged on at least once per month[13]. That surpasses the population of China.

The Suffocating Void

And it continues to grow.

As much as the mainstream celebrates social media, even attempting to posture it as the tool of liberation during the Arab Spring (though ironically demonizing it when it was used in the same way in the Ferguson Uprisings of 2014 and beyond), our sense of how radical this change in form really is becomes lost.

Marshall McLuhan famously made the case that the "Gutenberg technology," the printing press, had made universal change in the way its users and consumers saw the world. This pattern, beginning with the written word, cannot be overstated. Yet it is so often lost within civilization because everything we know is taught through the lens of symbolic culture: the internalized whispers of domesticators reinforcing our own perceived split from the wild world and necessary dependency on masters. This is how domestication works, but the purpose of technology is to update form and context. And as McLuhan famously observed: form dictates function, the medium is the message.

So his words for the impact of the printed word hold equally true for the updated technology: when a technology is introduced "if it gives new stress or ascendancy to one or another of our senses, the ratio among all of our senses is altered. We no longer feel the same, nor do our eyes and ears and other sense remain the same."[14]

Technology flattens our world by reducing our reliance on senses while over stimulating particular sensory input. Our brains are, to put it simply, overworked and underwhelmed. Mediation and representation as evidenced by blogs, Youtube channels, Facebook feeds and Twitter handles.

This is the form.

This is the form that creates a world filled with crushing depression, alienation, suffering and anxiety. A National Center for Health Statistics study found that by 2008 the usage of anti-depressants in the US had gone up 400% over the previous decade across all demographics.[15] The iPhone was released in 2007. The researcher's period of study from 2005-2008 saw an increase of Facebook users from 5.5 million to 100 million.[16] That is an increase of over 1700%. And this isn't even touching on the horrid and dire social and ecological consequences across the world.

The point isn't to say that Facebook caused these things, but, along with all other facets of the social network (both past, present and future), it exacerbates them. It amplifies on exponential terms.

The content and platforms drive each other. But they always have.

Hyper-internalized and portable technology is the form.

Domestication is the function.

As the domesticators developed technology to employ their will, the ability to make change with intentionality arose. No longer was power in the scythe and the stored grains. The agrarian curse of drudgery and toil for the perceived pay off in the heavens paved the way (literally) to updated industrial forms.

And the mythos evolved.

Collective consciousness was slowly channeled into individual consumerism. It is no surprise that the overstressed working class in early industrializing nations thought their liberation lied within possessing the machine collectively, nor is it surprising that the antidote to that notion was selling individual heavens on an increasingly closer horizon.

Progress remains. Mythos adapt.

Technology increasingly spread from the means to the purpose itself. The time clock led to the pocket watch to the wristwatch and now to the cell phone. We embrace the objects that confine our minds to think on an artificial sense of place and self.

Our world becomes both larger and smaller, so we turn to the machine, to this bartered identity. Even in a sea of flux, the technology itself increasingly becomes the constant. It becomes the savior.

Chellis Glendinning called this process by what it is: "techno-addiction." "In such a society people have historically become obsessed with anything that helps them to cope with the trauma of it all."[17]

We buy to know we're alive.

And, increasingly, we Tweet to remind everyone that we're still here.

Facebook's creator, Mark Zuckerberg, saw the writing on the wall. He didn't just sell it: he bought it. His rise from a computer programmer at Harvard up to the richest 20 people in the world is

The Suffocating Void

sadly well documented and pathetically emulated.

While not coming up from the bottom of the social ladder, his story is more of an emotional rags-to-riches triumph. The reader can relate. A teenager in the 90s, a product of great technological change and raised in an atmosphere where "play" went from being outside with friends to inside and playing video games. Or, in Zuckerberg's case, programming them.

This story is drenched in the turmoil of responding to adolescence through increasingly mediated means. The starting point for what would become Facebook was a site that rated other students by their looks. It should not be surprising that the origin point of Facebook is driven equally by a bully's entitlement and an unrelenting sense of insecurity. And that is the tone that carried on.

Facebook didn't arise in a vacuum. This is hardly even history at this point; we're talking about websites that increasingly dominated the social atmosphere over the past decade. It's hardly necessary for me to recant them.

What is important here is how and why Facebook took off.

The obnoxiously entitled "Blogosphere" matched with former Facebook contender, MySpace, both served, as necessary steps towards what social networking would become. The blogs were driven by an attempt at a, and I'm biting my tongue here, "grassroots" sense of giving voices and reporting. Often centered around contemporary topics, their necessary role was less in what was being said, but littering the fairy tale notion of the internet as an "information super-highway" with opinions equally weighed with actual reporting and research. A huge part of the lucrative Search Engine Optimization (SEO) field existing relied on the hopes for bloggers to have their posts on a subject get the highest ranked search results in Google or whatever else is currently being used.

Blogs quickly became an accepted resource. The internet is, after all, marketing. A blog is a brand for an individual. A public face: a personalization of a perspective that transfers the subject from content to provider. This is the cult of personality moving from the television, books, politicians and newspapers to overly excitable and entertaining personalities. These people were enthralling because they could be you, the spectator. This was a move driven home even further via Youtube not long after.

MySpace was the place to market the self under the guise of a place to keep in touch with friends. A place to sell the image of yourself that you wish to portray. Echoed along the lines of Twitter, where irrelevant quips of 140 characters, and in an increasingly entangled and over-sharing, yet selective, web, the social network became accepted enough that the nearly stalker-esque Facebook was ready to take its place.

The idea of posting your quips and selling yourself was worthless unless it was the main feature: the News Feed. This is a sea of words projected onto a constantly shifting wall as if it was news. From the hyper-personal to the irrelevant, it's laid out flatly for your selected audience.

And there are no mistakes here.

These moves are intentional. They are marketing.

Sold as a supplement to the life anyone wants to live, they have become the main course. And they become the platform for broadcasting the life you want others to see. Far from being a tight knit group of friends, social networking sites, as Jose van Dijck states in his critical history, "forge personal, professional or geographical connections and encourage weak ties."[18]

This is that urge that we all have within us: the need for community. It is your inner-hunter-gatherer and their band associations.

An impulse redirected for a reality supplanted.

We spread ourselves widely. We feel that having information about others is as good as having actual relationships with them. And every time we log on, we are selling ourselves.

The grotesque level of acceptance of the social network is apparent in how Zuckerberg basks in it: "Think about what people are doing on Facebook today. They're keeping up with their friends and family, but they're also building an image and identity for themselves, which in a sense is their brand. They're connecting with the audience that they want to connect to."

And to always end on a high note: "It's almost a disadvantage if you're not on it now."[19]

We buy this reality because we sell it. If you want to take part in this society, if you want to stay connected with friends and fam-

The Suffocating Void

ily, both close and distant: here is the platform, here is the place to do it.

It almost seems ridiculous to give this platform such intense scrutiny. In the timeline of civilization, it won't even be a fragment of a blip. But the spread, grasp and ramifications of Facebook, its intentional and unspoken uses, are monumental. You simply cannot escape them. It's not as simple as deactivating an account (it was years before deleting was even an option).

These have become the terms, the grounding on which this late stage of Modernity stands.

The narrative of Progress hardly needs to sell a distant future; it has created an eternal present. And in doing so, it has removed the presence. It removes the essence of being human.

This is change.

This is change at a rate and depth that is unprecedented even in the nasty, short and brutish history of civilization. Amongst all of the critiques of technology, this is something that was predicted in dystopian terms, but the reality is far scarier and by the time most of us noticed its effectiveness, we are at a loss for outlets and terms to even discuss this ongoing and worsening epidemic.

The News Feed ticks.

Against the backdrop of a 24 hour "news" cycle, it is a fitting backdrop: the techno-addicted need constant stimulation. Going outside hardly cuts it unless it's for taking selfies or a necessary part of the sale for the projected self.

The Self, driven by hyper-individualistic consumerism, takes a form and precedence that could make even the most rampant egoist blush. This isn't just posturing; it's an attachment to a projected and widely cast image. An online persona is increasingly less foreign to our sense of identity. McLuhan was hardly off base when he claimed, "schizophrenia may be a necessary consequence of literacy."[20] In the digital age, schizophrenia may very well be a prerequisite.

It is hardly surprising that cyber bullying has become such a massive issue. The bully and bullying are no longer physically confined to a psychical place. And the amount of information and sources of self-doubt of the victim are broadcast far more widely.

And these are the terms on which marketers and programmers think. The social network is the place where they act.

Mining the Shallows

> It is a common fallacy, though, to think of platforms as merely facilitating networking activities; instead, the construction of platforms and social practices is mutually constitutive.
>
> — Jose von Dijck[21]

The link between social networking and technological production is vital. The point is, after all, to find ways to keep participation constant and consistent: to be always on.

Capitalists are no strangers to malicious forms of aggressive marketing. For a technocrat like Zuckerberg, it's clearly a two way street. New phone technology allows for updates to his system and updates to Facebook sell new phones.

The mobile phone industry is, after all, a force to be reckoned with. An industry report projects revenues to pass $2 trillion by 2017. As it stands now, 3.2 billion people are active mobile network subscribers.[22]

This is a massive economic force. Planned obsolescence is no new concept in terms of acquiring wealth. As the technology advances, so does the life expectancy decrease. But as the cell phone and its programs become the only acceptable form of communication, their monumental costs simply become a begrudgingly accepted burden.

The average smartphone in 2013 cost $337.[23] Imagine running into you from a decade ago and saying that's what you would be paying for a phone and that it would only have an expected lifespan of 2 years, at best. The absurdity of it is lost both in the cost of owning and using a cellphone (the average 2013 bill in the US weighed in over $700 per year[24]) but, as we'll get to in the following section, the ecological and social costs far outweigh all others.

Beyond planned obsolescence lies functional obsolescence: the perception that a technology is no longer functional in comparison to its contemporary options. You see this rampantly in the cell phone world where even replacing a battery or charger on a 2-year-old phone can be a feat. Just as with the News Feed, if you can't keep up, you are left to believe that you will drown.

But the function here is key.

The technologies being actively developed and sold serve a single purpose: to further entrap the user into the social network.

To become the algorithm.

When Facebook finally went public in 2012, Zuckerberg spoke to investors like old friends: "Advertising works most effectively when it's in line with what people are already trying to do. And people are trying to communicate in a certain way on Facebook — they share information with their friends, they learn about what their friends are doing —so there's really a whole new opportunity for a new type of advertising model within that."[25]

The very notion of creating an all-encompassing platform for communication is to expand into previously unreachable areas. This is why Facebook bought Foursquare: an application that "checks in" and posts on your News Feed where you physically go. Not to be left behind, they also purchased Atlas: an application that tracks offline purchases.[26]

This information is key to automation.

Every time you ask Google or Siri a question, Google, Apple and the NSA are listening.

The goal of programmers is to track your movements, decisions, thoughts and statements to create algorithms to predict and influence your actions. The cell phone, an early platform for GPS tracking, is the perfect platform for this. It is on your person, it is your electronic leash and confidant. It's an object you can stare at with intent when you don't feel like making eye contact or uncomfortable small talk.

And it is a tool to continually gather information about you.

Little is telling about the power of the temporary and shallow nature of new information from the Void than how quickly the outrage over the exposed US government's far and wide reaching surveillance programs died. Nothing changed, but everything was accepted. If the alternative option was to give up on cell phones and social networking, then it was an uncomfortable, but possibly necessary evil.

The users could live with it.

Less surprising was the FBI's official call out to social media corporations and platforms requiring them to offer a "back door" to organize, gather and collect information that might have been unavailable through real world social networking.[27]

Though science fiction writers might have dreamed being the first to come up with a technology as absurd as Google Glass (a literal technologically infused lens) it is in the more common forms of technology that the programmers claim their victories.

We chose to take part in this inexplicably vast social experiment and database without seeing it as a choice.

Again, this comes down to a redirection of impulses. The world that we live in is one in which every decision, purchase and action that we make has dire consequences across this globalized, technologically dependent world.

This is not the connectedness that hunter-gatherers knew and felt.

This is far from the relationship with the breath that moves through all things which our wild souls are intertwined with.

This is a vast, intentional, disconnected hyper-dependence. Our minds are wired for nomadic movements within familiar landscapes. That is how we are shaped. Our hunter-gatherer minds are bioregional in practice and global in spirit, but not consequence.

The unnatural world that civilization has created and Modernity has accelerated are simply too large for our minds to even comprehend. Our inability to empathize with the consequences of our actions is literally out of our world.[28] Programmers and marketers know this.

And they prey upon it.

So it is hardly ironic when Zuckerberg famously proclaimed: "A squirrel dying in front of your house may be more relevant to your interests right now than people dying in Africa."[29] The use of the word 'relevant' obscures the horrific confluence of our realm of being and our realm of understanding. Zuckerberg, like all other programmers, knows that when faced with the challenge of addressing the consequences of our actions, it's far easier to sink back into the reality that they've sold us than to address the one we live in. We'll get back to this, but it's pertinent for understanding the pathological drive of the social network for directing our impulses and how they can do it.

And the reality here is frightening.

If there is a canary in this coalmine, it should be Nicholas Carr's excellent book, *The Shallows: What the Internet is Doing to our Brains*. As far as I'm concerned, it's the *Silent Spring* for the crisis of the further integration of the internet and technology into every aspect and moment of our lives.

There are many points he touches on that are crucial to understanding how our interactions with technology, particularly the internet, impact the function and development of our minds.

While programmers like Zuckerberg extol the faux-virtues of transparency and giving voice to individuals through their platforms, the subtext is about instilling their vision into our minds through channeling synapses. Literally.

When we buy into or accept their mythos that the internet exists to make the world a freer, better place, stuffed beyond recognition with information, we are accepting an argument on their turf. And that turf is a confusing place.

There is almost nowhere on the internet where you aren't being sold products: be it physical, ideological or cosmological. This is the message in the medium. Information, relationships, connections and so on are all consumable. Quantifiable in nature, ever expanding in form: this is the world stripped of life and coded in binary and algorithms.

That information that you were after, that pressing question you had to Google, that curiosity that you had? Those are all starting points. The internet does act like a web. Every point is measured in its relation to others. It is a multiple-choice adventure at all times and if you weren't aware, the hyperlinks can sell you on directions that flashing ads might not.

They want you to click. They beg you to click.

Once you do, you start down their rabbit hole: this fog of consumption of information and products, opinions and trivia.

There's no explanation for how you found these random factoids when you paste them in on your News Feed, but there's a science to it.

Click. Share. Integrate.

At its heart, this visceral assault is not a new concept. We've known from the inception and integration of the television how this external and contrived fantasy (especially when driven by fright) deeply impacts our fight or flight synapse. We are overwhelmed with options even if they all lead to the same complicity.

This is how our brains work.

And this is what the programmers know.

That is why they can adjust algorithms on Facebook as a social experiment to see how the tone of a News Feed can impact worldviews. They call this "emotional contagion." To date it's been clearly exposed at least once as part of a weeklong emotional experiment conducted through tweaking the tone of shared content in your News Feed on Facebook.[30]

This is your cage.

While we are told that life without civilization was a struggle, we ignore that while things can happen fast, our minds and bodies have evolved to cope with them. Should we suddenly realize that we're being tracked or should a hunt take an immediate turn: our bodies are built to respond.

On the other hand, we were not built for prolonged exposure to over-stimulation. If anything, our inability to process the overwhelming input from life in Modernity is testimony to how much more relaxed our nomadic hunter-gatherer life really was. And yet we continually attack and offend our sensibilities. The result is exhausting, stimulating, exciting, depressing, crushing, lost, and searching all at the same time.

In true form, that is what the internet looks like: a barrage of ads, information, stimulus, and options. It is a visceral and literal distraction.

Following McLuhan, being on the internet forces the use of some senses at the expense of others: "We can assume," Carr observes, "that the neural circuits devoted to scanning, skimming, and multitasking are expanding and strengthening, while those used for reading and thinking deeply, with sustained concentration, are weakening or eroding."[31]

And the biology behind this is worse.

Not only are we impacting what senses are being used; we are altering the way our brains take in information. To move from short-term to long-term memory, a particular event or piece of knowledge requires a sense of depth, a memorable moment. It stops the flood of input in our waking lives long enough for the mind to find a reason to hold on to it.

As enraging as your online arguments can get or as off-putting as something might be, when read on the internet, the form dictates function in the mind. In a sea of distraction, all things are given equal footing. And our minds don't take the sensory overload of one site more seriously than others.

We are losing the ability to remember.

Our brain treats the internet as an external source: the very warehouse of information that the programmers have sold to us. We don't need to retain this full information because we can access it at any time through our computers or, more commonly, our phone. To say, "Google it," is hardly a passive phrase, it is an intrinsic change in the way they we find information.

We no longer gather it; we just seek it out when we need to reference it.

And then it is released again into the internet. This is not an intentional process on our part, but it is absolutely underpinning the nature of our relationship with the world through the megamachine. This is the suffocating void: that fogged sense of place, filled with the pressures to maintain existence while always searching for another reason to prolong the presence.

As Carr states, we are "outsourcing memory" and, in doing so, we are outsourcing function. This is our integration with the machine, our delusional participation in the Spectacle and yet it's as though we're not even there.

It's worth quoting Carr at length here:

> *The influx of competing messages that we receive whenever we go online not only overloads our working memory; it makes it harder for our frontal lobes to concentrate our attention on any one thing.*

> *The process of memory consolidation can't even get started. And, thanks once again to the plasticity of our neuronal pathways, the more we use the Web, the more we train our brain to be distracted – to process information very quickly and very efficiently but without sustained attention. That helps explain why many of us find it hard to concentrate even when we're away from our computers. Our brains become adept at forgetting, inept at remembering. Our growing dependence on the Web's information stores may in fact be the product of a self-perpetuating, self-amplifying loop. As our use of the Web makes it harder for us to lock information into our biological memory, we're forced to rely more and more on the Net's capacious and easily searchable artificial memory, even if it makes us shallower thinkers.*[32]

The machine is not controlling your mind: the machine is absorbing it.

This eternal present comes at the death of memory while the future hangs in the balance. It is widely noted that nomadic hunter-gatherers lack a sense of anything other than cyclical time. Living within the realm of an immediate return subsistence, it's easy to conflate our sense of immediate gratification. These are two greatly opposing realities: one lives in honor of the past and the future, the other exists at their expense.

The real world struggles to keep up. Amazon, the largest internet retailer in the US, pushed Sunday delivery as an option, is working on same day delivery, always offers one or two day shipping, and is just one of many corporations trying to cash in on streaming and immediately available content.

While our nomadic hunter-gatherer lives are typified by immediate return interactions, this sad repackaging of immediate gratification is an entirely different beast. It sacrifices long term relationships and sustainability for short-term acquisition. Another impulse to feed. Another plug to fill. A furthering of our integration with technology.

We are addicts.

But we wind up here for the same reason, every single time: we are lost. Our minds are wandering instead of our bodies, but they remain untethered and the internet provides an oasis for the search.

This is the restlessness.

The search is trying to find a light within the void. But the search is complacency. As long as we are lost, we are logged on. Our memory is as long as our News Feed. Our feelings are as deep as our memories.

Our tragedy is that as our world burns, we lose the very ability to even remember it was there.

And so civilization pummels along. Taking all of us with it.

Producing the Void

> *In the event of non-accidental injuries (including suicide, self mutilation, etc.), I agree that the company has acted properly in accordance with relevant laws and regulations, and will not sue the company, bring excessive demands, take drastic actions that would damage the company's reputation or cause trouble that would hurt normal operations.*
>
> – Foxconn's required anti-suicide clause for employees.[33]

It's easy to see the abyss of nothingness that is being sold to us as a First World problem, yet the fact that nearly a quarter of the Earth's population regularly uses Facebook indicates the depth of its pervasiveness.

Our daily lives, now more than ever, the fabric of our "social" lives, are soaked in blood.

While our ability to comprehend or empathize wanes, our footprint spreads exponentially.

Let's start with those phones.

Most of our phones are made in Shenzhen, China. And it is a city built on cell phones. "Twenty-five years ago it was a fishing village surrounded by rice paddies. Today it is an urban sprawl of 12 million people" observes journalist Fred Pearce.[34]

This is the home of Foxconn's now notorious sweatshops.

Foxconn runs the leading technological production facilities. This is currently where most Apple and Sony products are made, Blackberrys as well in their heyday. The reason they got some news was shocking: employees were forced to sign an anti-suicide clause. According to Wikipedia's numbers, up till 2013, at least 24 workers had killed themselves: the wretched working conditions, exposure to toxic chemicals, monotony of industrialized production, and overall depression being the clear common causes.

The most common method of suicide was jumping from the rooftops of the factories and corporate housing (if we can use the term that liberally), so the response of the corporation? Install netting around the rooftops to catch jumping workers.

Foxconn, for many living beings, sounds like hell.

The marketers promote the myth throughout civilization that you have a choice. And to some degree it is true. You can not purchase a smartphone, the catch is that it is that you are expected to. Consumers laud this as a choice: you lose your right to complain once you bought in. This is the Litmus Test for compliance in the Void. The presumptions here, however, are disgustingly off.

The presumption carried on is that people go to sweatshops because they want jobs. This may be true for some, but there's a long standing colonial and imperial legacy that is endemic (predominantly, though not exclusively) throughout the southern hemisphere whereby subsistence societies live in areas that would otherwise be useful for, let's say, the production of rare earth metals.

In some places, it's just easier to demolish any access to subsistence just to build factories and create a work force. If you can no longer harvest from the land directly, then you need to buy food.

But back to the rare earth minerals example (believe me, there are many options), your phone would not exist without them. Here in Shenzhen, tantalum is used to help make phone batteries lighter and last longer. That tantalum, however, comes from Congo, where forests are cleared by military leaders (often not on the State's side) to build what can only be considered shanty-mining villages.

And who works there? Prisoners, those caught in the crossfire, and, quite often, children.[35]

And these places are horrifically dangerous.

But for your phone to be lightweight and last longer off the charger, a constant and ongoing civil war will find bodies to fill, dig, and exhume those mines.

Then those materials are processed and assembled by overworked and tired hands in China before being sold to you. And while this new phone has a separate light to notify you when something is happening on your Facebook News Feed, every part of that contraption was possibly the worst part of another dozen people's lives.

And this goes on for every single piece of technology that you have in your pocket.

Never mind that those metals are both rare and irreplaceable.[36] Or on that they are on the verge of non-existence.[37] Or that they and their processing are absolutely toxic.[38] We are killing the earth, poisoning water ways, driving species to extinction, forcing labor, keeping sweatshops open, and on, for a device that allows nearly half of the earth's population to remain constantly in contact without ever just being there.

And this is how civilization ends: consumed by an uncaring and unfeeling impulse to reach out to those who are strangers surrounding us.

Lest you think the problem is simply capitalism, those operating the mines, work camps, poppy fields and mono-cropped farms are quite often socialist revolutionaries. No matter who is in control: this is the point that Modernity has gotten us into.

It is a quagmire of drifting along on limited resources with a sense of infinite wants and no fulfillment.

And it is here that our lives, the lives of all beings on this planet and the earth itself are bound. And as we sheepishly reload our News Feed, this is the world that is passing us by.

It's not okay.

We're not okay.

The problems that surround us, the emptiness of Modernity, the thing that has us looking at screens instead of into eyes is a distraction. It is life automated. As you shudder away from that frightening noise, the clutter, the crowds, the moment you look up mindlessly from your phone; you are confronted with all of this.

And it is too much.

It is suffocating. It is an endless nothingness, a weight on the lungs, a turning in the stomach, an unidentified repulsion.

The temptation is to look away. That is why we don't even have the words to address this plague, to address how the hardwired matrix became an invisible leash. We aren't confronting it. And the programmers, the domesticators of Modernity, are counting on the fact that we are losing the very ability to even situate or reconcile our loss and context.

They are counting on our inability to recognize the world around us.

And yet this is not the world as it exists.

The earth is suffering from the consequences, but it is still alive. The wildness refuses to be tamed. It refuses to succumb to the machine.

Our hunter-gatherer minds and bodies know this, despite everything that we have been taught. These misdirected impulses and synapses linger amidst the confusion. That is why we still reach out in the first place.

That is why these caged birds Tweet.

In that moment, that second when we look up, that second when we feel the crushing realness of our circumstance, we are human. We are afraid. We are scared. We are lonely.

And we do have a choice.

If given the chance, these realities will never be reconciled. These words might be etched forever in silicon and roam electrical feeds so long as the power lasts, but that feeling is real. This world is real.

It is our work to smash the distraction. To pull the plug. To render the machines useless.

To see this world the way our bodies feel it and our minds know it, there is no other option but the annihilation of civilization. We have guides. We have instincts.

We have our wildness.

So before we are lost in a sea of unending, constant nothingness: to take the first step, we must first look up. Breathe deep.

And fight back.

Endnotes

1. Zygmunt Bauman, *Liquid Modernity*. Blackwell: Malden, MA. Pg. 8.
2. http://www.wired.com/2011/06/internet-a-human-right/ Retrieved 12-29-2014.
3. This vastly increasing occurrence does have a name: "Phantom Vibration Syndrome." A word first used in print in 2003 by Robert Jones who reiterated his earlier thoughts ten years later with the following comment: "Whether PVS is the result of tissue over-stimulation, neuro-psychological unconscious bias, a genuine mental health issue, or all of the above, this persistent phenomenon indicates that we long ago crossed the line in the sands of privacy in this "always on" society." From: http://inclusiveworks.com/cn-executive-coaching-corner/phantom-vibration-syndrome-update/ Retrieved 12-29-2014.
4. See Paul Shepard, *Nature and Madness*. University of Georgia Press: Athens, GA. 1998 and *Coming Home to the Pliestocene*. Island Press: Washington DC. 1998.
5. Lewis Mumford. *The Myth of the Machine*. Harcourt, Brace & World: New York. 1966, Pg. 3.
6. Jerry Mander. *In the Absence of the Sacred*. Sierra Club Books: San Francisco. 1992, Pg 190.
7. The link between domestication and religion is vital. I've touched on it elsewhere and will be elaborating on it in upcoming works. A solid book on the subject is Morris Berman's *Wandering God*. State University of New York Press: Albany, 2000.
8. See John Zerzan's on-point essay "Faster!" in *Black and Green Review no 1*.
9. According to a PEW Research survey: http://www.pewresearch.org/fact-tank/2013/06/06/cell-phone-ownership-hits-91-of-adults/ Retried 12-29-2012.
10. Lee Rainie and Barry Wellman, *Networked*. MIT Press: Cambridge. 2012, Pg. 12.
11. http://www.textinganddrivingsafety.com/texting-and-driving-stats/ Retrieved 12-29-2014. That's 23% of car accidents in case you were wondering.
12. http://readwrite.com/2012/02/01/zuckerbergs_letter_to_shareholders_personal_relationships_are_the_fundamental_unit_of_our_society Retrieved 12-31-2014.
13. http://www.telegraph.co.uk/technology/facebook/11194049/Facebook-profits-pass-1bn-as-more-users-log-on-every-day.html Retrieved 1-1-2015
14. Marshall McLuhan, *The Gutenberg Galaxy*. Signet: New York. 1969, pg 35.
15. http://www.cdc.gov/nchs/data/databriefs/db76.pdf Retrieved 1-2-2015.
16. http://news.yahoo.com/number-active-users-facebook-over-230449748.html Retrieved 1-2-2015.
17. Chellis Glendinning, *My Name is Chellis & I'm in Recovery from Western Civilization*. Shambhala: Boston. 1994, Pg. 101.
18. Jose van Djick, *The Culture of Connectivity: A Critical History of Social Media*. Oxford University Press: Oxford. 2013, Pg. 8

19. http://www.wired.com/2009/06/mark-zuckerberg-speaks/ Retrieved 12-31-2014.
20. McLuhan, 1969, pg. 32.
21. Ibid, pg. 6.
22. http://www.gsmamobileeconomy.com/GSMA%20Mobile%20Economy%202013.pdf Retrieved 12-31-2014.
23. http://www.idc.com/getdoc.jsp?containerId=prUS24461213 Retrieved 1-2-2015.
24. http://www.dailytech.com/Average+Mobile+Phone+Bill+in+US+is+Growing+Despite+Competition/article34485.htm Retrieved 1-2-2015.
25. http://content.time.com/time/business/article/0,8599,1644040,00.html Retrieved 12-31-2014.
26. http://www.wired.com/2014/12/facebook-atlas-google/ Retrieved 1-3-2015.
27. http://www.cnet.com/news/fbi-we-need-wiretap-ready-web-sites-now/ Retrieved 12-30-2014.
28. I touch on this point in more detail in my essay 'Everywhere and Nowhere: the Pathology of the Machine' from my book, *For Wildness and Anarchy* (Black and Green Press, 2009). It's also, ironically, easy to find online.
29. David Kirkpatrick. *The Facebook Effect*. Simon & Schuster: New York. Pg. 181.
30. http://www.theatlantic.com/technology/archive/2014/06/everything-we-know-about-facebooks-secret-mood-manipulation-experiment/373648/ Retrieved 12-30-2014.
31. Nicholas Carr. *The Shallows*. WW Norton: New York. 2011, Pg. 141.
32. Ibid, Pg. 194.
33. http://shanghaiist.com/2010/05/26/translated_foxconns_employee_non-su.php Retrieved 1-1-2015.
34. Fred Pearce. *Confessions of an Eco-Sinner: Tracking Down the Sources of My Stuff*. Beacon Press: Boston. 2008, Pg. 200. Despite it's liberal guilt sounding title, it's actually a really great book.
35. Ibid. Pgs 203-206. Kevin Bales' *Disposable People* (University of California Press: Berkeley. 2000) is also an indispensible source on the matter.
36. http://gizmodo.com/the-metals-in-your-phone-arent-just-rare-theyre-irre-1477904295 Retrieved 12-28-2014.
37. http://www.sciencedirect.com/science/article/pii/S0360544212008055 Retrieved 12-28-2014.
38. http://www.theguardian.com/sustainable-business/rare-earth-mining-china-social-environmental-costs Retrieved 12-28-2014.

Hooked on a Feeling:
The Loss of Community and the Rise of Addiction

> *Bored, miserable creatures are more likely to seek altered consciousness than engaged, contented ones. Animals in captivity, for example, are much more likely to use intoxicants than those in the wild. And one could say that civilization itself represents a state of captivity.*
> - David Courtwright, Forces of Habit[1]

> *Addiction, in one form or another, characterizes every aspect of industrial society*
> - Morris Berman, The Re-Enchantment of the World[2]

His body was found hours after life had escaped it.

Lying against the wall between two bedroom windows there were two options for what might have been his last sight. One was looking out the window into the night sky. Perhaps it was peacefully calm and the sky was filled with stars. Possibly it was covered in a late fall haze from passing storms. Either of which would feel serene in comparison to the alternate view: the junkie's toolbox; a metal spoon bent at the tip of the handle, a lighter, a syringe, and a belt, his belt, strewn about the floor. Beyond that kit was the false hope of a closed door and its potential for life saving help.

Before this particular night, the door opened. Someone was there or someone came in to respond, to pull him back to life, to stop his body from shutting down forever as heroin invaded his blood stream, inhibiting endorphins and overwhelming the body with such a euphoric relaxation that the body can literally forget to breathe.

This time the door didn't open. No one was there to stop this well-rehearsed play from reaching its logical and biological conclusion.

As he slumped against the wall, a fatal dose of heroin overtook his body. His respiratory system shut down. Life loosened its grasp for the final time and Mike was gone.

He was my brother.

And I want to believe his last sight was looking out the window.

That he might have seen something, anything, other than the empty room where he died alone.

Some wounds never heal. Within civilization, some are never given the chance.

We have taken the unfortunate position within Modernity to treat addiction, a chemical or social dependency upon substances or activities, as a personal flaw. A stigma: a sign of failure. We point to the most extreme examples of addiction to feel superior, to take pride in our own polite complicity.

But it's not that simple.

Particular addictions might be more obvious than others, but the impulse for addiction in general is something that we all carry within us. As eco-psychologist Chellis Glendinning contextualizes it, "addiction is an attempt to avoid confronting the pain that lies at the heart of the traumatic experience."[3] That experience: the domestication process, the universal experience within every civilized society. The tie that binds us.

Domestication in terms of plants and animals is an external force. It is a tinkering on the genetic level to breed out "undesirable" traits and increase those that conform. It is something put upon them.

For humans, the process isn't as simple: human domestication is social in nature. Our captivity is a matter of circumstance, not breeding. The domestication process in every single society where it is present attacks the same elements of our nature: the need for community, the need for place, the need to feel like a part of something. All needs that move beyond the simple axiom of food, clothing and shelter. Domesticators, priests, politicians, and programmers all recognize that if they want our obedience they have to divert our bodies and our minds. If you look at the circumstances for humans outside of First World privileges, it becomes increasingly clear that force is the primary method. But even in the slums, shanties, and missionary camps, you catch the glimpse of the other side of the equation, the part those of us in the First and Second worlds are more familiar with: the illusion of choice. The dream of prosperity and wealth. Hopes for a better life ahead.

We look to the propagators of our misery for handouts. But the trauma that Chellis speaks of is the intuitive feeling, the deep-seated want for something more: for substance over subsistence. We may not be able to name it, but we seek it out.

And some of us are less able to keep that search under wraps. Looking back to Chellis again, the "hallmark" of addiction "is an *out-of-control, often aimless, compulsion* to fill the lost sense of belonging, integrity, and communion with substances like alcohol and food, through experiences like falling in love or gambling. The addicted person is trying desperately to satisfy real needs—but since either the external situation or the internal climate does not allow for satisfaction, she turns to secondary sources."[4]

We don't chastise the addicts because they are failures. We chastise them because their excesses are a reflection of our search, our escapes. Addicts are the dirty laundry of domesticated societies. We admire them when they hit bottom and wake up. When they overcome their addictions and fall in line like the rest of us. They become the subjects of movies, talk shows, and gossip columns about their success in attaining complicity.

Externalizing their situation, we continue in desperation to satisfy our own real needs. Alone together, we quietly find ways to fill our void.

And we continue to perpetuate the trauma of meaninglessness as we further internalize the domestication process.

Mike was neither the first nor the last relative or friend to die from an overdose, but the words "death by acute heroin overdose" on the death certificate in my hands were absolute. He was the first person that I had lost to heroin just before the current national heroin epidemic would fully take root. Between 2002 and 2013, there was a 286% increase in deaths caused by heroin overdose. This came alongside a doubling of the number of actual heroin users in the same time period.[5]

According to the Center for Disease Control, heroin claimed 8,200 lives within the US in 2013. It quickly spread across all demographics.[6] Ushered by a surge in Oxycodone, a pharmaceutical opiate widely sold as OxyContin, a highly addictive and fast acting pain reliever, opioids found a new audience amongst the dispossessed.

The seekers.
The lost.
The bored.
Those who can't tolerate the crushing despair and disappointment that modernity has left us with. That is a percentage of the population that is growing exponentially. Even with a quadrupling of heroin related deaths in just over a decade, heroin is just a fraction of the 2013 average of over 100 fatal opioid related deaths *per day* in the US in 2013.[7]

And that number continues to rise. Quickly.

In 2014, that number rose to 125 opioid related deaths in the US daily.[8]

Heroin may be the more dramatic of addictions, but it promises its users a quick escape. As our technologically infused lives speed up, increasingly drastic measures deliver the promise of immediate gratification. For most of us, our addictions may appear slower: addiction to sugar, to alcohol, to social media, to an unending stream of 24 hour news or gossip, to video games, to misery, to shopping, to legal or illegal substances; all of us are looking for that distraction. We can escape into the vices of domestication to ignore the empty feeling, that longing deep within.

We crave that moment where giving in doesn't have to feel like giving up.

We crave that moment where dopamine hits our blood stream and spreads throughout our bodies. That moment where we can feel something. We crave feelings of euphoria. And we have shown that we will seek it out at any cost.

Despite everything that we have experienced in the shill of a life that civilization has brought us, we were not programmed by millions of years of evolution to desire nor to thrive in misery. The nomadic hunter-gatherer written into each of us knows this.

The forager's band is where our social life evolved. That place where life is a known rather than a question. Where we don't have to second-guess our purpose and significance. That place where we can exist, where we can share space, experience and presence.

This community is the place where we belong.

This is the place where we can air our vulnerabilities and give our fears an outlet so that together the community, the band, the society, can move on with life. It is here that wildness is embraced, that egalitarian relationships flourish, and that the complexities of life are understood without delusion.

It is our nature, as living beings, to be cautious. But it is not our nature to become absorbed by fear, to want and to seek out diversions. That is what domestication brings.

When we seek diversions, when we seek euphoria and ecstasy by whatever artificial means we have chosen, we are searching for that piece of ourselves that we find within each other. As animals, we have needs. And those needs extend beyond the tooth-and-nail material necessities that survival requires. Within each of us is that yearning: the want to see beyond survival, to live.

As humans, as animals, as a part of the community of wildness: we want to feel and live our purpose rather than to merely think it.

In lieu of direct experience, the domesticators have learned that we will take substitutes.

Their greatest fear is that we will realize that we don't have to.

Narcotics, sedatives, and other intoxicating substances aren't new. Modernity did not create them, but isolation drives us to them. Exponentially.

What these substances are is an indicator. As domestication, sedentary life, and civilization increase, so too does the reliance upon intoxicating substances within societies. The immediacy and integrated existence of capable individuals working as a cohesive group enmeshed into the landscape can itself bring about those ecstatic states to heal worn bonds, to cope with the stress that life can bring, and to ease social tensions that arise when animals constantly interact with each other.

It is the removal from that place and circumstance, that connectivity, where doubt creeps in and the substances become the first of many necessary escapes. They become the instigator of specialization. The spirit of the warriors. The metaphysical justifier of hierarchs. The numbing fuel for workers, soldiers and consumers.

The history of domestication runs parallel with the ritual and habitual use of intoxicating substances. A by-product of alienation, exacerbated through war and technology, something like the current global heroin epidemic where people are literally injecting venom into their veins is a stinging reminder of our own removal. Our inability to cope with or recognize our own disconnect from the world and each other is the invitation.

For us to exist in this world as sane, functioning and healthy beings, we need to have relationships that give us the space to be joyful, enthusiastic, miserable, grumpy, sad, ecstatic, and whatever other emotion we are going to cycle through. The sense of isolation that we carry is a direct result of the sedentary lives we live as civilized people.

We are products of circumstance.

The gaping hole that addiction fills begins here: at the unresolved tensions of existence. Of not being given the place to express fear, anger, and joy without losing the ground we stand on.

The ingenuity of nomadic hunter-gatherer societies doesn't lie in some mystical sense of New Age Oneness embodied by all of its participants. Hunter-gatherers, like us, are human. That means they, like us, are far from perfect. They, like us, don't have to be.

What is most telling about these societies is that they are *functionally* egalitarian in a sustainable manner. This state of primal anarchy works. And it works because their societies are pragmatic.

To highlight the pragmatism of nomadic hunter-gatherer societies might seem at odds with our understandings of the world. Within civilization we uphold our hyper-rationalism and etiquette as virtues. This is our presumption, but we mistake diplomacy for balance.

Civilization places politeness over honesty.

"Niceism," as John Zerzan aptly called it, "keeps us all in our places, confusedly reproducing all that we supposedly abhor."[9] Civilization can endure atrocity and the horrific because it needs atrocious and horrific things to happen so that flicking on a power switch yields results. What it cannot endure is endemic negativity. We must always act "civilized" because we are forced, by proximity, to have to deal with each other.

The fragility of our society is most apparent in its incessant need for all of us to internalize its failings. If we didn't, then the whole sham falls apart. So we uphold politeness as a virtue even as we suffocate each other. I think all of us have seen how effective that method really is.

Conversely, one of the primary reasons that immediate return hunter-gatherer societies, that is nomadic hunter-gatherer societies who do not store food,[10] function is because they're built around our imperfect reality: to state it clearly, hunter-gatherers know that we can't always get along and they act accordingly.

Mobility is the greatest factor here. In terms of reducing social (alongside ecological) stress, hunter-gatherer bands simply move often. Hunting and gathering is a system of procurement that requires going off into the surrounding world, in groups or alone, often daily. It gives people time away.

Movement is the greatest form of conflict resolution.

Flux, as observed by Colin Turnbull amongst the foraging Mbuti of the Congo and the Ik of Uganda, Kenya, and Sudan is a "highly effective social mechanism." Groups and camps have no overarching identity or organization, which encourages the movement of individuals between them. This creates "a fluid band composition, a loose form of social structure" that allows individuals to simply remove themselves from social tension rather than to force proximity.[11]

James Woodburn adds to this that the Hadza (hunter-gatherers in Tanzania) "make use of environmental explanations to justify nomadic movements which ease conflict."[12] Some disputes are best resolved by simply walking away.

The importance of this is emphasized in how *mobility as virtue* is ingrained early in life. Amongst the Mbuti, there's effectively an internal society of children, the *bopi* (loosely translated as "children's playground"). Within it:

> *children will find that mobility is one of their prime techniques for avoiding or for resolving a dispute, for once they move elsewhere their spheres move with them and the dispute is discarded. ... Chortles quickly become laughter, and this laughter becomes the Mbuti's prime weapon against conflict, aggression, and violence.*[13]

It cannot be overlooked that for many, like the Mbuti, "the one really strong cohesive factor is simply the forest itself."[14] The forest, the desert, the plains; whatever the wild community is that surrounds a group is vital to the health and well-being of the individual. Wildness is an actor in these societies, not merely a backdrop.[15] That adds another dimension to the curative powers and the conflict resolving nature of movement.

On the Importance of Healing

Mobility is just one form of conflict resolution.
    Bonding is another.
    Healing, group activity, playing, singing, and dancing: these are the tools that a functioning community has at hand. When the individuals are participants rather than mere spectators, tensions can dissolve. The community pulls itself together. It confronts tension by putting it front and center, by enacting ritualistic displays of conflict.
    Looking again to the Mbuti, children and adolescents engage regularly in group games, some rougher than others. Tug-of-war is a prime example. A game that we almost all recognize, but in this context there is a ritualization of conflict resolution through enacting it. Turnbull observes that it "is expected that the conflict will arise within the age grade of adulthood, to some extent it is their role to manifest such conflict, and it is the role of youth to resolve such conflict if they cannot avert it."[16]
    These kinds of games interweave an ongoing thread throughout hunter-gatherer life: to blur the lines between entertainment,

healing and conflict resolution. If games can mitigate conflict, then there is no reason why life shouldn't err on the side of fun, of happiness, and enjoyment. That is a sad reminder for those of us afflicted by Modernity.

So what does this have to do with addiction, with intoxication?

This is where the ingenuity of function within immediate return societies comes back into play: their rituals, those daily or weekly outbreaks of communal healing and bonding, work because they make people happy. Mobility can resolve tension, but attaining euphoric states as a community can dissolve them.

The healing dance is a near universal amongst nomadic hunter-gatherer societies. Variations are relatively minor, but the form is almost universal. Dances are largely unorganized, unplanned. They can be started or stopped on a whim. They encourage group involvement and often centralize around ritualistic enactments of causes of group tension; sexuality, relationships, aging, and the like. They often begin as the sun goes down and can last all night or as long as the participants get joy from them.

The purpose is to achieve ecstatic states. To experience mutual derived joy. While the dances can occur around illness and their participants largely attest to their ability to heal or comfort the sick, the healing spoken of here is social and psychological in nature. Anthropologist James Woodburn reiterated of the *epeme* dance of the Hadza in Tanzania "that the point of the ceremony is to heal rifts and bring everyone together."[17]

But what is telling is that ecstatic states are reached through the combination of singing and dancing (with or without a fire). Historically speaking, it is the lack of substances used to attain these states that makes them particularly relevant here: healing requires communal engagement. Intoxicants serve to bring individuals to euphoric states, but the dances take an entire community there. The want for an individualistic indulgence largely does not exist within these societies prior to contact and conquest by neighboring or intruding societies.

In his 1971 survey of hunter-gatherer societies, anthropologist Carleton Coon observes that until "outsiders began bothering them" nomadic hunter-gatherer societies were notably free from the use of intoxicants.[18] Intoxicants exist in the wild, but the circumstances for using them largely do not.

But it is worth making a further clarification.

It is improbable that nomadic hunter-gatherers never had interactions with intoxicating plants, as we shall see with peyote, a number of them are used for medicinal reasons, typically below the threshold of intoxication. I'm specifying habitual and ritual use because they are cultural phenomena: a reflection of what communities find of value. Among nomadic hunter-gatherers, that indicates an implicit disregard for intoxicating substances prior to colonization or settlements. It is the correlation of the habitual and ritual use of intoxicating substances with domestication alongside the lack of substances in attaining group ecstasy that is most telling.[19]

I have to take a step back here.

Looking further into the details of communal healing and methods of resolution, it is no wonder that isolation within hunter-gatherer societies is a non-issue.

And at the same time it is no wonder that isolation is such an issue within Modernity. We literally build walls around ourselves. We live amongst strangers. We bury ourselves within a society that "is made up of vast numbers of traumatized individuals" where the only universal is an unspoken, unaddressed and on-going trauma.[20] Our tension isn't met with joy; it is catered to with *violence as entertainment* in movies, video games, or the faceless bullying of the internet.

We can see the power of community through healing dances because the absence of our own community, of place, of touch, weighs so heavily on each of us. Even addressing that void directly tears at my soul: this is domestication, this is our lives redirected. This is the human animal, removed from context, just destroying itself, over and over and over again trying to find that piece of us that only exists within each other.

And as we walk past each other in unthinkable numbers, each of us carrying our personalized traumas, the community we need is literally all around us, but at the same time so buried in constant socialization and the virtues of commodification that we just don't reach out until after we break. That is if we ever reach out at all.

Healing, that term so bastardized by self-help gurus and conferences, offers us real grounding. And yet we give it no real outlet unless it's just another commodified attempt to find solace in the cracks of complacency.

For hunter-gatherers, healing isn't a *retreat*. It is an *engagement*. Among the Huaorani of Ecuador, tensions surrounding gender are ritualized not as "an expression of hostility" but "as a means to overcome potential conflict and transform social division into necessary complementarity."[21] Unlike the religious rituals of priests, communal healing is an outpouring of the anarchistic spirituality of life integrated with the community of wildness.

It is accessible to all.

As we will see in two immediate return hunter-gatherer societies, it is the bonds of community that allows the 'healing energies' (*n/um* for the Ju/'hoansi, *be* for the Pygmies) to arise.

N/um[22]

> *Community is at the dance, and the dance establishes community. … In a real sense, it is the community, in its activation of* n/um, *which heals and is healed. … And there are no restrictions in the access to* n/um. *In egalitarian fashion, all receive healing.* N/um *is shared throughout the community. It is not meant to be hoarded by one person; perhaps it never can be.*
> — Richard Katz, *Boiling Energy*[23]

The true spirit of egalitarian societies is exemplified by the healing rituals of the San, hunter-gatherers of the Kalahari. That ritual is called *kia* and its purpose is to attain "an altered state of consciousness, enhanced to the degree and quality of transcendence."[24]

As the San see it, *kia* is meant to activate *n/um*, a "substance that lies in the pit of the stomach of men and women who are *n/um k"ausi*—medicine owners" which "becomes active during a healing dance." The dancers heat *n/um* through dance and song induced trance until it boils and "rises up the spinal cord and explodes in the brain."[25] The !Kung consider it to have been passed on through their culture, a claim they can easily verify through depictions in their ancient rock art.[26]

The ritual is initiated by healers, beginning at night and lasting as long as it takes for the *n/um*, or "boiling energy," to do its work. It is important to distinguish healers from shamans. Healers lack specialization, their role isn't to interpret the world but to take part in collectively giving in to it. It has not been uncommon to find that most of the adults at any given location consider themselves to be healers.[27]

N/um is available to everyone. As Nisa, a !Kung woman and healer, puts it: "Both men and women learn how to cure with it, but not everyone wants to. Trance-medicine really hurts!"[28] The physical and emotional toll of leading that transcendent state isn't to be taken lightly. There is nothing personal about *n/um* and no expectation to take on the role of a healer. Healers take on *n/um* for the sake of the group, the culture and themselves simultaneously and without contradiction.[29]

The dance itself starts off spontaneously. Unless it is meant to cure or comfort someone with a serious illness, the planning is largely non-existent.[30] It begins at night and takes place around a fire. There is a semblance of sexual division of labor with the roles, but, like all things in a truly egalitarian society, they have room for flexibility and lack any pretense of sex-based values. During the *kia* ritual, it is men that dance and enter trances. Women sing and tend the fire, yet the "men insist that it is the women who are crucial to the success of the dance. Without their sustained singing, the *n/um* cannot boil."[31]

Women entering the dance or entering trance isn't unheard of within the context of *kia*. But there is an equally important women's dance, *!Gwah tsi*, where the roles are reversed. *!Gwah tsi*, like *kia*, lacks planning and either can occur without conflict as needed, upwards of multiple times per week.

Both dances center around the creation and sustaining of involved rhythms with drums, instruments and, most importantly, vocalization. The ritual has two parts, the first is about getting the dancers to that trance state, which permits the second, a "process of curing and the collective emergent sense of fellowship."[32] The Nharo "deny any connection between *dagga* [a native plant similar in effect to marijuana that began to be used after the Nharo were settled] and the trance ritual. Instead, trance is achieved through the vigorous, sustained, and physically exhausting activity of dancing around a nocturnal fire, to the chanting of women—both the fire and the chanting producing hypnotic effects."[33] This is something that I think most of us are familiar with: the enchantment of music, friends and fire is something we are arguably drawn to on a very primal level.

The curing aspects of the ritual come through the emphasis of physical touch. Nisa describes the experience of healing:

> *As you being to trance, the n/um slowly heats inside you and pulls at you. It rises until it grabs your insides and takes your thoughts away. Your mind and your senses leave and you don't think clearly. Things become strange and start to change.*
>
> *You touch people, laying on hands, curing those you touch. When you finish, other people hold you and blow around your head and your face. Suddenly your senses go "Phah!" and come back to you. You think, "Eh hey, there are people here," and you see again as you normally do.*[34]

It is important to shake loose any notions of "ritual" that we may carry with us. I use the term because it is technically fitting, but the context shifts everything. The egalitarian, free-flowing nature of these healing rituals is as absolutely contrasting with religious ritual as virtually any civilized person would know it. So it's easy to transpose our biases and experiences. But to do so would be to miss the point entirely.

The trance element of a ritual is taken very seriously, but the gathering is far more informal (something we will see further exemplified amongst the Pygmies). It is, in effect, a "social gathering" more akin to a party than a religious ceremony. It is a "time of general excitement and festivity, a time for people to ensure their safety, to suspend conflicts, and to act out and verify the common bond that unites them." Not unafraid to ruin the vibe, people "talk, joke, flirt, and comment on everything that happens."[35]

After the trance is reached, the mood shifts to playfulness. During *kia*, all join in the dance, including women and children. While expressing *n/um* may be painful for the healer, the ecstatic joy of the group is infectious. The bonds are healed to dance another day.[36]

It is worth pointing out the relationship between mobility and healing rituals. It has been noted that the "actual frequency of dances is influenced by ecological and sociological factors."[37] Namely, the longer bands have stayed around water holes or at times of increased population density, the more often dances occur.[38] When new bands join up at a waterhole, dances can happen nightly.

This brings home an important point: hunter-gatherers are capable individuals. They learn early on how to survive, how to forage, how to hunt, how to sustain their own lives.

From an individualistic perspective, they have no real reason to seek other people out, but that fractured perspective is our own baggage. It simply doesn't exist outside of the world that domestication has created. This is further evidence of the innate needs for community that we, as humans, as animals, carry within us.

The tragedy is that it needs to be reiterated.

Be

> *I tend to consider that when people partake in a collective act, the participants behave with propriety and affinity to the group or social gathering.*
>
> - Daisuke Bondo[39]

Be among the Baka (a branch of the Pygmies of the Congo) is reminiscent of both *n/um* and the healing rituals. *Be* "as a noun means both 'song' and 'dance'."[40] Among the Mbuti, it is reflected in the *molimo* and *elima* rituals, reflecting a "community festival" led predominantly by men and women respectively.

Be and *molimo* are in some ways even less of a ritual. *Molimo* "consists of singing daily to the forest." Both men and women within the Mbuti love singing, often even more than dancing. Compared to the desert and plains dwelling San, the forests of the Congo can be filled differently by the songs of birds and calls of other animals. Anthropologist Jerome Lewis has argued convincingly that it is this ongoing symphony of the forest that language arose from, first as song and then as speech.[41]

This is something that should again sound familiar. Among the Huaorani it was noted that they were always chanting in a way that takes on a central role in their society and "plays an active role in the creation and life of society itself".[42] Melodies fold into the songs of the forest, but the lyrical content can be as mundane as just talking about the tasks at hand. But those chants also "constitute a form of cultural knowledge through which it is their very personal autonomy that co-residents come to share."

For the Mbuti, this aspect of *molimo* "is an attempt to awaken the living and benevolent forest to the band's misfortune, and to make the forest a cheerful place again."[43] The community of the wild takes on a very real and active part of daily life. It grants solace and healing. It is the essential backdrop for the more lived elements of the Mbuti ritual.

That is a lesson that is instilled from birth. Primal anarchy is built into the play of children. Within the *bopi*, the world of the Mbuti is reflected:

> *While they are learning the fun and beauty of working and playing with not against other, they are in a positive way learning by prescription rather than proscription, by being told what they should do rather than what they should not do. There is the essence of cooperative, communal life, of which competition is the antithesis. With cooperativeness in action comes community of spirit, and with community of spirit the foundation for truly social behavior is secured; social order becomes possible without law, as we know it, and without the threat of physical coercion, and without anything even approaching a penal system.*[44]

The children have their own ritual dance, *bina*, which mirrors the dances of adults and the sexual themes that will make more sense in adolescence. The *bina* is considered a social dance. It is a form of play where children are replicating the behavior of adults, preparing for the cultural world that they will be inheriting themselves.

Within the Baka, children can even take part in the *be* rituals, which are innately more spiritual and communal in nature, purely for the fun of it. For adolescent women, the rituals carry over into the *elima,* which celebrates the onset of menstruation among young girls. Menstruation is something that the Mbuti celebrate loudly. The *elima* festivals begin when two girls in a band begin menstruating within a few days of each other.[45] The ritual lasts for days and involves the entire band and extended kin.

There is an air of freedom here, the girls are not kept in secrecy nor subject to a litany of ritual restrictions in terms of diet and behavior, which we see quickly vanish as domestication arises. There is a distinct and painful chasm between how the Mbuti treat *elima* and how their neighboring agricultural villagers see it: "as far as the villagers are concerned, evil spirits emanate from the forest."[46]

For them, there is little more evil than the wildness inherent in the menstruation of women.

For the civilized, wildness and any other reminders of our animality must remain hidden. That is how weak the veneer of domestication is.

Among the Baka, *be* rituals are far more concise than the lengthy *elima* or the daily singing aspects of the *molimo* festivals. And yet, here again, we find a notable lack of formality.

Dances begin at night and take as long as is required. Unlike the San, they have no fires: only dancing and singing in the darkness of night.[47] The Hadza take that further, whose *epeme* dances "usually occur every night when there is no moon in the sky."[48] For the Hadza, *epeme* is slightly more formal in nature; it is a dance that reflects on the killing of large game. The men dance stiffly here, while the movement in other nightly dances "they can move so gracefully and beautifully" dancing with women and emulating the sounds and movements of animals.[49]

For *be* to commence, dancers simply start dancing to see if others will take part or not. The "social relationships of the Baka society" are "embodied in the performances."[50] It is telling that taking part is completely voluntary. If the energy isn't there, dances simply stop and no hard feelings are held.

There is a distinct lack of ego to any of this. If the group wants the healing, wants the dance, it happens. Otherwise camp life goes on without it. There is no residual or social tension after a dance dissolves, it either happens or it doesn't.

Community gives us the outlets necessary for attaining ecstatic joy and also gives the space to just comfortably absorb into the wild surroundings.

Without force.

Without punishment.

What we see here are intact communities that learned to mitigate conflict, to experience joy as they remain enmeshed with the world of wildness. This isn't coincidental. These societies embraced the imperfections of being human, of being animal; they danced, sang, argued, or moved their way through it. Violence wasn't unheard of but oppression, coercion, and hierarchy did not exist.

When times got tough they turned towards each other and they turned towards the wild.

There is no doubt that hunter-gatherers, foragers by their very nature, would have knowledge of intoxicating substances. But it becomes clearer why they didn't turn to them. The circumstances for addiction, the need for escape, simply weren't present. The power of community, the ability to heal bonds, to move further into the landscape, to be integrated with wildness; all of these things offer so much to define and celebrate our lives as humans, as animals.

It becomes more obvious that the question at hand has less to do with why hunter-gatherers, by and large, didn't use intoxicating substances, but why anyone else did.

Intoxicants and Interpreters: the Rise of the Shaman

> *Spontaneous healers, usually women, have always accompanied humans. But the shaman is a latecomer—part of the agricultural fear of curses and evil spirits, the use of intoxicants, the spread of male social dominance, the exploitation of domestic animals (especially the horse) as human helpers, and the shift of sedentary peoples toward spectatorship rather than egalitarian participation.*
> - Paul Shepard, *Coming Home to the Pleistocene*[51]

The myth of Progress tells us that humanity took certain steps on the way from hunter-gatherers to post-modern consumers. It would appear that humans made a conscious choice to settle, to garden, then to farm and take up warfare, expanding with increasing speed until we got in the mess we're currently in.

To state it bluntly, that never happened.

Most of the "stages" between immediate return hunter-gatherers and civilizations are unrecognizable to each other. As radically different as the societies between nomadic hunter-gatherers and hyper-technological civilizations may be, the domestication process works effectively the same way: it pulls apart our needs as human beings and redirects them. This is not to say that all of the societies in between are one in the same. That absolutely is not the case: it was almost universally sedentary *hunter-collector* societies that created civilizations. Outside of a tiny handful of examples, it wasn't gardeners.

Hunter-collector societies are hunter-gatherers who become reliant on a surplus of hunted meats (to be carried by pack animals), dried fish, or wild grains. Hunter-collector societies reflect the widest range of variation of all hunter-gatherers, going from the largely egalitarian dog-sled using hunter-gatherers of the Arctic to the hierarchical native states of sedentary hunter-collectors in the Pacific Northwest of North America or to the sedentary grain harvesters who would develop agriculture in Mesopotamia, around the Mediterranean Sea, in Ethiopia, India, and China.[52]

We'll come back around to hunter-collectors shortly, but to really understand how we've diverged from communal celebrations of ecstasy, it's worth looking at the horticultural and delayed return hunter-gatherers who began to part ways with them to understand what happened.

It must be stated clearly that this is a process that most likely happened slowly or imperceptibly. We're talking about changes that came over decades or generations unless neighbors spread their vices quickly (a tragic reality of colonization, as we will see).

What we will be focusing on here are the circumstances under which the use of intoxicants, namely in ritual, arise. This is our grey area, but it is necessary to understand how the role of the healing dance is specialized, further ritualized, and, most importantly, increasingly aided by the use of intoxicants. It's a side step in the story of addiction, but in looking closely at this spread of societies where remnants or intact pieces of our ancestral lineage of healing remain, we catch glimpses of the resilience of community and the exceptional impact of civilizations.

As most of the societies that we discuss were hit the hardest and most abruptly by the flooding spread of civilization, it's the unfortunate reality that the use of the substances left a door open, only to be followed immediately by the incorporation of the colonizer's alcohol, tools, and processed foods, often just amplifying the reality of colonization.

The results of that process are something we will return to. However, there are no secrets here, this is the living, breathing tragedy of civilized life: there is no way to have been prepared for the onslaught that civilization carries.

And it never ends well.

The link between the use of intoxicants and domestication begins with stored foods.

Societies with storage are considered *delayed return* which contrasts with the *immediate return* societies of nomadic hunter-gatherers. This might seem like a minor point, but I don't say this to damn horticulturalists and delayed return hunter-gatherer societies. I make it to understand how domestication functions.

And to that end, the distinction works.

Nomadic hunter-gatherers live in mobile bands; they are, by the nature of their subsistence, never physically removed from their land-base. They are foraging daily, hunting or fishing most days, and travelling between camps fairly often. They have no want or need for long-term storage because it's more they would have to carry or plan around.

This is an important point for understanding how egalitarian societies function: sharing is implicit. If you can't or won't store meat, fish or anything else then there is no reason not to share. This is why nomadic hunter-gatherers were personally capable of sustaining themselves in physical terms and it underlies the importance of their social relationships. It makes sense that they lacked specialists, that they had many healers instead of a few shamans: there was no real mediation between individuals, the group and the wider community of wildness.

As storage arises, either in terms of storehouses or literally being buried in gardens, so too does property. The focus slowly begins to shift from daily treks through the forest to relying on grown and stored foods. The population check afforded by "the contraceptive on the hip" (carrying and exclusively nursing a child combined with the later age of first menses among nomadic peoples) begins to fade and population pressures rise alongside ecological and social ones.

It is here that two new roles emerge: the Big Man (a precursor to the chief) and shamans (a precursor to the priest). A Big Man's role is to mitigate conflict socially; a shaman's role is to mitigate conflict spiritually, it is not uncommon that the positions overlap. Both roles arise as the first specialists in the human timeline. There was neither a place nor a need for them in nomadic hunter-gatherer bands.

The shaman becomes tasked with both healing and cosmological interpretation. While it was common for all nomadic hunter-gatherers to have interactions with spirits,[53] Mircea Eliade, in his definitive overview on shamanism, noted "'Seeing spirits,' in dream or awake, is the determining sign of the shamanic vocation."[54] The shaman took up residency between the worlds of the living and the dead. Which is why in horticultural societies throughout South America the shaman's initiation was a "ritualistic death:" "the shaman must so die that he may meet the souls of the dead and receive their teaching; for the dead know everything."

The Jivaro, Amazonian horticulturalists, exemplified this initiation rite by subjecting the shaman-to-be with intoxicants, restrictions, and blows until they lost consciousness "in a manner assimilated to a ritual death."[55] Along the west coast of North America, among the semi-sedentary and sedentary hunter-collector tribes of "the Kawaiisu, the Luiseno, the Juaneno, and the Gabrielino, as among the Diegueno, the Cocopa, and the Akwaala, the aspirant awaits the vision of the tutelary animal after becoming intoxicated by jimson weed."[56]

The shaman as a specialist had an increasing demand put upon them by their patrons for resolution. Among Inuit communities (among the most egalitarian of delayed return hunter-gatherers), the demands upon shamans arose for a cosmology "existing out of the quest to resolve moral dilemmas, simultaneously offers an account of why misfortunes occur, and how they can be rectified."[57] It was in the shaman's own interest to "constrain how cosmologies are elaborated and represented."[58]

The position of the healer arises from community; the position of the shaman arises from a need for communal accountability. It makes sense that the pathways taken would necessarily be different or far more extreme. As the healer can't attain a trance on their own, the shamans almost universally require an external source.

That came, by and large, from intoxicants.

It is worth clarifying that the point here isn't to equate shamans with hucksters. By specializing in healing and transcendence as a career, they are certainly going to master their craft. It is probable, if not likely, that their worlds often overlapped and that a shaman might impose their own self interests, but it would be wrong to presume that this possibility negates their intents and effectiveness as spiritual and social mitigators.

It is also apparent that as the societies shifted, so too did the methodology. Removed even slightly from the conditions that foster egalitarianism in band societies alternative narratives must originate in a sense of cosmic hierarchy.

The needs we have as individuals or as community still come about in dances, but a new role of spectator, of consumer, creep into view.

Our want for place and connectivity becomes a story over an experience. Even in its earliest stages, domestication begins by substituting our needs, by channeling them through arising social institutions. That is the requirement for power. It is as true amongst delayed return societies as it is for those of us living in a post-industrial glut of hyper-consumerism.

The second domesticators fail in reinforcing their worldviews, either psychologically or physically, the entire veneer crumbles. Our minds search out the cracks, our bodies suffer from regiments and drudgery, but it is the ability of civilization to offer alternative visions and means for euphoria or a sense of connectivity that has us turning towards addictions. Guzzling the alternatives to fill that void.

It is worth reiterating that domesticators largely didn't invent intoxicating substances (until relatively recently at least). We just didn't have a need to seek them out.

But sadly we know that circumstances changed.

We see a shift between the opening of doors through shamanic-induced-trance and the incorporation of outside sources for intoxicants.

Eliade argues that Inuit shamans induced trances through exposure to freezing temperatures along with self-imposed thirst and hunger. He found that Ugrian shamans of north-central Asia and the Lapps of northern Europe began using mushrooms to induce a trance in relatively recent history.[59] Stating further:

> *Intoxication by mushrooms also produces contact with the spirits, but in a passive and crude way. But, as we have already said, this shamanic technique appears to be late and derivative. Intoxication is a mechanical and corrupt method of reproducing "ecstasy," being "carried out of oneself"; it tries to imitate a model that is earlier and that belongs to another plane of references.*[60]

The mushroom in question is Fly Agaric, which isn't the most lucid of intoxicating mushrooms. The technique employed by shamans to induce a trance was to eat the mushrooms then drink their slightly fermented, mushroom laced urine that increased the hallucinogenic potency.[61]

Psychedelics such as Fly Agaric would eventually become a powerful means of shamanic vision, but their prevalence and availability arose alongside agriculture.

A more notable psilocybin mushroom, *Psilocybe cubensis*, may likely not have spread widely until the introduction of cattle farming.[62] It shares an ecological niche with its relative *Psilocybe seminlanceata*, or Liberty Cap, in that it "favours acid upland pastures and grows in the kinds of conditions where the only viable form of agriculture is sheep- or cattle-farming."[63] That form of agriculture involves the removal of dense forests to clear room for pastures, this is the ecology that *Psilocybe* grow in. A similar psychedelic mushroom, *Straphoria cubensis*, has been linked so closely with cow-dung that it has been called a "weed" for "high-technology cattle-raising cultures."[64]

Glorified though psychedelic mushrooms have become within our culture, Andy Letcher writes in his history of the "magic mushroom," that it "would be quite wrong of us to assume that just because a magic mushroom is abundant now it has been so throughout all of human history and prehistory."[65]

Likewise, cultural preoccupations with psychedelic mushrooms may cause us to overstate their impacts: Psilocybin is "about a hundred times less potent than LSD."[66] *Cubensis* is the basis for the "magic mushrooms" that are sold on the street, which itself may be a source of misunderstanding. A lot of reported experiences within civilization have actually been with store bought mushrooms, laced with PCP, LSD, or MDMA, dried and sold as "magic mushrooms." When a team of scientists undertook an 11-year study of 886 samples that were said to be "psilocybin," they discovered that only "28 percent of these were hallucinogenic mushrooms, while 35 percent were other drugs, mostly LSD or PCP and 37 percent contained no drug at all."[67]

The fanfare surrounding psychedelics has led to misconceptions about their universality. Among the Kuma from the Wahgi Valley of the West Highland region of New Guinea the consumption of a mushroom called *nonda* before trance-dances led to false reports of its hallucinogenic qualities. Upon further inspection, *nonda* comes from the *Boletus* family and "no trace of any hallucinogenic compound has ever been found within them."[68]

What we see here is how fast cultural change can occur. Within decades or less of contact, the role of healers can quickly be supplanted and replaced by shamans. The role of the trance-dance begins to wane as the use of intoxicants arises.

This shouldn't be surprising.

Contact is context. New diseases and new technologies go hand-in-hand with the colonizers who bring them. Forests are cleared, mountains are destroyed, lands are seized, and people are killed. These aren't the circumstances in which healers have thrived, they are beyond the realm of understanding for grounded and rooted cultures. They need answers for questions that would have never been asked before and crisis dictates the new narratives.

The role of the shaman takes root to help reconcile the eradication of community as civilization increases its grasp and expands further into the forests.

The non-shamanic curers and healers of the hunter-gatherer Netsilik of what is now the Nunavut territory of Canada, *krilasoktoq*, were within range of contemporary times and practicing a "head lifting" or "touching" approach to healing soon after they began to settle.[69] This was a practice that began to fall by the wayside as the role of shamans increased after contact. Likewise, the Ese Eja (hunter-gatherers of Bolivia and Peru) would have their *eyamikekua* hand-based healing displaced by the introduction of *ayahuasca* (a native intoxicant) by neighbors. Representing a transition that "is consistent with the transformation of a society being symbolically and materially centered around animals and hunting to one more centered around agriculture and plant based extractivism."[70]

The Huaorani shamans called *meñera*, "parents of jaguars," turned towards manioc beer for their rituals and dances. A change in line with moving from hunting and gathering to shifting cultivation, which as "we know it today is the product of the steel axe, and also the machete."[71]

It becomes clear that the waters get murky here. The Western infatuation with shamanism and trance-inducing drugs obscures elements of great recent historic change and colonization. So there are instances where seemingly minute differences in subsistence reflect in far greater differences in how trances are induced.

More to the point, that line, particularly under outside pressure, can blur easily between when the substance is assisting the trance and the shaman is becoming addicted.

Epene use by Yanomami shamans drives that point home.

Epene[72]

> *Hostile demons, scattered in various locations, haunt the different levels of the universe. They are busy devouring souls, which they capture by surprise inside the dwellings. If they are vigilant, if they have knowledge and power, the protecting shamans recognize them immediately thanks to the fact that each demon has his own particular path and odor. The shamans know how to avoid the perils that threaten those who approach supernatural beings and*

> *how to restore their souls to the sufferers; if they fail, the soul is "eaten" and the body, deprived of its energy, of its "center," gradually wastes away and dies.*
>
> *Transformed into* hekura, *the shamans travel through cosmic space to recover a soul from a demon or from enemies, or to steal one in order to "eat" it.*
>
> - Jacques Lizot, *Tales of the Yanomami*[73]

The Yanomami came to fame for what can only be considered a tragedy at the cross roads of Modernity and colonization.

Anthropologist and utter scumbag Napoleon Chagnon drew them into a public spectacle, a case point to establish his socio-biological theories about the innate violence of humans within a state of nature. He wrote about the extensive and enduring traditions of warfare within this horticultural society within the Amazon. He didn't create that warrior culture: that is another by-product of settlements and property, it typifies horticultural and hunter-collector life-ways.

What he did neglect was to include his own role in what can only be considered genocide.

It has been argued that the degree of horticulture amongst the Yanomami is itself a recent historical condition. The ecocidal decimation of the Amazon by civilization forced the Yanomami deeper into the forest or to settle nearer to trade posts and missions.[74] It was missionaries, colonizers and Chagnon himself that had introduced steel tools, Western foods, and guns into the equation alongside diseases that the Yanomami would have had no immunity towards.[75]

This is a story that repeats itself throughout the history of civilization.

And it is gut wrenching.

Like the Jívaro mentioned earlier, the steel axe made gardening manioc easier. And like the Jívaro, the Yanomami used it to make manioc beer. Paired with the crushing reality of the colonial frontier and an already existing warfare complex, the alcohol no doubt added to the fierceness with which Yanomami groups fought each other, also increasing the tensions within the *shapono*, or communal living structures.

This would have been ample cause to amplify the role of the shaman. And here the role of the shaman is absolutely tied to *epene*, a native intoxicant. *Epene* wasn't used exclusively by shamans, but it would become anticipated that the more they crossed that line between the world of the *shapono* and the world of the dead, the more they had to offer in terms of metaphysical explanations for the rapidly deteriorating state of the world.

The anthropologist Kenneth Good spoke of one Yanomami shaman as "a great shaman": "He took drugs each day, powdered *epene* seeds, a powerful hallucinogen that the Indians took turns blowing into each other's noses through a three-foot-long drug-blowing tube." In that trance-like state, it was their responsibility to interact with the spirits to heal the sick and protect the village from evil spirits.[76]

We can see that the spirit of the communal dance lingers here. The shaman didn't act alone. Good recounts a particular story in which a person was sick and in need of healing. The shaman "had taken the *epene* drug and was being assisted by five or six other men who had also taken the drug and were painted and decorated with feathers." The "shaman was drawing the sickness out of the patient, transferring it to others, then reviving them."[77]

This doesn't sound unfamiliar, but we see the level of communal involvement wane as the specialist arises. *Epene* isn't the property of the shaman, but a signature of sorts. It was expected that the shaman would chant and seek *hekura*, the world of the spirits, often. That is an expectation that may have pushed the shaman closer to addiction. In the middle of the night as the shaman awoke and began chanting at an hour when no one was awake to blow the *epene* into their nose, "he'd inhale the *epene* powder like snuff from his hand."[78]

This is a point I don't take lightly. The connection here is an absolute correlation between the external stress on a society and the internal demand for answers from the shaman. What may have originated as a vocation becomes an occupation in response to encroaching turbulence. In the case of the Yanomami, contact remains the antagonist in this equation.

As social and political tensions rose, *epene*, mixed with alcohol, would lose its spiritual side completely and become the pathway to an intoxicated state for fighting over property and territorial disputes. Helena Valero, who had been kidnapped as a girl by the Yanomami and raised within their culture, told a story of a dispute between Namoeteri and Konakunateri bands while hunting boar. They entered one *shapono* and all ingested *epene* while arguments mounted until they began to beat each other with the blunt end of an axe.

In this case, that was enough to bring resolution. They concluded their battle saying: "We have beaten you hard and you have beaten us hard. Our blood has flowed, we have caused your blood to flow. I am no longer troubled, for our anger has passed."[79]

There's something to be said about that kind of conflict resolution and perhaps in times of less pressure and outside incursion maybe that's how many disputes ended. Unfortunately the correlation stands: intoxicating substances are used in societies that may already have taken on some degree of domestication. As the threads that ignite egalitarian resolution of mobility and communal healing are pulled, intoxicated states will amplify the potential for violent outcomes.

And civilization requires expansion. Tensions arise from social, ecological and psychological pressures. As the paths to resolution are removed, the potential for decimation and/or further isolation become the only options.

As alcohol, guns and steel tools flooded the world of the Yanomami, the role of social intoxication had already been opened. The stage was set.

The results were absolute.

Emboldened with Western goods and weapons, the warfare that the Yanomami practiced fed the illnesses and stresses of contact. Starved as forests were felled, as game were displaced and killed, Yanomami warfare took on a new level of lethality. The West watched with a harrowed fascination as the bodies piled up as though they were mere spectators of some primeval process.

We simply removed ourselves from this situation as we justified the carnage as tribal war.

That story, as we know it, as they know it, as they struggle against their extinction in the face of Modernity, are familiar paths. Domestication deals in distraction because it trades in tragedy.

Without those pressures the Yanomami may have never settled at all, the tensions may have never required a culture built around warfare.

It may well be that their tensions could have resolved themselves without notice on a global scale, but what happened to the Yanomami is a problem the world over: civilizations did arise. Horticultural societies rarely ever grew into agriculture. Their scale was minor compared to what it could have been. Domestication has its consequences, but its presence doesn't ensure civilizations or States will arise.

The problem is that civilizations did arise.

Ethnocide goes hand-in-hand with the ecocide of contact and colonization.

But this is not a uniquely modern problem. This is the pattern that all civilizations follow, that all civilizations must follow. What might have happened to the Yanomami in time has a precedent: the Uto-Aztecan societies that ran through what is now southern North America. These societies are arguably the only cluster of civilizations to arise from horticulture.

And it is here that the use of intoxicants, mirrored in the distancing from and decimation of the earth, become deeply entrenched in the day-to-day lives within these societies.

Creating Gods and Eating Them

If there is a single plant that can sum up the complex relationship between intoxicants and subsistence, it is peyote.

Long before Carlos Castaneda used Don Juan to introduce peyote to the West, the spindly cactus had a deep and significant role in the societies that existed throughout the deserts of what is now the Southwest of the US into Mexico.

However, that is a role that was attained not as a hallucinogen, but as a medicinal plant.

This isn't an uncommon situation. In lesser doses, nearly all intoxicating plants contain curative properties. That they become central to societies through ritual should come as little surprise given the curative power of healing dances and trance rituals. The space for overlap is clear. As the trance-dance becomes specialized, the mildly intoxicating plants used medicinally could become an easy transition for inducing trance for the shamans and priests.

The Uto-Aztecan people are defined by a mutual language group with widespread roots. By 1519, the Uto-Aztecan language family spread nearly 2000 miles from the Aztecs through the Shoshone in the prairies of what is now Idaho and Wyoming.[80] It has been argued that, if you go back far enough, the entire swath of Uto-Aztecan speakers was all one society.[81] That group includes the native civilizations of the Aztecs in Mexico and the Hopi, Anasazi and Pueblo of the American southwest. Intricate trade routes permeated from the Incas in Peru and spread north from there.

Of the substances that would become abused by the civilizations within this massive trade network, most of them originate in their curative powers. *Datura* was used as an analgesic. *Nicotiana rustica* was used as a poultice and fumigant. *Peyotl*, as it would be called by the Aztecs, were no exception.[82] Among the Tarahumara, Huichol, and Tepehuane people, peyote was used externally for rheumatism, wounds, burns, snakebites, the stings of scorpions, and skin diseases.[83]

Early explorers such as Ortega and Hernandez made no mention of the hallucinogenic aspects of peyote, while writing about it extensively as a medicinal. In his 1938 account of the initial accounts of peyote usage amongst indigenous societies, Richard Evans Schultes writes "the principal appeal of peyote has been and continues to be centered around the therapeutic and stimulating properties of the plant and not around its vision producing properties." Its visions, he surmises, "were incidental."[84]

If you live in the desert, an ecosystem that necessitates quick and long movements, peyote is a pretty perfect companion. Among the Huichol and Tarahumara, whose ritualistic and long distance running (respectively) would become emblematic, peyote is a cure-all. It wards off sleep and hunger, reduces body temperature, decreases pain perception, is a mood stabilizer, and improves sensory perception.[85] It's not hard to see how a plant such as this wouldn't be widely used.

The different relationships with a plant that we widely understand as a hallucinogen might seem at odds with the interpretations that Castaneda or drug enthusiasts like Terrence McKenna offer. But it's important to note that mescaline, the primary chemical within peyote, fluctuates greatly. The potency of peyote buttons depend on age, location and season of harvest, it is greater in the top half of the button, lesser in the bottom and almost none in the root. The levels of mescaline are tied directly to the rains, typically going up in content in the winter and down in the summer. Dried buttons can have as much as 5-6% of their total weight in mescaline content, though it is commonly found in the 1-2% range or less. The high percentage of mescaline in dried buttons owes itself directly to the high water content found in fresh peyote where mescaline content is as little as 0.2-0.3%.[86]

In light of this, the argument for incidental visions starts to make more sense.

However, we know that the relationship with peyote changes. The visions become a vital part of Uto-Aztecan religious culture. The role of peyote doesn't diminish: among the Maya and Aztecs it becomes ritualized as the civilizations grow and expand into warring, cannibalistic empires.

So what happened?

Even prior to the advent of agriculture, it would appear that the vast trade networks that would come to transport things like peyote for ritual and obsidian for ornate sacrificial blades had deep roots. None of these people are fully isolated from each other.

When domestication originates for one society along this line, it is not surprising that it would spread relatively quickly throughout the continents. In this case, that points to when the oldest cobs of domesticated *teosinte*, or what would become maize or corn as we know it, start showing up in southwestern Mexico 8,700 years ago.[87] It starts to be seen in South American caves around 4250 BC.[88] The seeds would spread south through the Incans in Peru from the Olmec and Mayans, distributed by Uto-Aztecan cultures, possibly carried by ancestors of the Huichol and Tarahumara to the Anasazi, eventually travelling to the northeast coast of what is now the United States by way of a series of relatively short-lived civilizations along the Mississippi and Ohio River Valleys.[89]

Compared to the settled hunter-collector societies that built the civilizations that overtook the entire world (which we will discuss in the following section), the origins of civilization among the Mayans and those that spread from there seem modest. Living in the forest, without the open valleys and nutrient dispersing flood plains, they practiced horticulture, or slash-and-burn agriculture as it is also known. This swidden system involves:

> *clearing a patch of jungle with stone axes during the dry season between December and March and then setting fire to the area just before the start of the rainy season when maize and beans would have been planted with a digging stick to be harvested in the autumn. The cultivated patch would have been abandoned after a couple of years as weeds reinvaded and made clearance too difficult.*[90]

This is an extremely common form of horticulture that is used widely throughout the world, though the crops were different, it's what the Yanomami practice as well. While this form of horticulture can potentially long outlast agricultural systems, it doesn't escape their trappings. The Mayans, like the Aztecs and Incans that follow them, certainly fell into them.

And they did not fare well.

The problem with horticulture is that it could potentially work well, but only for small populations. Small populations are something that nomadic hunter-gatherer societies learned to check largely through mobility. Once that is removed, populations start to rise. Slowly at first, but they inevitably pick up. The slow movements of gardens begin to result in running into the gardens of other tribes. The decreased level of movement results in over-harvesting wild game. In an all too familiar situation, resources (as they eventually come to be known) start to dry up. Competition arises.

What happened in Mesoamerica was an amplification of production. Horticulture, with its slow movements, could no longer keep up with the population growth and the move to agriculture begins. The geography here matters: the Petén forests of the Yucatán Peninsula had only two permanent rivers, waterholes would become the basis for settlements which greatly limited the size of the populations that could be supported through hunting and gathering, much less agriculture. The region was so ill suited for agriculture that even stones sufficient for grinding corn had to be imported.[91]

Unlike the large watersheds of the Nile or the Tigris-Euphrates, these societies were forced to build waterways, cities and farms with far less space to work with. They also notably lacked domesticable animals to use for food and labor.[92]

The usual suspects come into play. We have Divine Kings and Priests, we have a divided society with peasants and elites. To appease them all, alcohol made from maize becomes a mainstay.[93] Alcohol from maize, honey, and saps, intoxication through plants and mushrooms sway between ritual and habitual usage.[94] But as populations grow and nutrition declines, a new part of the religious society emerges: human sacrifice.

The architecture begins to accommodate. With the temples of the Mayans, Aztec and Inca, you see steep stairs leading up to altars. This is where captives of war, encaged and fattened with corn, would be ritualistically sacrificed and eaten, their scoured bodies rolled from the altars.[95]

I don't think there can be a more straightforward way to show how civilization always devours community. But the rite is important, for all its gruesomeness, cannibalism, like warfare is a response to what has been called the "ecological extremities of the Valley of Mexico."[96]

That's both true and false. Compared to the situations where civilizations typically arose, these valleys are extreme. Outside of agriculture the picture looks greatly different as nomadic hunter-gatherers had inhabited these forests for thousands of years prior. This is the epitome of a created tragedy: civilizations must conquer and cannibalize just as peasants must be soothed with alcohol and elites must invoke the divination of hallucinogens.

Warfare, and cannibalism as an extension of it, is a response to self-imposed ecological boundaries. Among the Aztecs, what wild game remained beyond the realm of their sedentary and rapidly deforesting cities was hunted for consumption by the elites. Commoners were barred from eating human bodies, a privilege that was bestowed upon elites and warriors. The dire need to gorge on human flesh was enough to lure "the lower class to participate in these wars since those who single-handedly took captives several times gained the right to eat human flesh."[97] If you captured enough enemies, you could bring your family into the elite ranks.

We run into intoxicants again here, but in a different light.

The priests and elites of the Aztec doused the sacrifice of captives in religious ritual. Their might was furthered when the sacrifices appeared to walk willingly onto the altar. And they did. With a little help from a plant called *Datura*, or as it is known today, *Devil's Breath*.[98] In our scientific terms, this is Scopolamine, which the hipster-voyeurs of Vice Magazine came to dub "the scariest drug in the world."[99]

Datura contains potent hallucinogenic seeds that, when distilled and powdered can be merely blown into the face of a would-be victim. Too much and they will overdose. But, given a small amount, they become "zombies", or a walking and willing participant in whatever their assailant suggests. It's a pretty logical part of the arsenal for street gangs in Columbia where it grows wild. The victim will have no recollection of the perpetuators, no memory of what happened, and often long term effects. To an outsider, nothing looks abnormal about the victim's participation as they hand over their lives, identity, money, and anything the gangs want.

In the Aztec case, long term memory wasn't an issue. Under the spell of *Datura*, the captives would sit upon the altar themselves as a ritualistic obsidian dagger tore open their chests and their heart was removed.

It would be a hard sell to try and debate the sustainability of these civilizations. Not surprisingly, they mostly collapsed prior to European contact. The remnants of these societies moved on, splintering at times into other existing societies, or starting new ones. Though the civilizations may have collapsed, the religious culture of the Aztecs did not fade entirely, nor did their earlier horticultural practices disappear.

In the case of the Aztecs, we will focus on two societies that outlived them: the Huichol and the Tarahumara. Both are indigenous societies that arise from the same group as the rest of the Uto-Aztecan lineage and their deeper hunter-gatherer roots, but they both developed cultures that incorporate and respond to elements of Aztec reality. Becoming farmers in their own rite, but also outcasts of Olmec and Aztec wars and refugees of a thriving military of raiders seeking captives.

And it is within these societies that the ritualization of intoxication and escape becomes central.

Huichol and the Peyote Hunt

To the Aztecs, the Huichol (or *Wixdrika* as they call themselves), were the *Chichimeca*: "the northern barbarians who lived as nomadic hunters and collectors in the high deserts to the northeast of their present home" in the Sierra Madre Occidental range.[100]

Their ancestral home was in San Luis Potosi, where Aztec and Spanish colonizers and conquerors exiled them. They practice *milpa* agriculture, not unlike the swidden agriculture of the early Aztecs and Mayans, which centers on maize and beans. They carry on a strong religious tradition that centers around the "trine divinity", the connection between three of the most important Huichol gods; Corn, Deer, and Peyote.[101]

For the Huichol, corn, deer and peyote are one in the same. A central part of the Huichol identity lies in the "peyote hunt", which is what they have become known for. As sedentism and deforestation would have decimated the wild game populations within range of the Aztec civilizations and their outliers, the role of the hunter within these societies would have been elevated, not unlike warriors, possibly as high as that of chiefs or priests.

Within the Huichol, that role of authority lands on the *maara 'akdme*, the shaman-priests. These singing shamans lead the annual peyote hunts that are a peyote-driven ritualistic journey through 500 miles to hunt the sacred deer, embodied as peyote.[102] Though the peyote hunt takes place only once per year, the pilgrimage is the universal theme throughout all Huichol ceremony and symbolism. The pilgrimage itself appears to be connected to the role of the Huichol as runners on the Mesoamerican trade routes[103] and it moves further beyond that in reviving their hunter-gatherer past.

What is particularly relevant to the peyote pilgrimage for our purposes here is how direct the tie is between the use of peyote and the identity of the community. Despite sharing so much cultural and religious affiliation with the world that the Aztecs created, the memory of nomadic hunter-gatherer life runs rampant through Huichol identity.

For the Huichol, hunting and gathering, as much as they may be absent from their lives, is what defined them.

Their cultural obsession is with a ritualistic resurgence of life within community. But lacking the proximity and fluidity that nomadic hunter-gatherers possess, the dance is not enough. Instead, a perpetual ritual of dance and song is channeled into shamanistic indulgences of with peyote as an intoxicant. Peyote established its central role in their hunter-gatherer days for its cure-all abilities for their desert ecology. Here it is used to attain a ritualized re-enactment of hunting and gathering life.

"The Deer-Maize-Peyote complex," typified by the peyote hunt, writes anthropologist Barbara Myerhoff, "functions to achieve a series of unifications by presenting, then embracing, many of the contradictions, oppositions, and paradoxes of Huichol life."[104] During this time, non-egalitarian divisions associated with age, sex, ritual status, regional origins, and family affiliations are disregarded ritualistically for the duration of the rite.[105]

The hunt follows the path of exile from their ancestral lands. That is a place where there was no perception of separation between "man, plants, animals, and "gods." Identity becomes fluid and the participants can move between being human and deer, just as peyote, maize and deer all merge with each other.[106]

The participants must take peyote to open their "inner eye", which is necessary so "he will recognize the tracks of the Deer-Peyote and see the brilliant rainbow-soul of Elder Brother *Wawatsári*, the Principal Deer, rise from the peyote plant as it is "slain" by his arrows."[107] The sacrificial and ritual deer, represented by peyote, is a symbolic stand in for the life they once lived immersed in the wild as nomadic hunter-gatherers. A life lived in community, where the ritual of participation would have been experienced without this kind of formality.

It is likely in earlier times that this re-enactment surrounded the use of young peyote to stave hunger and push the body further as Aztec hunters decimated deer populations, pushing Huichol hunters further out. This is a point highlighted by the current reality, where the introduction of the rifle only increased the decimation of deer populations and forced the Huichol to sacrifice cattle in their place.[108]

There is something innately primal to this ritual.

Entrenched though it may be with the trappings of agricultural and civilized reality, it seeks to reconcile the distaste for the anti-community of agrarian life. You can catch glimpses of how the power of the nomadic hunter-gatherer community still lives on in their mythology as an ideal, a place where separation between community and wildness doesn't exist. In a way, this is a reflection of the allure that peyote has gained within hippy and drop out cultures.

However, there's something definitively encouraging knowing that this universal understanding of our own primal anarchy exists so strongly in an agrarian tradition, especially compared to the emptiness and forward-obsessed perspectives inherent in Modernity. And yet even here, we see that this is about escape, about a purging of uncivilized wants, which ultimately perpetuates complacency with civilized life.

The Huichol ritualistically indulge back to their hunter-gatherer ways so that they can continue farming: so that they will work and so they won't focus on their own trauma of domestication.

The peyote hunt is therapeutic.

In reality, it only reflects on the dis-ease of civilized life and its inability to fulfill our innate needs.

And it is that reality, that acknowledgement that civilization will destroy, denude, and decimate wildness, both externally and internally, that perpetuates our drive to find substitutes and escapes for what it is we so desperately seek. It is that impulse that has sent the Tarahumara running and, sadly, has kept them on the run.

Tarahumara

The Tarahumara, or *Rarámuri* as they call themselves, live further northwest of the Huichol, in areas now known as Chihuahua and Talu in Mexico. Their culture was seemingly closer to the semi-nomadic hunter-gatherer Basket Maker cultures of the American Southwest who had started to farm corn.

Between 1000 and 1500 AD, as the Mayan civilization was collapsing and the Aztec Empire emerged, they began to intensify their horticulture in lieu of decreased hunting. As a part of and partner to the Mesoamerican trade route, it is probable, if not likely, that overhunting was the primary cause of this cultural change.[109]

Of their crops, corn and gourds seemed to be the most impactful.

They shared in the Huichol veneration of peyote.[110] Considering the medicinal uses of peyote mentioned above, the roots here shouldn't be a mystery: the reason the Tarahumara have come to the forefront in recent years is because of their long distance running. Their endurance is absolutely extraordinary: often trekking distances upwards of 200 miles.

How much of that movement is a result of taking part in trade and how much of it is solely related to the harsher ecological conditions of the Copper Canyon of Mexico where they live is hard to say. What we do know, without question, is that the rise of civilized colonization into the region has forced Tarahumara to stay on the move.

And their culture reflects that.

The Tarahumara live in *rancheros*, widely spread encampments and gardens. There are many elements of their lives that seem to hark back further into their own nomadic hunter-gatherer lives and their choice of shelter (not uncommonly, caves) is one reflection of that. But their use of running pulls on an even more primal aspect of their lives: the persistence hunt.

Persistence hunting is arguably the oldest form of hunting. It refers to the act of hunting by literally running an animal down. It's a process that requires speed, but above all else, endurance. But there is a huge problem there: archeologically speaking, you can't physically find evidence of it.

In his Tarahumara influenced book, *Born to Run*, Christopher McDougall points out that persistence hunting "leaves behind no forensics—no arrowheads, no spear-nicked deer spines."[111] Anthropologically speaking, we know that it is still (or has recently been) practiced by some San hunter-gatherers of the Kalahari.[112] We have evidence in cave art that the practice was widespread among hunter-gatherers, but living cases of it are rare. The Tarahumara are among those few cases.

What we can glimpse from this is an indication of cultural change. The rise of domesticated maize in the region, the expansion of empires, the elaborate trade networks; the collective and primal memory and community that the Huichol ritualistically call upon seems to echo throughout the ancient subsistence methods of the Tarahumara. The remnants of a nomadic hunter-gatherer life way, of nomadic hunter-gatherer community, lingers.

Its direct opposition comes in the form of domestication.

The impact of expanding civilizations decimated the region and its wild communities. The rise of protein scarcity forced communities to spread further apart. The increasing reliance upon grown and stored foods fostered hierarchical social relationships: relationships that were pressed harder through trade relationships with civilized societies.

While peyote may lack the prerequisites necessary for a chemical-level addiction, alcohol does not.

Tesguino is a thick, milky beer made from fermented corn. And the Tarahumara consume it religiously.

The process for making *tesguino* is not a simple one. It takes three days to grind, cook, and ferment the corn. Its shelf life is incredibly short, 12 to 24 hours, so it must be consumed quickly. This doesn't stop the Tarahumara from making batches as large as 50 gallons at a time.[113] In the 1960s, anthropologist John Kennedy estimated that "the average Tarahumara spends at least 100 days per year directly concerned with tesguino and much of this time under its influence or aftereffects."[114]

The brew is relatively low in alcohol content, but drank in such quantities doesn't negate the effects. Being drunk is akin to religious intoxication: "Drinking, to the Tarahumara, is a social rather than an individual activity."[115] True as that may be, it cannot be overlooked that the alcohol comes from maize that comes from settlement and trades with horticulturalists and civilizations. The social drinking here is a reaction and response to the physical distancing and the loss of ancestral food sources.

Community becomes a relic, upheld in the ritual of drinking. Likewise, contemporary Tarahumara drink *tesguino* daily, only to drink more heavily during religious celebrations.[116] Just as the maize-centric elements of Tarahumara reality are a historical creation, so too are their amplifications. As we shall see shortly, it is the presence of civilizations that grabs a hold of any level of intoxicating ritual among indigenous society to use them as an entry point for colonization.

Just as the intoxicated trance supplants the communal trances attained through dancing, singing and hand touching, the interpretation of colonization on an unprecedented scale can only be understood through increasing intoxication.

This is why addiction rates are so much higher on reservations: the religious and spiritual council of the shaman seeks to reconcile the tensions within settled societies. The level of decimation and emptiness that those of us unfortunate enough to have been raised within civilization are simply used to make even less sense in the shadows of fractured community. Nomadic hunter-gatherers approached increasing tension through healing dances. If that didn't work, they moved.

The same circumstances that the Tarahumara faced which pushed them towards becoming maize farmers has kept them from subsistence farming in recent times: the civilizations that pushed on their lands only became more militant, more technologically assisted and more ecocidal.

This is the sad stage that has been set for indigenous societies the world over: civilization grows; its threats and consequences amplify exponentially alongside it.

In the case of the Tarahumara, Aztecs lost out to the Spanish. Their ancestral homelands became Mexico and they the subjects of its government.

The pre-historic Mesoamerican trade routes remained intact and yet the demand for trade items shifted immensely. By the 1980s, the Aztec and Spanish warriors would come to be replaced by drug cartels that forced the Tarahumara to cultivate marijuana and opium. Choice and mobility become fleeting options when faced with armed cartels that couldn't care less about anyone's life.[117] Climate change induced drought directly impacts the Tarahumara corn crops, pushing them further into the arms of the cartels by making drug growing operations the only way left to eat.[118]

The mountains of the Sierra Madre are increasingly subjected to intensified logging and mining. The erosion that results washes away the thin topsoil. Cattle and goats overgraze what fertile land exists. The waterways are awash with the waste from all this along with the chemicals used in marijuana and opium production. And on top of all of this a United States backed "War on Drugs" funds the Mexican government to spray herbicides from planes onto the fields where marijuana and opium are grown: the very same fields where the Tarahumara plant their corn, beans and squash.[119]

As we shall see in the coming sections, this kind of cannibalistic clusterfuck defines civilization.

It doesn't improve from here.

We simply hide away. In lieu of community, we shrink further and further into ourselves and lose the ability to even have a baseline understanding about the span of our impact. I don't say any of this to fault or blame on an individual level, but there is absolutely no end in sight to any of this if we don't recognize the link between our own narcissistic indulgences with intoxicants, with social media, with technology, with consumerism, whatever escape it is we personally turn to, with the fate of the Tarahumara, the Huichol, with the Earth.

In looking at the Uto-Aztecans, we get a glimpse of what horticulture amplified can attain in its worst-case scenario through the Aztec and Mayan civilizations. That is not an inevitable fate, but it is a reality of domestication. The rise from horticulture to agriculture is the exception, not the norm. The self-imposed bounds of carrying capacity may have resulted in another millennia or two of civilizations popping up and collapsing throughout the Americas, just as it had in the thousand years prior to European colonization.

The difference is scale.

And it is in the nature of domestication within the rest of its points of origins that we get a clearer picture as to how things have gotten to where they are now.

But the Uto-Aztecan case cannot be overlooked nor surpassed without further examination. The plight of indigenous societies still under the oppression of proxy European powers bares the violent and brute face of Modernity that those of us in the First World rarely see.

A Cultural Survival report on the struggle of the Tarahumara puts it bluntly:

> *As modern industrialized Americans sit in their living rooms each evening and watch their flickering screens, a war of survival is being fought just south of the border. Nearly 400 Rarámuri have been murdered in the last decade.*[120]

And in the end, it is the euphoric dance of intact community that we all seek.

That feeling of place.

That feeling of belonging.

We may lack the ritualized revival of nomadic hunter-gatherer life that the Huichol and Tarahumara maintain, but that primal urge within does not die. It gets buried.

And it gets buried beneath mass graves.

The Conquests of Bread, or, Cheers to Industry

> *Researchers have often dealt with the process of sedentarization without understanding the true nature of the sedentary way of life. The stereotypical thinking has been that technical progress of subsistence made possible the efficient acquisition of food, which in turn made it unnecessary to be nomadic, or possible to be sedentary. Such a scenario is undoubtedly based on the mindset peculiar to sedentary people, that man must have chosen sedentarization whenever it was possible.*
>
> — Masaki Nishida[121]

The history and presence of intoxicants among horticultural societies is in some ways anecdotal.

Among settled and settling societies, their presence is central.

So our focus begins to shift here.

The focus on cross-cultural differences between varying degrees of domestication and sedentism is important to understand how the grey area between the use and abuse of intoxicating and addictive substances arises. To a large degree, this is sifting the fine details, but sadly we know how this ends. We know the shaman isn't the bastion of domesticated life. We are far too aware of programmers and politicians and the history that we have collectively taken part in to not acknowledge that a historical shift set us off in an endemic direction by way of civilized life.

At this point, we are no longer looking at other societies to understand our own; we're looking directly at our own history, at the lineage of civilizations that brought us to this point. The link here is in how familiar the domesticating process is, how this innate that sense of being, disemboweled and repackaged for our consumption, has always been a necessary prerequisite for compliance. For our labor: for active participation in our own drudgery.

These worlds may arise imperceptibly from semi-sedentary hunter-gatherer bands, but the presence of temples, mounds, and altars, the turn from digging sticks to plows, herding animals instead of following their migrations, the change in the landscape from streams and rivers to diverted waterways and rows of crops; all of these things are absolute. They are basis for the history that civilization has written into each of us, that it has written into the earth.

Agriculture doesn't represent a new level of alienation; it is itself a cataclysmic shattering of relationships, reframed onto the needs of a rising state. It requires the subjugation of community just as it requires the subjugation of the land and all its relationships.

To have any discussion about addiction, agriculture is the defining point: these are societies built upon the original trauma of domestication.

Nomadism wasn't simply a matter of ecological necessity among hunter-gatherers: it was a cultural necessity. Ironic though it may sound, movement ensured rooting in a place. It brought and encouraged interactions and awareness not only with other humans, but also with the entirety of life.

The presumption that humans would have chosen settled life, if given a choice, is a narrative of domestication. The same narrative that tells us that civilization brings us joy. A story that directly conflicts with the reality that nomadic hunter-gatherer bands danced in ecstatic joy as much as they wanted while our society is riddled with rising levels of addictions, suicides and over-the-counter mood altering medications. Where freedom is equated with the freedom to shop. Where we exemplify the advancements of our own lives with devices made in sweat shops from rare metals extracted from warzones and the existence of life-prolonging drugs, neither of which most of humanity can economically afford.

The question that digs at my mind about how some hunter-gatherer bands settled 10,000-12,000 years ago isn't why they may have settled, but why they stayed.

We know this: civilizations, by and large, did not emerge from a path of horticulture and pastoral societies banding together to start farming and move from there. Outside of the previous examples, civilizations were started by sedentary hunter-collectors, who were still technically hunter-gatherers. Presumably for ecological reasons, they temporarily "started to utilize starchy seeds as on the of the major foods, such as wild wheat, acorn, chestnut, and water chestnut." These small seed heads required a lot of processing and technique to make what nomadic hunter-gatherers apparently considered "extremely undesirable and low-value foods."[122]

It is only through the lens of history that we can look back to this era and presume change was a matter of choice. Even with the few places where hunter-gatherers settled and became what archeologist Lewis Binford labeled hunter-collectors the timeline spreads over decades and generations, likely resulting in an imperceptible level of change for those taking part.

These societies did not immediately begin to domesticate. They had no need to. The grains grew in abundance naturally and most hunter-gatherers opted to just let them be. The meat that came from animals that grazed those fields was universally more valuable.

The difference lies in a change of strategy. I'll allow Binford to define this phenomenon: "In contrast to foragers, collectors are characterized by (1) the storage of food for at least part of the year and (2) logistically organized food-procurement parties."[123]

Agriculture is not a necessity for these societies to arise. Hunter-collectors arose in handfuls of areas seemingly at the same time when the domestication of grains begins to take root in other parts of the world. The results were remarkably similar: State-level societies arose with rampant inequality.

The difference is that agriculture allowed the manipulation of carrying capacity, or the size of the populations that can be supported by a land base. The domestication of grains, the expansion of their preferred habitats, the artificial redirection of water and use of labor (both human and animal) to turn soils, to tear down forests and stretch fields, create circumstances where you could almost buy the underlying principles of civilized life: might makes right.

Convoluted as it may be, our current reality would like to give the impression that we have truly conquered *nature*, that we have cracked its boundaries and limitations, giving rise to our hyper-technological present and future. But it doesn't take a weatherman to tell you which way the winds blow, or, more to the point, to tell you that the ecological instability we currently face is evidence that our actions are not without consequence. Agriculture doesn't shift carrying capacity in favor of supporting civilization (though it and the industrial systems it supports can certainly reduce it drastically), it merely prolongs and worsens the pitfall when a system of unlimited wants overstays its place in a world based on limited means.[124]

All civilizations inevitably collapse under the weight of this basic mathematical reality. The difference comes down to scale.

The limitation for hunter-collectors who focused on proteins is the animals themselves.

In the Pacific Northwest of North America, that looked like hunter-collector societies built around annual runs of salmon to be smoked and stored. Even with the limitations imposed by finite fish runs, these societies created warring political states complete with slavery. The Tsimshian, Tlingit and Haida tribes shared political structures of rank and inherited leadership positions.[125] The *potlatch*, an organized ritual of sharing amassed foods and cultural objects, was central to these states.

Despite it's focus on sharing, the potlatch is about the "absolute power" given to chiefs.[126] As representatives of the group, individuals "potlatch in order to validate their own position": asserting their own power as emblematic of the group. The chief, like the priest, must ground their asserted rights in terms of subsistence. Being so close in proximity to the means of nomadic hunter-gatherer subsistence, the fragility of power risked becoming even more apparent. If the shaman was the interpreter, the chief and priest are the manifestations of god/s. As Timothy Earle writes,

> *The cultural and economic landscape was transformed to create a new physical world in which the chiefs existed as owners of the productive facilities and the earthly manifestations of the gods. The materialization of ideology transformed the legitimizing beliefs of the ruling elite into concrete, cultural things that could be controlled through the labor process within the local community.*[127]

The complexity these states developed is often spoken of as evidence of abundance, as though it was something non-existent for the nomadic hunter-gatherer. But the nature of these societies, the strict order that they attained is evidence of a more fragile reality here. There were times of "plenty," but "it was not constant." As anthropologist Wayne Suttles observes, "Abundance there consisted only of certain things at certain times and always with some possibility of failure."[128]

In the plains and tundras, collectors looked like hunter-gatherers who began to domesticate or to herd pack animals to carry their surpluses permanently or seasonally. The Caribou Inuit and Plains Indians of North America are examples of this. Sedentary hunter-collectors are only limited by the size of fish runs or how long any food item can be stored, but for the mounted hunter-collectors, their limitation was based on how much they could carry. It should come as little surprise that these societies were, by and large, much more egalitarian in nature than the sedentary, collector societies.

There is a spectrum of hunter-collector societies from egalitarian to absolute hierarchy. While extremely hierarchical and state societies emerged from fish-dependent, sedentary hunter-collectors, civilizations did not.

Those were dependent upon grains.

Without grains, we would have no civilization.

Period.

In the places where civilizations arose, domestication was a consequence of settlement. We tend to treat it as a historic achievement, a part of our rise from savage animality. But hunter-gatherers didn't lack the knowledge of propagation. Every time a forager picks one berry over another and then excretes its seeds, they are taking part in that cycle, just like any other animal. Their knowledge of botany was unquestionable. They simply had no need for domestication.

The wild plants that humans settled and built civilizations around share a "weedy tendency," an ecological adaptation to "'open', disturbed, or unstable habitats with bare soil and less competition from other plants."[129] A circumstance that arises from heavily travelled paths and settled areas. It is likely that the origins of agriculture's spread arose as "plants with weedy tendencies colonized kitchen middens and rubbish heaps and were thus gathered … and, imperceptibly perhaps, brought into cultivation."[130]

Domestication, as it applies to humans, arose largely from our settlements.[131] Our slow change in social circumstance, amplified and reflected in a fragmentation of the world into economic, religious, political and social realms, each carrying its own self-serving narrative of hierarchy.[132] "Community" becomes an idea rather than a known reality: our sense of connection and belonging center around production of a surplus and its social expressions.

So while we will only ever have some degree of assumption around why certain hunter-gatherer societies settled around wild grains, we also have an indication as to why they stayed. Greg Wadley and Angus Martin broke the news in 1993:

Recent discoveries of potentially psychoactive substances in certain agricultural products -- cereals and milk -- suggest an additional perspective on the adoption of agriculture and the behavioural changes ('civilisation') that followed it.[133]

They became addicted.

The diet of nomadic hunter-gatherers relied heavily on fat consumption, unlike civilized diets that are based predominantly on sugar and carbohydrates. Short of sporadic gorging on honey and seasonal access to berries and other fruits, sugars were relatively uncommon. Grains, were, at best, seen as secondary food sources.

In the extreme, Arctic and Sub-Arctic hunter-gatherers seasonally bordered on carnivorous diets, at times only having the vegetation within the stomach of animals available to them. They ate the organs, muscle and fat of the animals and thrived from it even in harsh environments.[134] Complex carbohydrates, such as grains, legumes, along with simple sugars, act like intoxicants in the body. As Nora Gedgaudas explains:

Neurotransmitters are our main mood and brain regulators, and surges of blood sugar generate surges—and subsequent depletion or dysregulation—of the neurotransmitters serotonin, epinephrine, norepinephrine, GABA, and dopamine.[135]

We get flashes of joy from these complex and simple carbohydrates, but they are fleeting. To borrow an analogy from Gedgaudas, fat burns for fuel in the body like a log on a fire, glucose (from sugars or from grains) burns like twigs on a fire. That is why hunter-gatherers had no problem spending hours to days dancing in ceremony or far less hours focused on procurement than agricultural societies. Breakdowns of caloric intake presume that all calories are equal which is simply false.

Sugar dependency breeds and amplifies addictions because it requires constant maintenance: "A brain that is dependent on glucose for its functioning will experience considerable compromise during those fluctuations, and moods, together with cognitive functioning, will tend to be unstable and at the mercy of blood sugar availability."[136] Bled of persistent nutrition, our need and wants for community and the connections it brings are amplified by a starving body.

Starches were hardly absent from nomadic hunter-gatherer diets, but the unnecessary complexity of harvesting and processing grains kept them at bay. The addictive nature of grains goes far beyond their transformation into glucose and stored fat in the body. Grains contain exorphins, a morphine-like compound.[137] Exorphins compound with opioid receptors in the body creating "a sense of euphoria, happiness, and sleepiness tends to be activated, as well as a reduction in pain sensation."[138]

It should be little surprise that the grains that spurred domestication and that underpin so much of our daily reality are not only addictive, but that they're not seen as intoxicants themselves despite the fact that our bodies treat them that way. When removed from the diet, individuals "often exhibit cravings, addiction and withdrawal symptoms" in ways that are not dissimilar to drug addicts.[139] This isn't a coincidence, wheat contains 5 types of opioid peptides; dairy (which outside of breast milk, only comes with domestication) contains a similar amount.[140]

Grains, the staples of all agrarian and civilized life, are themselves intoxicating. They are the true opiate of the masses. We crave in mind, we crave in body, and so addiction becomes a defining aspect of our reality.

But there is one more aspect of grains that has given them the upper hand since the dawn of agricultural life: they can be fermented.

Enter alcohol.

Liquid Conquest

Alcohol holds an unquestionable throne within civilized life. It is the center of social interactions, synonymous with unwinding from tense situations. A reputation gained despite its direct relationship with increased violence.

This isn't a new situation in any way. Alcohol is arguably the engine that fuels civilizations.

Alcohol covers up drudgery, has been used for subsistence, and has become an outlet, a means of escape from the monotony of domesticated life. It is an excuse for "uncivilized" behavior, a signifier and unifier of cultural identity. It can induce ecstatic states and euphoric escapes.

But it is both the carrot and the stick for domestic life. Civilization may have never existed without it.

One of the earliest domesticated crops, and seemingly the most universal, was not meant for consumption. The domestication of *Lagernaria siceraria*, the bottle gourd, dates back 10-11,000 years before present. It has been adopted more widely than any other domesticated plant for thousands of subsequent years.[141]

The gourd was domesticated for storage, likely for cultivated wild grains.

It is worth noting that those wild grains that were cultivated and eventually domesticated early on were contemporaries or relatives of grain crops as we know them now: wheat, millet, barley, rice, and maize. All of which likely fermented in gourds creating alcohol. Sedentary hunter-collectors weren't just addicted to grains; they were getting drunk off of them.

The absence of carbonized or burnt grains and seeds in the areas where domestication originates seems to indicate that the first widespread use of the grains came from fermenting them for alcohol, not cooking them. Soaked grains are easier to process and any exposure to heat would have caused yeast to form. This is the recipe for alcohol.[142]

Alcohol is a mainstay of village life.

We see this among the pastoral Nuer of contemporary Sudan and Ethiopia, the brewing of beer from millet was relegated to village life over nomadic camps. Porridge and beer were dietary and social staples.[143] As steel axes spread manioc farming through horticultural societies, so too did manioc beer: made largely by women stirring a mash of boiled and chewed manioc until it ferments. By the late twentieth century, the Jívaro considered it "a basic part of their diet" and "consider it to be far superior to plain water, which they drink only in emergencies such as when their beer canteens run dry while they are out hunting."[144]

This use of alcohol has a deep history that extends all the way back through the origins of sedentary and agriculture life.

A combination of porridge or mashes of grains and alcohol become a mainstay of labor from the first cities through industrialism and, as most of us can attest, remains within Modernity. That same mash was used to wean children at a younger age and opening the cradle to be filled with additional fodder for production. Tools and containers meant for the preparation of alcoholic drinks go back 10,000 years before present. In China between 7000-6600 BC, evidence of fermented drinks made from rice, honey, grapes and hawthorn berries become common. Through the Fertile Crescent and the Middle East, domesticated grapes for wine dates back to 5400-5000 BC. Uruk, one of the first cities, brewed alcohol on "an epic scale."[145]

Defining agricultural life, beer "was treated principally as a kind of food" while the wine trade "was a stimulus to civilization in the Middle East."[146] The Old Testament exalts wine. Priests took part in a long-standing duty of brewing.

Civilization was literally carried on the shoulders and backs of drunks. A religious devotion to production required a degree of inebriation to take root. Agriculture, the necessary fuel of civilization, defines drudgery. It defines work: monotonous, pain-staking, dull, and unending work.

Humanity would have never lifted its hand for surplus production if it weren't holding a raised glass.

This holds equally true for industrialism.

The production of alcohol itself didn't just fuel the Industrial Revolution, it was one of its first services: "Breweries were among the earliest modern industrial enterprises."[147] Workers filled factories to earn wages used to get drunk and escape the monotony of drudgery. This is a hamster wheel that comes to define Modernity: the relentless pursuit of moments of elation, no matter what it takes to attain them.

In the 1840s, a young Friedrich Engels observed:

> *It is not surprising that the workers should drink heavily. ... It is particularly on Saturday evenings that intoxication can be seen in all its bestiality, for it is then that the workers have just received their wages and go out for enjoyment at rather earlier hours than*

on other days of the week. ... And when the revelers have no money left they go to the nearest pawnshop with whatever they have...[148]

History also shows a painful trend where the more removed a society becomes, the more extreme the escapes will be.

While beer remained a source of fuel for industrial workers, that escape increasingly required a larger push. That came in particular from distilled spirits. Originally arising as anesthesia in the standard Western military kit to ensure that soldiers acted more like machines than living beings, liquor became a regular part of modernized life. As soldiers left the battlefield and came home, the taste for liquor that they brought back with them flooded industrial society. In many ways liquor "represents a process of *acceleration* of intoxication, intrinsically related to other processes of acceleration in the modern age."[149]

If efficiency was the learned goal, liquor fit the times.

The need for escape among industrial workers was met with another stimulant promoted to the middle class and driven by a Protestant work ethic: coffee. Addiction to alcohol was a target of religious devotees to the Progress that a rising middle class upheld. It wasn't a target because of the addictiveness of alcohol, but because of the uncontrollability of drunks. Alcohol could be targeted because it could be replaced.

And for an industrializing world, coffee fit the bill perfectly.

Despite religious groups early ban on coffee (notably as Christians didn't want to partake in the perceived drink of Muslims), its role in increasing production placed it front and center in the Industrial Revolution. It allowed humans to act like machines:

Medieval man did physical work, for the most part under the open sky. The middle-class man worked increasingly with his head, his workplace was the office, his working position was sedentary. The ideal that hovered before him was to function as uniformly and regularly as a clock.[150]

The class divide over the stimulant of choice: either to promote production or to inhibit escape, only furthered a sense of class camaraderie: a distinction that Engels and fellow socialists would ironically grasp onto. Liquor became the target of socialists while beer became their unifier for the working class.

Gin was a clear threat to proletarian identity. As historian Wolfgang Schivelbusch observes: "It provided alcoholic stupefaction, not social intoxication."[151] Despite the words from a young Engels, socialists saw that it was the tavern that would launch a socialist revolution. Karl Kautsky, a socialist and contemporary of Engels, took no qualms stating: "Without the tavern, the German proletariat has not only no social, but also no political, life."[152]

On the face of it, such a statement might seem contradictory. But that would only be true if the socialists had intended on freeing workers from the drudgery of industrial and agrarian life.

That is what they absolutely did not want.

Socialism catered to that same false sense of community peddled about by religious and political elites since the dawn of civilization: production for the sake of society is rewarding in and of itself. The link between individuals was their sacrifice for the greater good. Engels was aware enough to recognize the importance of an unquestioning sense of place to the human experience.

But he didn't dig deep enough and settled on the drudgery of production.

The prospects of Progress could be liberated beyond the binds of Capitalism. The success that socialists, communists, and anarcho-syndicalists achieved during the industrial era were due to the fact that their notion of community could arguably be found within a rising class-consciousness.

Proletarian identity was observable. There was a sense of belonging. But this was doomed to failure because it was a sense of belonging that was based on escapism, a mutual sense of dis-ease with the misery of work. That distaste lingers back to our hunter-gatherer minds, but could never take root fully because they were limited in their scope to never shed domestication.

Instead, they just blamed the current management. And there is some palatability to that, as anyone who has spent their free time with co-workers complaining about work can attest. And, again, the ritual of complaining about work with co-workers is one that most often revolves around alcohol consumption.

Our domestication requires a sober assessment; which is never an easy task when you realize how horrifically entrenched the values of civilization are within our psyches. If we seek to break the cycles of addiction and patterns of escapism, then this is where we must begin.

From here, the cycles continue to worsen.

None of these things happened in a vacuum. Alcohol wasn't the sole affliction of working class Europeans and Americans. The coffee that fueled the arising middle class came from colonies. Those coffee cups were filled by the forced labor of slaves, plantation systems, and the brutality of the frontier.

They still are and they will continue to be.

It's impossible to look at the sources of our addictive substances while being divorced from reality. The globalized world of this techno-industrial civilization has always come with a body count. Forests are destroyed to make way for cash crops. Societies are torn apart to create labor. Debt-systems are created to build railways, to enlist soldiers as cannon fodder, to perpetuate the maintenance and expansion of a civilization that must grow to survive.

Coffee consumption among the middle class in the industrial age was mirrored in the introduction of sugar, arguably one of the most deadly addictive substances in the world today. As Sidney Mintz unapathetically points out:

> *England fought the most, conquered the most colonies, imported the most slaves (to her own colonies, and, in absolute numbers, in her own bottoms), and went furthest and fastest in creating a plantation system. The most important product of that system was sugar.*[153]

Though sugar becomes one of the most vital substances within modernity, it was hardly alone at the time. Workers in Russia were fueled by vodka. Chinese migrants were lured and addicted with opium. Given the opportunity for work abroad, Chinese migrants would arrive in distant lands carrying a debt that they would never be able to repay. But their brokers would gladly credit their labor with opium, only furthering their debts.

This too should sound familiar. Gangs and politicians run the world of immigration in a constant scheme that involves drugs, cash, and the arms trade. The promise of economic freedom ends in prostitution, trafficking, and industrial slavery today as surely as it did at the dawn of the Industrial era.

So as you hear that more "than a few sick and despairing Chinese finally stepped off the treadmill by the same means used to keep them on it: they took an overdose of opium"[154]: we can find the contemporary correlations in Third World farmers subjected to International Monetary Fund (IMF) and World Bank Structural Adjustment Policies where they are coerced into growing cash crops that require intensive applications of pesticides. Unable to escape debt and sick from contact with toxins, it is not uncommon for them to commit suicide by ingesting the pesticides directly.[155]

On the other side of that equation, you have more and more individuals willing to take extreme drugs like heroin, krokodil, crack, cocaine, and meth.

Our disconnect is unilateral in its impact. The further we are from each other, the more willing we are to turn towards drastic measures of escape. The more we indulge in those escapes, the less aware or caring we are of how those systems even arise and function.

In our attempts to escape misery, we further the reach of domestication.

And there are few places where that is more apparent than where intact communities are thrust into and met by our hollow and hallowed Modernity.

Forced Settlements

> *The Bushmen sat in the dunes, wondering, frustrated and angry. In their frustration, they had begun to turn on each other: there had been a lot of drinking and violence. Rikki, Jakob, even old Dawid, were beating up their wives almost daily, and the children were asking Belinda a question she couldn't answer: 'Why do the grown-ups drink?'*
>
> *Sillikat, who had come back from Kagga Kama for a while, had answered the question one night: 'You want to know why I*

drink? I drink because I feel like a caged animal. In the old days this clan, when we disagreed, would have split up, different families going off to live where they pleased, coming together again as they pleased, no problems, no fighting. So we drink, and when we drink, the anger comes, and we fight.'
- Rupert Isaacson, *The Healing Land*[156]

Civilized narratives go to great lengths to bury the point of contact.

It is here that genocide is simply the norm. It is unironic to speak of domestication in terms of addiction, because there is no greater addict than civilization itself. It must consume life to perpetuate itself: to perpetuate its unchecked growth.

We repackage the wanton extermination of peoples under the guise of "tribal war." We chastise the "savages" for having the repugnant position of choosing the joys that they know from their own existing communities over the perpetuation of our need for resources to fuel our addiction-riddled wallow through apathy. We uphold the virtues of fillers as evidence of our superiority, taunting indigenous societies with sugar and steel, while we destroy everything that they know.

The Huaorani, whose perpetual singing to the forest I spoke of earlier, have their entire world threatened by the presence of oil that would account for thirteen days of oil for American consumption. Thirteen days worth.[157]

The realities of life for intact communities have always been tormented by the inability to rationalize the depravity and extent to which civilized societies will kill, rape, enslave and steal everything. Decimation of a culture, of a place, for nearly all of these peoples, both hunter-gatherer and horticultural alike, was literally unthinkable.

So you see how their worlds are contorted and it makes you sick.

The intoxicated state of shamans amongst native North Americans gave the colonizers an entry point. Drunkenness, which was "perhaps more destructive than any other European influence besides epidemic disease" was met with familiarity. It was treated as "akin to ritually entering an inspired altered state and met with little initial cultural resistance."[158]

By the time the impact of substances were obvious, the damage was already well underway. Alcohol was used to lure Native Americans into a barter system that was absolutely foreign to them. Their land was being stolen, their people raped, tortured and systemically killed, while negotiations over property, a framework that they didn't share, resulted in one of the greatest episodes of land theft in the history of the world.

Alcohol became a tool of escape in the same way civilized societies had always used it.

A situation that was not unacknowledged as this early recorded interaction shows:

> *"When I come to your place with my peltry,"* one Pennsylvania Indian rebuked a trader, *"all call to me: 'Come, Thomas! Here's rum, drink heartily, drink! It will not hurt you.' All this is done for the purpose of cheating me. When you have obtained from me all you want, you call me a drunk dog, and kick me out of the room."*[159]

There was no illusion as to what the colonizers were doing here. A colonial era letter from a Canadian agent of the Hudson Bay Company shows how different native societies were "tamed" by their barter system and how to approach those that hadn't been.

> *In the plains, however, this system will not do, as they can live independent of us, and by withholding ammunition, tobacco and spirits, the Staple articles of Trade, for one year, they will recover the use of their Bows and spears, and lose sight of their smoking and drinking habits; it will therefore be necessary to bring those Tribes round by mild and cautious measure...*[160]

Approached as a bait-and-switch view of civilization, the idea of introducing barter systems sought to give colonization an air of credibility, as though the joys of civilized life were universals. Australia in the 1890s undertook a vast and intentional policy of moving from military force to a policy of rationing. The government specifically targeted peripheral groups in ways to destabilize their self-sufficiency. Baited with free bread, the Aborigines were brought into settlements and then rations turned into barter for labor. Cash, naturally, bought alcohol and tobacco as well.[161]

Sugar is an introductory substance of choice. Its distribution has been synonymous with the spread of Progress throughout the world. First offered by missionaries or "charities", the enticed recipients are then drawn into labor to purchase more.[162] Along with "store food", this is the key reason why diabetic rates among Native Americans, particularly the previously near-carnivore Arctic and Sub-Arctic hunter-gatherers, are among the highest in the world.

Slowly or quickly, civilization settles for nothing less than the complete abolition of hunter-gatherer and horticultural societies by death or assimilation. It is their very existence, the mere possibility of another way of life outside of civilization that threatens the narratives that make the domestication process possible.

Even in a defeated, withdrawn, and corralled state, unless they succumb to the vices of Modern life, they remain a too familiar semblance of what life can be. A reminder of what community can look like and how it can persevere.

Any reminder of the thing that we are all so desperately searching for must be eradicated so that we keep on seeking it out ourselves. So we go to work, so we consume, so we embrace and perpetuate our own misery and emptiness.

It is probable that there is no more of an apparent point of diffusion and forced settlements than roads.

Cutting through forests, opening up deserts and prairies, increasing traffic or increasing access for mining, logging, and hunting, while expanding the reach of governments, corporations, and missionaries, roads carry the means of civilization and its spoils.

For the San of the Kalahari, the presence of roads made it more permissible for neighboring BaTswana tribes to take over more land, putting up fences that block wild migration patterns and keep grazing domesticated animals in their way, sinking boreholes to supply water for livestock. The animals they would otherwise hunt end up dying along agricultural fence lines on what becomes "private property" or, worse, land preserves that bare their names, where they are persecuted for subsistence hunting.

The situation is dire.

With the exception of a few clans still living outside the grasp of the ranchers, most of the Bushmen had found themselves, within a few years, enclosed by wire, their age-old food source gone, reduced to serfs looking after other people's cattle on land that had once been their own.[163]

The roads carry in tourists who bring cash with them. It's a horrid fate that their want to see people living as the whole of humanity is rooted: as nomadic hunter-gatherers, are contributing to the death of their cultures. Tourists brought marijuana into the Kalahari, which has become heavily used by the San.

Among San settled in farming villages, anthropologist Mathias Guenther observed that the economic dependency that arises resulted in the commodification of the healing dance itself. The trance dancer becomes a professional just as the trance is gutted of sharing, that "central mode and spirit."[164] It is the reality of cash "as a medium of exchange and remuneration" that cements "the context of the wage economy."[165] In light of the commodification of the sacred, the San only turn further towards intoxication and addiction as their escape.[166]

This fosters a tense reality, these nomadic hunter-gatherer societies by large knew of intoxicating substances and avoided them. Yet as roads tore into previously uncontacted or inaccessible areas, they brought the scourge of domestication with them. They brought drugs, they brought alcohol, but, more importantly, they brought a reason to use them.

Roads tear apart communities as they bring in the outside world. Miners, workers, armies, missionaries, tourists, governments; the road brings civilization closer and the need to escape that reality rises. And the intoxicants flow in. Arab traders introduced the Pygmies to marijuana. Plains Indians knew of peyote but didn't begin using it ritually until contact had already started to fray their culture. The hunter-collector Ainu of Japan began drinking alcohol after they started growing millet around settlements.[167]

Tobacco, at times symbolic of American exploit, spread from

the agrarian tribes of the south and east of what is now the United States. For the hunter-collector Tlingit of the Pacific Northwest, tobacco was the first crop that was grown.[168] Smoking tobacco was a different acculturation spreading from the point of contact. Amongst the Inuit, they were taught about smoking tobacco from neighboring Russians.[169]

These newly acquired substances can become a source of cultural identity.

Among the Australian Aboriginal cultures, it is widely reported that the use of tobacco and alcohol were long standing native traditions. Alcohol, typically a mild version made of the fermented, sweet sap of the Palm and Miena Cider Gum trees from their crevices, became in some ways emblematic of Aboriginal tradition.[170]

This presumption comes from the fact that Aboriginal societies had such intense reactions to the liquor of the Europeans. Leading to rampant alcoholism, rapidly increasing levels of domestic violence, eventually building a movement that would be countered by contemporary native "anti-Grog" (anti-alcohol) campaigns. However, this method of cider making bares exact resemblance to the Arrack that the Macassan trepangers (sea cucumber fishers) from Indonesia brought to Australia and Tasmania alongside a tradition of smoking tobacco. Like the fermented sap of palm trees, Arrack is a saccharine juice made from fermented sugars and saps.[171]

The Macassan impact on native culture was widespread; the substances that were acquired made their way into the indigenous identity and culture as ingrained traditions.[172] Yet they are overlooked because of the Western bravado around first contact. This occurs despite the fact that cave art depicts the presence of Macassan trade relations as early as the mid-1600s, a timeline that is backed up with the remains of Macassan goods.[173]

It is not improbable that these relationships encouraged coastal Aboriginal societies towards semi-sedentary lives, complete with a loss of social egalitarianism between ages and sexes. Egalitarianism here is not fully buried. As Elder Rosalind Langford stated, "Traditionally, our mob has used plant medicines, healing hands, and spirit to help us move through that and heal." Unfortunately, "nowadays most of our mob use alcohol and drugs to suppress our pain and grief or we use pills."[174]

Intoxicants don't simply arrive on the scene and get added to communities. They become replacements, substitutes. Healing dances wane in lieu of individual intoxication. And it is the communities that suffer.

Pain becomes personal. The social identity of the society and their means of resolution are lost to forced settlements and arguments fueled by alcohol. Dances sometimes are revived for tourists, almost mocking the original form and purpose.

Like us, fragmented lives are subjected to fragments of escape.

In the shadow of community, addicts arise.

Where there is money and defeat, there will be alcohol and escape. As Frank Marlowe observed among the Hadza, tourism within the last two decades increased 10-20 times over. The tourists are eager to pay the Hadza for any cultural relic to take home with them. But once the tourists leave, "neighboring tribes waste no time bringing the Hadza alcohol and leaving with all the tourist money. ... Drinking leads to arguments and fights and injuries and murder. A few recent alcohol-related murders have caused the murder rate to soar."[175]

For the Jarawa of the Andaman Islands, the road has turned them into a tourist attraction. They become a sight seeing trip for the morbid fascination of wealthy Indian travellers. Expensive hotels offer the road through the Jarawa territory as a must see exhibit. The Jarawa were once known for the reclusive behavior and militancy against settlers. But as roads are cut and loggers clear the forests and settlers poach game, they are left coming to the road for handouts.

This has brought alcohol, tobacco and a narcotic betel leaf into their society, but it has also brought endemic disease, such as a measles and pneumonia outbreak, in 1999, that impacted up to half of the population. Poachers, settlers, bus drivers and tourists have notoriously abused, assaulted and raped Jarawa women.[176] It has become a form of drive-thru frontier.

In a global overview of hunter-gatherer and hunter-collector cultures, Carleton Coon states without question that "Drugs, along with new diseases and new foods such as flour and rice, share the principal honors for the decline of hunting populations throughout the world, plus the social disturbances caused by the presence of traders and colonists in recent times."[177]

Roads simply facilitate those interactions.

It is the certainty of genocide that draws indigenous societies away from the road, but it is the reality of ecocide that forces them closer. The illusions of Progress, preached from a sugar-coated pulpit that creates the desperation where hope for survival overcomes the fear of assured cultural assimilation.

The uncomfortable back and forth of this reality is best spoken of by the Awa of Papua New Guinea, who share suffering on both sides of this ambiguous colonial reality:

To them, however, the road remains a metaphor for culture change and 'development.' Men talk about it feverishly and insistently point to the high rain forest where it will eventually come. The road-to-be is a symbol of salvation, of endless economic gain, a path toward material wealth and increasingly accessible consumerism.

But not all of the villagers find this talk comforting. ... Still others, mainly of the older generation, know that a road will be their final death cry. They could already see the end coming in the past several decades of contact with the uninvited arrival of pale, gum-booted Australian kiaps (patrol officers), Western currency, trade stores, and wage labor migration that carried their young sons on airplanes to the coastal plantations that they themselves would never see.[178]

Perhaps sharing in the delusion, my hope is that the civilization building these roads bleeds itself dry before any more can be built. But this is the reality of our shared situation that we also must face.

Our lives are not without consequence.

Drugged Warriors, Drug Wars

Of all of civilization's occupational categories, that of soldier may be the most conductive to regular drug use.

— David Courtwright, *Forces of Habit*[179]

A history of drugs, like any other facet of civilized life, cannot ignore a primary antagonist: warfare.

There is perhaps no greater truism than anthropologist Stanley Diamond's statement that "Civilization originates in conquest abroad and repression at home. Each is an aspect of the other."[180]

Liquor was distilled through military personnel before it found its way into mainstream society. The same can be said about nearly every other hard drug. Heroin and cocaine are perhaps the worst of it, but just as soldiers bring their newly formed addictions home, so too do those addictions fuel war.

There is no distinction to be made here. The further civilization carries on, the more intoxicants become another resource to war over. Warriors arise early in the trajectory of domesticated societies, as we've seen among the Yanomami and other horticultural societies. But here warfare becomes social in nature. The cult of the warrior serves to limit populations by creating a preference for having boys instead of girls, resulting in higher rates of female infanticide. Brutal though it may be, when the ecological benefits of slow population growth within nomadic societies are lifted, that is a pattern that is largely efficient in limiting numbers.

But warfare within horticultural societies is a very real thing.

And we see that in some regards the rituals surrounding horticultural warfare run contrary to warfare as we know it. Amongst horticulturalists in Papua New Guinea, for example, battlefield warfare was mired in ritual. Pigs were slaughtered and feasted upon before battles, warriors gorged on food, and there were ritual limitations on drinking water. Parched and overstuffed, these moves reduced the potential duration of battles. Death tolls were reduced. This, however, isn't to give the impression that horticultural warfare was less violent: the flipside of battlefield warfare was a shorter and nastier pattern of raiding which involved sneak attacks, a massive loss of life and abduction of women and children.[181]

It becomes clear how things like steel tools and manioc beer, or its localized equivalent, alongside epidemics of new diseases exponentially increased the drastic impact of contact.

Unfortunately, we don't need imagination to see what that looked like.

Unlike the horticultural warrior, the soldiers of civilization became intoxicated to prolong their rampages, not to shorten them.

The arsenal of soldiers, specialists in killing and subjugating populations, contained intoxicants as rations. In contrast to the methods of horticultural warriors, civilized soldiers were meant to be more deadly, fiercer: more machine-like. Liquor allotments in the era of industrializing military forces were required for anaesthetization, or, "to make the soldier an integral member of the mechanical corps."[182] It shouldn't be surprising that the use of those same intoxicants would be used "to allay the boredom and fatigue inherent in military life."[183]

The problem with soldiers is that they're still human.

Killing is no easy task, but it is the involvement in mass killing and mass destruction, often in areas or places removed from what one may call home, that fragments an experience of the world. Post-Traumatic Stress Disorder (PTSD) is most discussed as it impacts soldiers. Traumatic experiences were created by war, but removed from any communal background and then often put back into civilian life; there is no way to process those traumatic experiences.

Soldiers may be examples of this, but they're not alone. PTSD is often a gateway to addiction and with the trauma of the domestication process, none of us are exempt from it. Logically, soldiers tend to face PTSD the most and they're also on the frontline of addictive substances used to self-medicate.

A mixture of trauma and intoxication was crucial in the cathartic transformation of warlords and their ranks, often including children. Themselves outcasts of horrific violence and civil wars, refugees left to wander alone after witnessing the death of their families and the destruction of their homes. Child soldiers were initiated through acts of horrific violence. Their first kills, sometimes their own family members, were never with bullets, but often hacking with a machete or equally brute and direct forms of violence.

Taking part in this brutality actually allowed them to "psychologically distance themselves from it." As individuals involved in campaigns to rehabilitate former child soldiers saw over and over again: "The children suffered more trauma from seeing someone hacked to death ... because they were witnesses, not the executioners."[184]

A former child soldier of the Revolutionary United Front of Sierra Leone, Ishmael Beah, spoke of the role drugs played in coaxing this initiation into an altered reality:

> *We walked for long hours and stopped only to eat sardines and corned beef with gari, sniff cocaine, brown brown, and take some white capsules. The combination of these drugs gave us a lot of energy and made us fierce. The idea of death didn't cross my mind at all and killing had become as easy as drinking water. My mind not only snapped during the first killing, it had also stopped making remorseful records, or so it seemed.*[185]

Brown brown is a drug of choice amongst African warlords. Often considered to be a mixture of gunpowder and cocaine, it is more often than not gunpowder mixed with heroin or amphetamines.[186] Heroin increasingly became an option through the region as it spread from Afghanistan following its rise to opioid-fueled prominence in the early 2000s.

This relationship between intoxication and war overrides all religious and political boundaries. It has been found that radical Islamic militants will promote and lethally enforce Sharia Law on one hand and drug their warriors without hesitation on the other.

Boko Haram's involvement in the drug trade and use of drugs is well known.[187] While jihadist fighters within the death cult of ISIS use a drug called Captagon, "an amphetamine pill that can cause a surge of energy and a euphoric high."[188]

Like every aspect of domestication, we cannot cease to be humans, but domesticators will seek to use our needs against us. Diverting our want for belonging and place into jihadist death cults or imperialist forces fueled by nationalism serves no different force.

In the end, it all looks the same.

Heroin use among Vietnam Veterans was an epidemic. While GIs were restricted from liquor and marijuana on bases, heroin could be mixed with tobacco and smoked without notice from superior officers. But even more importantly, heroin was accessible.

> *Heroin was available at roadside stalls on every highway out of Saigon, and on the route to the main US army base at Long Binh, as well as from itinerant peddlers, newspaper and ice-cream vendors, restaurant owners, brothel keepers and their whores and domestic servants employed on US bases.*[189]

It is estimated that in 1971 over 10 percent of enlisted US soldiers in Vietnam were addicted to heroin. That equates to at least 25,000 men.[190] In the same year, there were roughly 10,000 Veteran addicts at home in New York City alone.[191]

This trend didn't end with the Vietnam War.

The destabilization of Afghanistan caused by the current and now long running war there resulted in its ascendancy to the number one producer of opioids in the world. As millenials are shuffled into the military, their lives shaken by the nationalistic fervor of their youths surrounding the September 11, 2001 terror attacks in the US, they have found a pipeline for heroin akin to what was seen in Vietnam.

If you compare the contemporary maps of the highest per capita use and overdose from heroin with a map of active military bases, they overlap exactly.[192] This cannot be coincidental. And as we shall see, it never has been.

The United States government has a long-standing tradition of its own involvement in the international drug trade. In the 1950s, in an attempt to subvert the rise of Communist China, the CIA had been backing anti-communist opium producers to destabilize the region. Communism was not thwarted, but the Golden Triangle was created. While this is often attributed to the CIA turning its head for an enemy's enemy, it was a far more insidious involvement: "In short, the CIA became inextricably entangled with the Golden Triangle opium trade, handling opiate consignments, flying drug runs and tolerantly turning a blind eye to the affairs of their criminal allies."[193]

Cocaine was arguably even worse.

Gary Webb shined a light on the involvement of the CIA in

what became the crack-cocaine epidemic that overtook largely African-American low-income neighborhoods, leading to higher involvement in the criminal system and steeper punishments for possession of crack than possession of cocaine, another form of the same drug used more heavily by whites.

Webb's reporting did not go unnoticed even though official government confirmation came out silently in the media just as the Clinton-Lewinsky sex scandal took over the headlines. Webb himself would be found dead a few years later, his death ruled a suicide despite having died with two bullets to the head.

What came of this was that in Nicaragua the US was funding the Contras, a particularly vicious paramilitary group, in their war against the socialist Sandinistas. Unable to give direct funding, the CIA built a pipeline for funding through the trafficking of cocaine. In the process creating intricate networks of stateside drug gangs and international drug cartels.

Not unlike the viciousness inherit in targeting indigenous populations; the CIA "had assisted the transformation of the powder cocaine market to crack cocaine in the early 1980s." Cheaper and now widely available, crack tore communities apart.[194] And as it remains a cheap high and offers quicker escape through smoking, it still does.

Ironically, though the intent was to defund socialist revolutionaries, cocaine has since become a primary funding source for FARC, a merciless Communist army in Columbia, among others. As the Columbian drug trade originated in the 1970s with marijuana, FARC denounced the trade under Communist Party principles, resulting in burnt plantations and running their owners out.

Cocaine, a higher priced commodity, was different. For FARC, "the benefits were too big to ignore, and the guerillas' logic shifted. Soon, what was against their ideals became "just another crop" that the rebels decided to tax."[195]

The presumption of war for ideological reasons falters constantly under a reality that all lines cross. All civilizations, regardless of stated religious or political affiliation, require resources. And here cash is a secular king.

And it is all of us, with our incessant search to fill the void within, who are footing the bill.

As the former President of Columbia, Virgilio Barco Vargas accurately stated: "The only law the narcoterrorists don't break is the law of supply and demand."[196]

The drug cartels that were a proxy of CIA counter-insurgencies during the Cold War didn't fade away. They grew. And they continue to grow more powerful and more deadly.

In Mexico, the lethality of these cartels is impossible to overlook. Between 2007 and 2014, there were 164,000 drug-related homicides in Mexico.[197] Mass kidnappings, executions, drive-by shootings; the United States market for marijuana, cocaine and methamphetamines pays for all of this carnage.[198]

Those 164,000 bodies are absolutely foreign to us.

We attribute them to violence between drug cartels, but that is only a fraction of it. The reality here is gristly. At times the morgues in Mexico City are overrun with bodies. Lives lost to organized and disorganized violence. There is no shortage of documentation here despite our aloofness and involvement in the entire ordeal.

The day-to-day violence can look like this: On May 13, 2012, 49 decapitated and dismembered bodies were found alongside a highway in Nuevo Leon. On September 26, 2014 gunmen opened fire on buses carrying students and soccer players in southern Mexico, leaving 3 dead and 43 missing. Those 43 were declared dead the following January.[199]

In two instances that amounts to 95 lives lost to drug-related violence, a drop in the bucket for that total number of 164,000. And these instances are happening daily.

But they are not confined to Mexico.

Mexican drug cartels use would-be migrants riddled with impossible debts to guard and maintain devastating marijuana plantations within US National Forests.[200] Josh Harkinson summed up the damage in around the San Bernardino National Forest in 2009.

Growers clear land year-round, plant crops in the spring, and haul out the harvest in the fall, often leaving behind mounds of trash and dead animals, denuded hillsides, and streams full of sediment and human waste. Last year, the community of Snow

Creek, California, traced feces in its water treatment plant to a grow in the nearby San Bernardino National Forest.[201]

These illegal growing operations have destroyed 10,000 acres of National Forest. All of this for marijuana: grown for and sold to Americans.

The lavish extravagance of the cartel's drug lords is so ridiculous that it can be best exhibited not in how they lived, but in how they were buried. The mausoleums of the cartels are well documented for their exuberance. Cemeteries for the cartels look like high-price gated condominiums.

Ignacio Coronel, a founder of the Sinaloa Cartel and the self-proclaimed "King of Crystal" for his role in the manufacture and distribution of methamphetamine in the United States, is entombed in a $450,000 mausoleum with state-of-the-art music and security systems, Wi-Fi, and air conditioning. Arturo Guzman Loera, brother of notorious drug lord El Chapo, is enshrined in a modest two-story, air-conditioned mausoleum with 24-hour surveillance, and en-suite bedrooms with a price tag of $1,200,000.[202]

This globalized, hyper-technological civilization distributes consequences, not wealth. Profit from misery is distilled into a small global elite and that is who the rest of us are busy producing for. And when we're not busy just trying to get by, we are buying substitutes for the community of nomadic bands that was our birthright for the 2.5 million years leading up to our lives as *Homo sapiens*.

We are the products of a historically created and horrifically malicious system that seeks to tear apart our being and sell it back to us piecemeal. And the price is complicity in our own enslavement and the enslavement of all other life on the planet.

This is the unforeseeable consequence of hunter-collectors settling around wild grains 10,000 years ago. A cycle perpetuated by unthinkable levels of violence and an inability to psychologically reconcile the consequences of our actions, worsened as technology casts our shadow further and deeper throughout the world.

So raise your glass in cheers to the conquest of nothingness: the endless pursuit of completion.

It only gets worse.

Modernity and Other Distractions

> *The peculiar, vomitorious genius of modern capitalism is its ability to betray our senses with one class of products or services and then sell us another to cope with the damage so that we can go back to consuming more of what caused the problem in the first place.*
>
> - David Courtwright, *Forces of Habit*[203]

If the goal of domestication is to subvert innate human desires towards consumed impulse, then there is no finer closing for civilization than our current era of late Modernity.

We, the children of Progress and Empire, have run the mill. Our lineages are divorced from place. Community is increasingly about many weak online connections rather than deep and meaningful interactions.

We take part in the dreams of programmers. Our hesitations for drudgery are reflected onto the potential of technology to take on mundane tasks and, seemingly, human action. If domestication were able to deliver on its promises of substitutes for ecstatic states, this would be it. We equate freedom with the freedom of choice between products. We believe that we are free to do as we please: that if we chose to we could walk away from civilization.

And we are miserable.

The myths of the domesticators ring hollow. They have offered to us the technology, the medications, the stuff, the sugar-laced foods, and the machines. We consume them in such frenzy that they get old quickly and we crave more.

Addiction defines Modernity because it must. The more our society offers the rewards of Progress, the more apparent it becomes that they are filler: the dreams of cyborgs.

And so we consume.

Everything.

Capitalists long ago recognized that dopamine, that source of joy that floods our brains quickly, brings about euphoric states. It gives us that feeling that we are getting what it is we need in life. Unfulfilled we come back for that hit, again and again.

This chronic need for fulfillment feeds into the role we have taken on as spectators. We no longer take part in the creation and exaltations of communal joy: we become voyeurs. Healing dances are replaced by stages, by mass spectacles of State power, or exhibitions of individual ability. Situationist Guy Debord referred to "the society of the spectacle" as "an epoch without festivals."[204] Barbara Ehrenreich follows on his sentiment: "Instead of generating their own collective pleasures, people absorb, or consume, the spectacles of commercial entertainment, nationalist rituals, and the consumer culture, with its endless advertisements for the pleasure of individual ownership."[205]

In the absence of community, indulgence of the Self takes over.

But we still seek and desire that sense of belonging, that sense of place: that moment of euphoria.

And so we consume it regardless of consequence.

I often wonder how anyone in our society could turn to heroin, crack or similar heavy drugs. There's no absence of information about what happens. How the brain can stop producing serotonin on its own and how this furthers dependency and worsens withdrawal.

But I knew Mike.

We grew up together and both of us were witnesses to how all problems could be solved by consumption. If you have a physical problem or any level of discomfort, there is a pill for that. Attention issues? Moodiness? Anger? Sadness? Each one had its pills. And the more pills you take, the more you must increase the dosage to feel the effect.

We see this in literally every aspect of life within Modernity. Our solutions are always to increase the synthetics and to amplify the effect. We expect immediate gratification. We expect to be entertained and coddled. Catered and comforted. We've reduced our needs to the chemical level and then reassemble them in pieces.

Oxycodone is a natural step in. Global poppy supply increases, first in Afghanistan, then in Latin America where the "War on Drugs" resulted in ridgelines of forest wiped out with glyphosate to combat coca operations pushing the growers into valleys where poppy grows easily. The cost of opiates drops and the drug companies react.

Opium use, in either heroin or painkillers, exploded simply because it was cheap and powerful.[206] Doctors began prescribing Oxycodone for increasingly less severe pain. Age was never a consideration; children and teenagers were and are being given opiates for relatively minor injuries.

I feel a sense of haunting over me after hearing the torn and pain-ridden words of a Massachusetts mother who lost two sons to heroin, an addiction that began as their high school football injuries were treated with Oxycodone. They were hooked and when the prescriptions ran out, heroin was there, and cheaper. In her words:

Back in 1999, Perdue Pharmacy spent 200 million dollars pushing opiates… What was supposed to be a life ending severe pain we start giving for wisdom teeth. Why are we pushing these drugs?[207]

On the streets, the cost of a single Oxycodone pill can run $80.

A hit of heroin can cost $10.

In the words of users: "I fell in love with the feeling. And it's cheap." "Heroin was amazing. It was like a fountain of warmth shooting out of the top of your head, covering you in a velvet blanket." "I don't shoot heroin to get high, I shoot it to get well. … I don't know how to have fun without drugs."[208]

There used to be a myth of Progress that pervaded the language of civilization: a notion that things were better and that they would continue to improve. As technology and social media use increase, we no longer talk of Progress: we live it. We expect the gratification of desires and it keeps us from even having to look up. Consequences take place in a time that isn't now, so it simply doesn't matter.[209]

This is the epitome of addiction: I will do what it takes to get this sensation immediately.

A new drug, Krokodil, drives that home. It is also appropriately called 'the zombie drug' and its name taken from the reptilian-esque skin users develop as a result of missing the vein while injecting, even slightly.

Krokodil has been an epidemic in Russia, but hasn't stopped there. Junkies use it because it is cheaper than heroin and a relatively similar high, but it is easier to manufacture. It is made from mixing codeine with "a brew of poisons such as paint thinner, hydrochloric acid and red phosphorus scraped from the strike pads on matchboxes."[210] Life expectancy for users is drastically short even compared to heroin users: typically one year, maybe two.

Where users inject the drug, "blood vessels burst and surrounding tissue dies, sometimes falling off the bone in chunks."[211] If you miss the vein, that area of flesh will die right away. If there is a worse drug out there, I don't think I can stand to hear about it.

A Russian krokodil user shares no illusion about the nature of this particular mix of poisons:

> *"You can feel how disgusting it is when you're doing it," he recalls. "You're dreaming of heroin, of something that feels clean and not like poison. But you can't afford it, so you keep doing the krokodil. Until you die."*[212]

Krokodil may be the more extreme case, but it is not abnormal.

Any place where the will to live is gone, this is what you'll find. For Inuit communities, they are losing their children to an addiction of huffing gas.[213] Indigenous societies in Canada that have been subjected to the decimation of their communities have a suicide rate ten times the national average.

The Guarani of Brazil have been committing suicide in droves. In 1995, suicide ended the lives of 56 Guarani. But suicide isn't what caused their death, the destruction of their culture did. The sentiment was not hard for remaining Guarani to understand:

> *Young people are nostalgic for the beautiful forests… A young person told me he didn't want to live anymore because there was no reason to carry on living—there is no hunting, no fishing, and the water is polluted.*[214]

The search for extremes in getting high has led to a flood of Western hipsters seeking *ayahuasca* for a new high. This has resulted in the deaths of European and American teens from using synthetic alternatives for the drug (native to South America) during sessions with faux-shamans.[215]

Not to be outdone, *Vice Magazine* wasn't going to miss out on this "new" trend, paying $230 per session with a "shaman" in Berlin, selling the trip as horribly as possible:

> *For late thirtysomething affluent vegans who don't go to clubs anymore and who spend Christmas in India so they don't have to visit their parents, it's about as hip as partner swapping.*

Confirming their own expectations, after elaborating on the violent sickness that comes hand-in-hand with this intoxicant:

> *In a way, it takes you back to your original essence in nature, and that's no bad thing if, like me, your regular connection with nature is watching your tomato plants slowly die on the windowsill each summer.*

Have no fear, that's not the only perk:

> *Oh, and seeing your dick as tall as a building, rendered from solid, impenetrable stone is something all insecure young boys, who grow into secretly insecure men, need to see at least twice.*[216]

"It is a measure of our general deprivation" states Barbara Ehrenreich, "that the most common referent for *ecstasy* in usage today is not an experience but a drug, MDMA, that offers fleeting feelings of euphoria and connectedness."[217]

For most of us, these extremes may come as unfamiliar. We can see them from the safety of a distance. We can judge and we can lie to ourselves.

The dopamine response that heroin users become addicted to lacks scrutiny with more acceptable social behaviors. As we mindlessly swipe the screen of a smartphone looking for updates, the mind releases dopamine in ways similar to receiving good news.[218] The hit of dopamine that comes from getting "likes" on Facebook "fools our brain into believing that loved ones surround us."[219]

A new trend has arisen in cities where there are "cuddle parties" or "snuggle buddies." These are explicitly non-sexual interactions where the purpose is simply to be touched. One company offers the service for $80 an hour and sessions up to 10 hours. Advertising the service as a cure all for everything from depression to aging, there is no question that the oxytocin released in our brains when we are in contact with another being creates a sense of joy.[220] But this industry is kind of a sad call back to the healing rituals we opened with.

There are moments when our search for community comes so close in form and function to those healing rituals, but deprived of context, it all becomes a kind of perversion. What we want, what we need, is right in front of us, but we are all too damaged to reach out. Paying for a service is far more in the comfort zone that has been provided to us.

It is consumable.

Addiction is a patterned behavior: a self-reinforcing cycle. Stripped of place, dopamine and its feelings of joy within our bodies becomes another drug. Psychologist Amy Banks explains our altered relationship with dopamine:

> *In an ideal world—one that understands the centrality of healthy relationship to health and wellness—the dopamine reward system stays connected to human connection as the primary source of stimulation. Unfortunately, we do not live in this ideal world. We live in a culture that actively undermines this precious dopamine-relationship connection. We raise children to stand on their own two feet while the separate self is an American icon of maturity. It is making us sick.*
>
> *This disconnection is a set-up for addiction as we search for other sources of dopamine. The "other sources" look shockingly similar to the list of common cultural complaints—overeating and obesity, drug and alcohol abuse, consumerism, chronic hooking up. Not only do these addictive, destructive behaviors get paired*

> *to the dopamine reward system but they create a feedback loop of isolation that pushes people towards more addictions.*[221]

The problem for domesticators is that we're still human. We're still animals.

We always have been and we always will be.

As depressing and hopeless as an exploration of addiction and civilization can feel, the common thread throughout all of this is that we never give up. The hunter-gatherer within us is not dead. We are captive animals. Distracted though we may be, it is the existence of our emptiness, the depravity of our search for that connection that keeps programmers awake at night.

Removed as we are from the world as we were meant to inherit it: our want for community struggles against all odds.

And it is that undying spirit that may ultimately bring the end of civilization.

Revival of the Spirit

> *The last communities do a ghost dance, and the ghosts of the last communities will continue to dance within the entrails of the artificial beast. The council-fires of the never-defeated communities are not extinguished by the genocidal invaders, just as the light of Ahura Mazda was not extinguished by rulers who claimed it shone on them. The fire is eclipsed by something dark, but it continues to burn, and its flames shoot out where they are least expected.*
>
> - Fredy Perlman, *Against His-Story, Against Leviathan*[222]

Rupert Isaacson sought out the San for his own reasons. He wanted to enter the Kalahari to find his wholeness, to take part in an ancestral society with its healing dances and intact community. What he found in his journeys at the turn of the twenty-first century was a radical departure from those expectations.

At this point, we know what happened to the San.

We know that forced settlements, an influx of intoxicants and an illegalization of subsistence hunting and nomadism took its toll on their culture. During his time with the San, Isaacson was forced to take a realistic assessment of what had happened and what future lay ahead for this captive society of hunter-gatherers as they struggle to fight for their land rights.

Before leaving the Kalahari, Isaacson witnessed a minor victory in the fight for land rights. An occasion met with the unthinkable: a healing dance. Outside of the world of tourists, this relic of their communal life had not vanished completely.[223]

Against all odds, the potential for healing, the potential for community survives.

It does no good to blame addicts.

That's not grounds for absolving or justifying behaviors. But the problem is that if we don't confront the nature and presence of our own addictions then we are simply denying our complicity with civilization, with the perpetuation of our own domestication.

We need a sober assessment of our situation and we need action to follow. It is not enough to blame the lack of community for indulgences. Rebuilding community is certainly no easy task, but it is the task at hand. Resistance against domestication, if it is not grounded in the world of the known rather than a philosophical notion of what could be, will never be successful.

This is also not the hippies call to the commune. Proximity alone is not enough.

Functioning community is a place where resolution comes from contextualizing conflict and handling problems on their own terms. Rooted in subsistence, community requires a connection to place and a basis in subsistence or, at the very least, a turn towards it.

We have to shed utopian and liberal delusions and the belief that we can and always will get along; we need to embrace those aspects of human emotion and behavior that only the primal anarchy of nomadic hunter-gatherer life can endure. And I say this knowing full well that nothing in life is this easy. We all have our conditioning and we are under assault on all fronts from the world that civilization has created.

But we have to start somewhere.

Like addicts, no one can make us change if we don't seek it out ourselves.

Like nomadic hunter-gatherers, engagement of community makes it immediately apparent that any illusion of freedom to leave civilization is a hoax. If it was simply accomplishable indigenous societies would have never taken up settlements or been forced to take up arms against armies, missionaries, developers, and corporations. To engage with the world, we can't carry delusions. Community begins with honest communication, with allowing ourselves to be vulnerable and emboldened at the same time.

This will not be a quick journey.

Rewilding can only be measured in terms of generations, not individuals.

Without resistance, there will never be the chance to see that through.

Our spirits need an awakening: a place to open up. A place where we can truly feel the crushing anguish and despair that suicidal Guarani peoples feel as they see the state of the world thrust upon them.

We need a place where our sense of comfort in conformity is challenged by sustenance.

And we will not get there alone.

Our ability to effectively bleed the machine that has stripped us of our community will be a rage born of healing: a euphoric catharsis within the context of the dispossessed.

Kia and *Molimo* are not ours for the taking, but they are part of a legacy of primal healing. Our dance has yet to be found, but it exists. That the seed of community hasn't been killed already should give us hope. As should the need of colonizers to target the healing dances. If the veneer of domestication begins to crack, the threat posed by communities of resistance arises.

"This is the real bone of contention between civilization and collective ecstasy:" Barbara Ehrenreich observes, "Ecstatic rituals still build group cohesion, but when they build it among subordinates—peasants, slaves, women, colonized people—the elite calls out its troops."[224]

The minor victory that Isaacson had witnessed did not last. The settled life of the San had carried on. *Kia* became a thing of memory. Or so it would seem. The anthropologist Charlie Goodwin living amongst the San happened to catch a group of drunk San engage in *kia*.[225]

The hope of communal survival springs forth again in dance.

Among present day Baka, hunting was a source of social cohesion: one that has been stripped away by the weight of Modernity. And yet when large groups gather, the songs and dances return.[226]

Despite everything that we have seen about the world that we have created, the world we were born into, it is resiliency that has carried humans as far and wide as we have moved. It is that same resiliency that allows the body to continue existing even as we assault it with chemicals, intoxicants, and poisons, subject it to sedentary life, and attack our senses with the sights and sounds of civilization instead of immersing ourselves in the wild.

For whatever reason, against all odds, our bodies still function.

It is easy to see that as a misfortune: to see what it is that civilization has done to this world, our home, and to be able to carry on. It's a privilege that we take for granted as we lose ourselves in screens and empty relationships, in production and consumption.

And yet it is that resiliency that keeps us searching.

Against all of the hopelessness in the world as it is, it is this constant nagging and want for life that gives me reason to fight.

To resist.

To undermine the logic of domestication.

The urge that led Mike to inject heroin into his veins lives on with me. Within all of us.

I can only imagine what may happen when our healing begins. What we may be capable of when we find our place again and are forced to confront the civilization that threatens to exterminate it.

May we one day dance in euphoria upon its ruins.

As wild beings freed from captivity.

As wild, euphoric communities.

Dedicated to Mike and Danielle.

Endnotes

1. David Courtwright, *Forces of Habit: Drugs and the Making of the Modern World*. Harvard UP: Cambridge, 2001. Pg 92. I can't speak highly enough of this book.
2. Cited in Chellis Glendinning, *My Name is Chellis and I'm in Recovery from Western Civilization*. Shambhala: Boston, 1994. Pg 99.
3. Ibid. Pg 98.
4. Ibid.
5. 'The Heroin Epidemic in 9 Graphs', US News & World Report. http://www.usnews.com/news/blogs/data-mine/2015/08/19/the-heroin-epidemic-in-9-graphs Accessed 12-24-2015.
6. 'Today's Heroin Epidemic' CDC, http://www.cdc.gov/vitalsigns/heroin/ Accessed 12-24-2015
7. 'Opioid Addiction Disease 2015 Facts & Figures' American Society of Addiction Medicine. http://www.asam.org/docs/default-source/advocacy/opioid-addiction-disease-facts-figures.pdf Accessed 12-24-2015
8. http://www.nytimes.com/interactive/2016/01/07/us/drug-overdose-deaths-in-the-us.html?_r=0 Accessed 2-25-2016.
9. John Zerzan, *Future Primitive and Other Essays*. Autonomedia: Brooklyn, 1994. Pg 137.
10. The distinction between immediate and delayed return hunter-gatherer societies is absolutely crucial to understanding domestication. For more on this, see James Woodburn, 'Egalitarian Societies'. *Man*, New Series. No 17, Vol 3 (Sept 1982).
11. Colin Turnbull, 'The Importance of Flux in Two Hunting Societies' in Lee and Devore (eds), *Man the Hunter*. Aldine de Gruyter: New York, 1968. Pg 132.
12. Turnbull, Woodburn, et al, 'Resolving Conflicts by Fission' in Lee and Devore, 1968. Pg 156.
13. Colin Turnbull, *The Human Cycle*. Simon and Schuster: New York, 1983. Pg 45.
14. Turnbull, 1968. Pg 156.
15. For more on this, see my essay 'To Speak of Wildness' in *Black and Green Review* no 2, Fall 2015.
16. Turnbull, 'The Ritualization of Potential Conflict Among the Mbuti' in Leacock and Lee, *Politics and History in Band Society*. Cambridge UP: London, 1982. Pg 142.
17. Cited in Frank Marlowe, *The Hadza: Hunter-Gatherers of Tanzania*. University of California Press: Berkeley, CA, 2010. Pg 60.
18. Carleton Coon, *The Hunting Peoples*. Nick Lyons Books: New York, 1971. Pg 187. Coon specifies in this line about the "vast majority of hunting and gathering peoples" and highlights "habit-forming drugs", but the book includes immediate and delayed return HG societies. As we see here, numerous delayed return HG societies do use intoxicants for ritualistic purposes, hence the qualifications in this particular line. The study does specify which societies do and do not use

intoxicants.

19. I have to admit my hesitancy in adding this clarification. I've spent the last decade trying to disprove the correlation between nomadic hunter-gatherer life and a distinct lack of intoxicating substances and cannot disprove it. However, I've chosen to leave this a bit more open and ambiguous because if someone were to find a skeleton of an individual Pleistocene-era hunter-gatherer with handfuls of opium somehow, the link between ritualistic and habitual use still stands. Egalitarianism is the nature of nomadic hunter-gatherer societies, in terms of individual behavior; this gives the space for true individual freedom should one wish to take that to whatever ends they imagine.

20. Glendinning, 1994. Pg 126.

21. Laura Rival, *Trekking Through History: The Huaorani of Amazonian Ecuador*. Columbia UP: New York, 2002. Pg 138.

22. Note that I have standardized all references to *n/um* despite some variation in how the term is spelled within the ethnographic record for the sake of consistency.

23. Richard Katz, *Boiling Energy: Community Healing Among the Kalahari Kung*. Harvard UP: Cambridge, MA, 1982. Pg 52.

24. Ibid, Pg 44.

25. Richard Lee, *The Dobe Ju/'hoansi (3rd edition)*. Wadsworth: London, 2003. Pg 130-131.

26. Mathias Guenther, *Tricksters & Trancers: Bushman Religion and Society*. Indiana UP: Bloomington, IN, 1999. Pg 181.

27. Katz, 1982. Pg 35.

28. Marjorie Shostak, *Nisa: The Life and Words of a !Kung Woman*. Vintage: New York, 2983. Pg 299.

29. Katz, 1982. Pg 52.

30. Shostak, 1983. Pg 296.

31. Lee, 2003. Pg 132.

32. Guenther, 1999. Pg 182.

33. Ibid. Pg 183. It is worth noting that Nisa claims that sometimes adolescents are given a root to help ease their transition into *n/um*, but I have not been able to find anything in detail about what the root is and whether it may be an intoxicant or an herbal remedy. Regardless, it is only used for "training" purposes, not to induce *n/um*.

34. Shostak, 1983. Pg 299.

35. Ibid, Pg 296.

36. Guenther, 1999. Pg 183.

37. Katz, 1982. Pg 37.

38. Lee, 2003. Pg 135 and Shostak, 1983. Pg 296.

39. Daisuke Bundo, 'Social Relationship Embodied in Singing and Dancing Performances Among the Baka'. *African Study Monographs*, Supp. 26: 85-101, March 2001. Pg 96.

40. Ibid. Pg 86.

41. Jerome Lewis, 'How Language Evolved from Singing'. https://vimeo.com/114605825 . For more on this subject, see my essay 'Subjects Object!' in *Black and Green Review* no 2 (Fall 2015).

42. Rival, 2002. Pg 101.

43. Kevin Duffy, *The Children of the Forest: Africa's Mbuti Pygmies*. Waveland Press: Prospect Heights, IL, 1996. Pg 54.
44. Turnbull, 1983. Pg 44.
45. Colin Turnbull, *Wayward Servants*. The Natural History Press: Garden City, NY, 1965. Pgs 132-133.
46. Ibid. Pg 72.
47. The absence of fire and even moonlight (during the Hadza's *epeme*) is worth further exploration. It seems probable that this dance is so primal that it incorporates a rejection of fire and a complete absorption into wildness without any element of mediation.
48. Marlowe, 2010. Pg 59.
49. Ibid, pg 68.
50. Bundo, 2001. Pg 96.
51. Paul Shepard, *Coming Home to the Pleistocene*. Island Press: Washington DC, 1998. Pgs 91-92.
52. Hunter-collectors are discussed in greater detail in the "Conquests of Bread" section, also see my essays 'The Forest Beyond the Field' and 'To Produce or To Not Produce' in Tucker, 2010.
53. For example, see Masato Sawada, 'Encounters with the Dead Among Efe and the Balese in the Ituri Forest: Mores and Ethnic Identity Shown by the Dead'. *African Study Monographs*, Suppl. 25:85-104, March 1998.
54. Mircea Eliade, *Shamanism: Archaic Techniques of Ecstasy*. Princeton UP: Princeton, 1974. Pg 84.
55. Ibid.
56. Ibid, Pg 109.
57. David Riches, 'Shamanism: the Key to Religion'. *Man*, New Series, Vol 29 No 2 (June 1994), Pgs 381-405. Pg 389.
58. Ibid. Pg 382.
59. Eliade, 1974. Pgs 222-223 & Pg 221.
60. Ibid. Pgs 222-223.
61. An act made famous enough in Siberia to channel animal spirits that it became a target during the onslaught of relentless Soviet persecution of Siberian shamans, see Piers Vitebseky, *The Reindeer People: Living with Animals and Spirits in Siberia*. Houghton Mifflin: Boston, 2005. Pg 261.
62. Andy Letcher, *Shroom: A Cultural History of the Magic Mushroom*. Harper Collins: New York, 2006. Pg 15.
63. Ibid, Pg 28.
64. O.T. Oss & O.N. Oeric, *Psilocybin: Magic Mushroom Grower's Guide*. Quick American Publishing, 1993. Pg 20.
65. Letcher, 2006. Pg 28.
66. Ibid, Pg 17.
67. Paul Gahlinger, *Illegal Drugs: A Complete Guide to their History, Chemistry, Use, and Abuse*. Plume: New York City, 2003. Pg 273.
68. Letcher, 2006. Pg 29.
69. Asen Balikci, *The Netsilik Eskimo*. Waveland: Prospect Heights, IL, 1970. Pg 227.
70. Miguel Alexiades and Daniela Peluso, 'Plants 'of the Ancestors', Plants 'of the

Outsiders': Ese Eja History, Migration and Medicinal Plants' in Alexiades (ed), *Mobility and Migration in Indigenous Amazonia*. Berghahn: New York, 2009. Pgs 235-236.

71. William Denevan, 'Stone vs Metal Axes: The Ambiguity of Shifting Cultivation in Prehistoric Amazonia.' *Journal of the Steward Anthropological Society*, 20:153-65. 1992.

72. Note: for consistencies sake, I'm standardizing the spelling of *Epene* and Yanomami regardless of sources.

73. Jacques Lizot, *Tales of the Yanomami*. Cambridge UP: Cambridge, 1985. Pg 124.

74. R Brian Ferguson, 'A Savage Encounter: Western Contact and the Yanomami War Complex' in Ferguson and Whitehead (eds), *War in the Tribal Zone: Expanding States and Indigenous Warfare*. SAR Press: Santa Fe, 1992.

75. This matter is covered extensively in R. Brian Ferguson, *Yanomami Warfare: A Political History*. SAR Press: Santa Fe, 1995 and Patrick Tierney, *Darkness in El Dorado*. WW Norton: New York, 2001. Both books are absolutely important.

76 Kenneth Good with David Chanoff, *Into the Heart*. Simon and Schuster: New York, 1991. Pg 66.

77. Ibid. Pgs 47-48.

78. Ibid. Pg 68.

79. Ettore Biocca, *Yanoáma*. Kodansha International: New York, 1996. Pgs 142-146.

80. Peter Bellwood, *First Farmers: The Origins of Agricultural Societies*. Malden, MA: Blackwell, 2005. Pg 240.

81. Ibid, pg 241.

82. Peter Furst, 'Intoxicants and Intoxication' in Evans and Webster (eds), *Archaeology of Ancient Mexico and Central America: An Encyclopedia*. London: Routeledge, 2001. Pg 372.

83. Richard Evans Schultes, 'The Appeal of Peyote (Lophophoria Williams) as a Medicine'. *American Anthropologist* October-December 1938, New Series 40(4/1):698-715.

84. Ibid.

85. https://www.drugabuse.gov/publications/drugfacts/hallucinogens

86. 'Peyote Dose" https://www.erowid.org/plants/peyote/peyote_dose.shtml

87. http://voices.nationalgeographic.com/2009/03/23/corn_domesticated_8700_years_ago/

88. Bellwood, 2005. Pg 156.

89. Ibid. Pg 174.

90. Clive Ponting, *A Green History of the World*. New York: Penguin Books, 1991. Pg 80.

91. Marvin Harris, *Cannibals and Kings*. New York: Vintage, 1978. Pgs 134-135.

92. Elman R Service, *Origins of the State and Civilization: the Process of Cultural Evolution*. New York: WW Norton, 1975. Pg 203.

93. Bellwood, 2005. Pg 154.

94. Furst, 2001. Pgs 371-373.

95. Michael Harner, 'The Enigma of Aztec Sacrifice'. *Natural History*, April 1977. Vol. 86, No. 4, pages 46-51.

96. Ibid.
97. Ibid.
98. Ingo Niermann and Adriano Sack, *The Curious World of Drugs and Their Friends*. New York: Plume, 2008. Pg 30.
99. Vice, 'World's Scariest Drug' https://www.youtube.com/watch?v=ToQ8P-WYnu04
100. Barbara Myerhoff, 'The Deer-Maize-Peyote Symbol Complex among the Huichol Indians of Mexico.' *Anthropological Quarterly*, Vol. 43, No. 2 (Apr., 1970), pp. 64-78. Pg 66.
101. Guilhem Olivier, *Mockeries and Metamophoses of an Aztec God*. Boulder, CO: University Press of Colorado, 2003. Pg 121.
102. Furst, 2001. Pg 373.
103. Stacy B. Schaefer, *Huichol Women, Weavers, and Shamans*. Albuquerque: University of New Mexico Press, 2015. Pgs 196-197.
104. Myerhoff, 1970. Pgs 73-74.
105. Ibid. Pg 66.
106. Peter Furst, 'To Find Our Life: Peyote Among the Huichol Indians of Mexico' in Furst (ed), *Flesh of the Gods: the Ritual Use of Hallucinogens*. Long Grove, IL: Waveland, 1990 (Orig 1972). Pgs 141-142.
107. Ibid, Pg 152.
108. Peter Furst, *Visions of a Huichol Shaman*. Philadelphia: University of Pennsylvania Museum of Archeology and Anthropology, 2003. Pg 25
109. William Dirk Raat, *Mexico's Sierra Tarahumara*. Norman, OK: University of Oklahoma Press, 1996. Pg 53.
110. Alfonso Paredes and Fructuoso Irigoyen, 'Jíkuri, the Tarahumara peyote cult: an interpretation' in Kales, Pierce and Greenblatt (eds.). *The Mosaic of Contemporary Psychiatry in Perspective* Springer-Verlag, 1992. Pgs. 121–129.
111. Christopher McDougall, *Born to Run*. New York: Alfred Knopf, 2009. Pg 229.
112. See Elizabeth Marshall Thomas, *The Old Way: A Story of the First People*. Sarah Crichton: New York, 2006.
113. John Kennedy, 'Tesguino Complex: The Role of Beer in Tarahumara'. *American Anthropologist*. 65, 1963. Pgs 620-640. Pgs 622-623.
114. Ibid, pg. 635.
115. Ibid, Pg 623.
116. See McDougall, 2009.
117. AC de los Derechos Humanos & Texas Center for Policy Study, 'The Forest Industry in the Sierra Madre of Chihuahua: Social, Economic, and Ecological Impacts'. 2000. https://www.nwf.org/pdf/Global-Warming/forestry.pdf
118. Kristian Beadle, 'The Drug Destruction of Mexico, Part II'. *Pacific Standard*, July 15, 2010.
http://www.psmag.com/nature-and-technology/the-drug-destruction-of-mexico-part-ii-19343
119. Enrique Salmon, 'Narco-Trafficking Sierra Tarahumara'. *Cultural Survival*. https://www.culturalsurvival.org/publications/voices/enrique-salmon/narco-trafficking-sierra-tarahumara
120. Ibid.

121. Masaki Nishida, 'The Significance of Sedentarization in the Human History'. *African Study Monographs*, Suppl. 26: 9-14, March 2001. Pgs 9-10.
122. Ibid.
123. Lewis Binford, 'Willow Smoke and Dogs' Tails: Hunter-Gatherer Settlement Systems and Archaeological Site Formation'. *American Antiquity*, Vol 45, No 1 (Jan 1980). Pg 10. It is worth noting that the original context here is with a nomadic hunter-gatherer society who stores food throughout the winter. I definitely appreciate Binford's point on the matter, but the term *hunter-collector* seems to take on a bit of a life of its own after its introduction, including in Binford's later work. I use the term more to signify the point at which hunter-gatherers become more invested in delayed return practices than immediate return.
124. For more on this, see my 'Forest Beyond the Field' in Tucker, 2010, and you can expect more from me on this subject in a number of current and future projects.
125. Abraham Rosman and Paula Rubel, *Feasting With Mine Enemy: Rank and Exchange Among Northwest Coast Societies*. Prospect Heights, IL: Waveland Press, 1971. Pgs 12-13 & 34.
126. Ibid, pg 36.
127. Timothy Earle, *How Chiefs Come to Power: The Political Economy in Prehistory*. Stanford: Stanford UP, 1997. Pg 192.
128. Wayne Suttles, 'Coping with Abundance: Subsistence on the Northwest Coast' in Lee and DeVore (eds) *Man the Hunter*. New York: Aldine de Gruyter, 1968. Pg 58.
129. J.G. Hawkes, 'The Ecological Background of Plant Domestication' in Ucko and Dimbleby (eds), *The Domestication and Exploitation of Plants and Animals*. The Garden City Press: Hertforshire, England, 1969. Pgs 18-19.
130. Ibid. Pg 20.
131. Peter Wilson, *The Domestication of the Human Species*. Yale UP: New Haven, CT, 1991.
132. Morris Berman, *The Wandering God*. State University of New York Press: Albany, 2000.
133. Greg Wadley and Angus Martin, 'The Origins of Agriculture: A Biological Perspective and a New Hypothesis'. *Australian Biologist* 6: 96-105, June 1993.
134. See, for examples, Weston A Price DDS, *Nutrition and Physical Degeneration (6th edition)*. Price-Pottinger Nutrition Foundation: La Mesa, CA, 2000 (orig 1939).
135. Nora Gedgaudas, *Primal Body, Primal Mind*. Healing Arts Press: Rochester, VT, 2011. Pg 226.
136. Ibid. Pg 227.
137. Ibid, Pg 15.
138. Eric Yarnell, 'Exorphins, Food Cravings, and Schizophrenia'. 2003. http://www.healingmountainpublishing.com/articles/exorphins.html
139. Ibid.
140. Sayer Ji, 'Do Hidden Opiates In Our Food Explain Food Addictions?'. May 3, 2012. http://www.greenmedinfo.com/blog/do-hidden-opiates-our-food-explain-food-addictions

141. Erickson DL, Smith BD, Clarke AC, Sandweiss DH, Tuross N; Smith; Clarke; Sandweiss; Tuross ,'An Asian origin for a 10,000-year-old domesticated plant in the Americas'. *Proc. Natl. Acad. Sci. U.S.A.* 102 (51): 18315–20 (December 2005).
142. Solomon Katz and Mary Voigt, 'Bread and Beer: The Early Use of Cereals in the Diet'. Expedition Magazine 28.2 (July 1986). Pgs 32-33.
143. E.E. Evans-Pritchard, *The Nuer*. Oxford UP: New York, 1979. Pg 82.
144. Michael Harner, *The Jívaro: People of the Sacred Waterfalls*. Anchor: Garden City, NY, 1973. Pg 51.
145. Iain Gately, *Drink: A Cultural History of Alcohol*. Gotham Books: New York, 2008. Pgs 2-10.
146. Ibid. Pg 6.
147. Ibid. Pg 237.
148. Wolfgang Schivelbusch, *Tastes of Paradise*. Vintage: New York, 1993. Pgs 147-148.
149. Ibid. Pg 153.
150. Ibid. Pg 38.
151. Ibid. Pg 159.
152. Citied in ibid. Pg 166.
153. Sidney Mintz, *Sweetness and Power: the Place of Sugar in Modern History*. Penguin: New York, 1986. Pg 38.
154. Courtwright, 2001. Pg 136.
155. 'Suicide by intentional ingestion of pesticides: a continuing tragedy in developing countries', *International Journal of Epidemiology*. 32 (6), 2003. Pgs. 902-909.
156. Rupert Isaacson, *The Healing Land: The Bushmen and the Kalahari Desert*. Grove: New York, 2001. Pg 152.
157. Joe Kane, *Savages*. Vintage: New York, 1996.
158. Jake Page, *In the Hands of the Great Spirit*. Free Press: New York, 2003. Pg 175-176.
159. Courtwright, 2001. Pg 147.
160. James Wilson, *The Earth Shall Weep: a History of Native America*. Grove Press: New York, 1998. Pg 60.
161. Tim Rowse, *White Flour, White Power: From Rations to Citizenship in Central Australia*. Cambridge UP: Cambridge, 1998.
162. Mintz, 1986. Pg 193.
163. Isaacson, 2001. Pg 21.
164. Mathias Guenther, 'The Professionalisation and Commoditisation of the Contemporary Bushman Trance Dancer and Trance Dance, and the Decline of Sharing' in Widlok and Tadesse (eds), *Property and Equality: Volume II*. New York: Berghahn, 2005. Pg 208.
165. Ibid, pg. 211.
166. For more on this, see Four Legged Human, 'The Commodification of Wildness and Its Consequences'. *Black and Green Review*, no 2, 2015.
167. Coon, 1971. Pgs 187-188.
168. The Tlingit started growing potatoes after contact with Russians in the 1820s. Andrei Val'terovich Grinev, The Tlingit Indians in Russian America,

1741-1867. Lincoln, NE: Univ of Nebraska Press, 2005.
169. Coon, 1971. Pgs 187-188.
170. Potts, Potts and Kantvilas, 'The Miena Cider Gum, Eucalyptus Gunnii Subsp. Divaricata (Myrtaceae): A Taxon in Rapid Decline' in *Papers and Proceedings of the Royal Society of Tasmania,* Volume 135, 2001. Pg 57.
171. Maggie Brady, 'Drug substances introduced by the Macassans: The mystery of the tobacco pipe' in Marshall Clark and Sally May (eds), *Macassan History and Heritage.* Canberra: ANU E Press, 2013.
172. Regina Ganter, 'Turn the Map Upside Down' in *Griffith Review Edition 9,* 2005. "Up North: Myths, Threats and Enchantment." Griffith University, 2005.
173. 'We Have Contact: rock art records early visitors', *The Canberra Times,* 24 July 2010.
174. Jillian Mundy, 'Good Times at Cloudy Bay' *The Koori Mail,* 446, March 11, 2009. Pg 42.
175. Marlowe, 2010. Pg 287.
176. Survival International, *Stories and Lives.* Survival International: London, 2004. Pgs 4-5.
177. Coon, 1971. Pg 188.
178. David Hayano, *Road Through the Rain Forest: Living Anthropology in Highland Papua New Guinea.* Waveland Press: Prospect Heights, IL, 1990. Pg 2.
179. Courtwright, 2001. Pg 140.
180. Stanley Diamond, *In Search of the Primitive.* Transaction Books: New Brunswick, 1987. Pg 1.
181. Andrew Vayda, *War in Ecological Perspective.* Plenum Press: New York, 1976 and Roy Rappaport, *Pigs for the Ancestors (2nd edition).* Waveland Press: Prospect Heights, IL, 1984.
182. Schivelbusch, 1993. Pg 153.
183. Courtwright, 2001. Pg 140.
184. Peter Eichstaedt, *First Kill Your Family: Child Soldiers of Uganda and the Lord's Resistance Army.* Lawrence Hill Books: Chicago, 2009. Pg 52.
185. Ishmael Beah, *A Long Way Gone: Memoirs of a Boy Soldier.* Sarah Crichton Books: New York, 2007. Pg 122.
186. I find the argument made here: http://www.microkhan.com/2010/04/12/the-lowdown-on-brown-brown/_to be compelling as to what *brown brown* is comprised of, but I have to note that the reason it is being examined here is repugnant: to question the validity of accounts of child soldiers and their memory. If they were told it was cocaine and not heroin, it changes literally nothing about the reality of it.
187. One such source: http://www.un.org/press/en/2015/sgsm16694.doc.htm
188. CNN, 'Syrian Fighters May be Fueled by Amphetamines'. http://www.cnn.com/2015/11/20/world/syria-fighters-amphetamine/
189. Martin Booth, *Opium: a History.* St Martin's Griffin: New York, 1996. Pg 271.
190. Richard Davenport-Hines, *The Pursuit of Oblivion: a Global History of Narcotics.* WW Norton: New York, 2002. Pg 423.
191. Booth, 1996. Pg 272.
192. For reference, I compared the following maps: 'The State of Drug

Use in America, in 9 Maps', Huffington Post, http://www.huffingtonpost.com/2014/10/22/america-drug-use-maps_n_5974592.html. Accessed 12-24-2015. With 'Military Bases in the Continental United States': http://www.nps.gov/nagpra/DOCUMENTS/BASES.PDF
193. Booth, 1996. Pg 256.
194. Dominic Streatfeild, *Cocaine: an Unauthorized Biography*. Picador: New York, 2001. Pg 324 and Gary Webb, *Dark Alliance: The CIA, the Contras and the Crack Cocaine Explosion*. Seven Stories Press: New York, 1999.
195. Steven Dudley, *Walking Ghosts: Murder and Guerilla Politics in Colombia*. Routledge: London, 2004. Pg 52.
196. Cited in Davenport-Hines, 2002. Pg 420.
197. Jason Breslow, 'The Staggering Death Toll of Mexico's Drug War'. July 27, 2015. http://www.pbs.org/wgbh/frontline/article/the-staggering-death-toll-of-mexicos-drug-war/
198. Tristan Reed, 'Mexico's Drug War: A New Way to Think About Mexican Organized Crime'. Jan. 15, 2015. http://www.forbes.com/sites/stratfor/2015/01/15/mexicos-drug-war-a-new-way-to-think-about-mexican-organized-crime/#c2413016ec535e4526ea6ec5
199. Mexico Drug War Fast Facts, updated Sept. 23, 2015. http://www.cnn.com/2013/09/02/world/americas/mexico-drug-war-fast-facts/
200. A fictionalized portrayal of this reality is a story line within the excellent 2010 Katie Arnoldi novel, *Point Dume*.
201. Josh Harkinson, 'High Sierras' *Mother Jones*. July/August 2009. http://www.motherjones.com/politics/2009/07/high-sierras
202. http://www.dailymail.co.uk/news/article-3139335/Inside-650k-tombs-Mexico-s-notorious-drug-lords.html
203. Courtwright, 2001. Pg 109.
204. Cited in Barbara Ehrenreich, *Dancing in the Streets*. Metropolitan Books: New York, 2006. Pg 250. Another book that has been of great help in following this thread of dance, ritual and the relationship of State control.
205. Ibid.
206. According to a 2014 United Nations report cited in 'Riding a White Horse into Hell', Susan Baldridge. Lancaster Online. http://special.lancasteronline.com/landing/special-report-heroin-lancaster-county/Accessed 12-24
207. 'Heroin Claims Two Sons in One Massachusetts Family', Here & Now, NPR. http://hereandnow.wbur.org/2015/09/08/heroin-claims-two-avitabile-sons Accessed 12-24-2015.
208. Three heroin users profiled in 'Riding a White Horse into Hell'.
209. For more on this, see my essay 'The Suffocating Void' in *Black and Green Review* no 1 (Spring 2015).
210. Simon Shuster, 'The World's Deadliest Drug: Inside a Krokodil Cookhouse'. http://time.com/3398086/the-worlds-deadliest-drug-inside-a-krokodil-cookhouse/
211. Ibid.
212. Shaun Walker, 'Krokodil: the Drug that Eats Junkies'. The Independent,

June 21, 2011. http://www.independent.co.uk/news/world/europe/krokodil-the-drug-that-eats-junkies-2300787.html

213. Survival International, 2007. Pg 28.

214. Ibid. Pg 24.

215. British teenager 'died after taking Yage drug in tribal ritual', The Independent, April 26, 2014. http://www.independent.co.uk/news/world/americas/british-teenager-died-after-taking-yage-drug-in-tribal-ritual-9291126.html Accessed 12-29-2015.

'Crappy Ayahuasca Shamans Can Kill You', *Vice Magazine*, April 30, 2014. http://www.vice.com/read/a-beginners-guide-to-ayahuasca Accessed 12-29-2015

216. Connor Creighton, 'Ayahuasca Will Make You Cry, Vomit, and Feel Amazing'. *Vice Magazine*, posted September 18, 2014. http://www.vice.com/print/ayahuasca-will-make-you-cry-vomit-and-feel-amazing-918 Accessed 12-29-2015.

217. Ehrenreich, 2006. Pg 255.

218. Bill Davidow, 'Exploiting the Neuroscience of Internet Addiction'. *The Atlantic*, Posted July 18, 2012. http://www.theatlantic.com/health/archive/2012/07/exploiting-the-neuroscience-of-internet-addiction/259820/ Accessed 12-24-2015

219. Eva Ritvo, Facebook and Your Brain. *Psychology Today*, posted May 24, 2012. https://www.psychologytoday.com/blog/vitality/201205/facebook-and-your-brain Accessed 12-24-2015

220. http://thesnugglebuddies.com/benefits/

221. Amy Banks, 'The Dopamine Reward System: Friend or Foe' on https://www.psychologytoday.com/blog/wired-love/201507/the-dopamine-reward-system-friend-or-foe Posted July 12, 2015.

222. Fredy Perlman, *Against His-Story, Against Leviathan*. Black and Red: Detroit, 1983. Pg 299.

223. Isaacson, 2001. Pg 270.

224. Ehrenreich, 2006. Pg 252.

225. Charlie Goodwin, *Fresh Field Data from my work among the Jai\\om and !Xun of Tsinsabis and Ekoka*. Lecture, CHAGS: Eleventh Conference on Hunting and Gathering Societies. Vienna, Austria. 2015.

226. Bundo, 2001. Pg 96

Society Without Strangers:
Conflict Resolution, Domestication and Systemic Violence

Sahlins has called the state a society especially constituted to maintain law and order. The vast administrative hierarchies of the state are, of course, absent in band and tribal societies. An alternative but complementary view is to regard the process of social evolution leading to the state as one of externalizing *violence rather than* controlling *or* eliminating *it. Such a view enables us to see the evolution of social control in a different light.*

- Richard Lee, *The !Kung San*[1]

/Twi was a dangerous man.

Living amongst the /Du/da clan of the nomadic foraging !Kung San of Namibia of 1940s, /Twi stood out. Violence amongst the indisputably egalitarian !Kung has been both well-documented and largely over-stated. But /Twi was particularly violent. By his own family's telling, he was possibly psychotic.

Amongst his contemporary !Kung this was well known.

Fed up, /Xashe, another !Kung man at /Du/da, one day ambushed /Twi, shooting him in the hip with a poisoned arrow, their preferred hunting weapon. They grappled and /Xashe's mother-in-law held /Twi and told /Xashe to run. Other residents at the camp gathered around /Twi as he pulled the arrow from his hip. Some tried helping him by cutting the wound and attempt extracting the poison out.

/Twi took advantage of the situation. He snapped. He flung a spear which ripped the cheek of a woman named //Kushe. //Kushe's husband, N!eishi, came to her aid and /Twi shot him in the back with a poisoned arrow.

At this point, everyone took cover, shooting arrows back at /Twi.

None sought to give aid to /Twi. They had decided, collectively, that he had to die.

/Twi walked out to the center of the camp and sat, calling out, "are you still afraid of me? Well I am finished, I have no more breath. Come here and kill me… Do you fear my weapons? Here I am putting them out of reach. I won't touch them. Come kill me."

As /Twi's younger brother, ≠Toma, recalled:

> *Then they all fired on him with poisoned arrows till he looked like a porcupine. Then he lay flat. All approached him, men and women, and stabbed his body with spears even after he was dead.*

/Twi was buried and the camp split up.

All going their separate ways.[2]

Within civilization, we have a very strange relationship with violence.

For anthropologists Nancy Scheper-Hughes and Philippe Bourgois violence "defies easy categorization. It can be everything and nothing; legitimate or illegitimate; visible or invisible; necessary or useless; senseless and gratuitous or utterly rational and strategic." It is a small term for a range of actions and provocations.

In their summation, "violence is in the eye of the beholder."[3] You know it when you see or experience it.

Violence is an outburst. It is a response to emotions, to anger, and to fear.

As animals, violence has a place.

As animals, violence also has its thresholds.

When we remove the distance between our lives and our actions: violence is just one part of our experience of the world. It is a trait, an ability, but hardly one that defines our existence. In the civilized perceptions of the world, *nature* is a passive place.[4] For the escapist backpacker or the spiritual zealot, wilderness is a place of peaceful reflection. We carry these voyeuristic perceptions of the world, of the ecology of life, because they are comforting. On a surface level they stand in stark contrast to the systemic, organized violence and anxiety of civilized life.

As technology intrudes, this contrast only becomes louder.

Our perception of wildness echoes our understanding of what it means to be an animal, of what it means to be human. Embracing that wildness is neither a simple nor an easy process, but it gives us the ability to know who we are, what we need, and what stands between us.

Wildness is a state where passivity is not an option. To borrow a phrase from Tamarack Song, wildness is a state of *dynamic tension*.[5] In this all beings are aware, ready, and reliant on the songs of birds, the movement of leaves, the sounds of the environment. Here we inhabit a state that is neither entirely peaceful nor warring, but of *being*.

This is a place where humans are neither angels nor demons.

This is a place where power, be it social, political, or economic, does not exist. And this is the place where our nomadic hunter-gatherer bodies and minds evolved.

This is also the place where the /Du/da camp of the !Kung collectively decided that /Twi must die.

He had become a liability.

And so they killed him. Immediately and without remorse or anger. It needed to be done so that life could continue on, as it had and as it would, without unnecessary violence.

Within civilization, our relationship with violence is schizophrenic.

Those of us unfortunate enough to have been born within this era of hyper-technological, modernized civilization live in the most violent society that has ever existed. And we have the fortune of almost never being confronted directly by any of it. We are so accustomed to not seeing the violence inherent in our daily lives that we can convince ourselves that it isn't there. We convince ourselves that we are better off: as individuals, as a society.

These are the lies that are sold to us by programmers, the architects of Modernity, like Steven Pinker. In his widely upheld 2011 book, *The Better Angels of our Nature*, he makes the claim that our past, human history, is "a shockingly violent one." He states that it "is easy to forget how dangerous life used to be, how deeply brutality was once woven into the fabric of daily existence."[6]

And yet we kill.

We subjugate and suffocate the earth, our home. We colonize the periphery, we tear down forests, we scrape the life off the bottom of the oceans while we pour toxins into the air and dilute chemicals into the soil. We wipe out entire species methodically. This happens every time we turn on the light switch. Every time we get into our cars, turn on our phones, buy food at the grocery store; as I write these words on a computer and as you read them in a book: the earth and all its inhabitants feel the consequences.

And so do we.

We've just been trained to not see them.

We use technology to distance ourselves from those impacted. We use the technology and politicking that Pinker upholds to feel as though we've braved the worst of our own humanity, our primal animality, to become civilized.

In the eyes of the State, violence is a violation of our supposed codes of conduct: a transgression from law and order. It happens when individuals act without involving the government-sanctioned mediators.

In the hands of the individual, violence is an unjust, uncivilized response to conflict.

All institutions, all vestiges of political power, require a monopoly on control. They require a monopoly on the justness or unjustness of violence. They must control it. They determine how an act of overt force fits with prescribed rules of conduct for any given society. And in doing so, they create *systemic violence*: the violence considered just and necessary to maintain a civilization.

What is happening in this process is the reification of violence. We turn it into an external entity, a *thing*. Violence becomes the property of the state; mitigated by its military and police. We remove violence from human emotion because, as Pinker's forbearers have told us, our innately nasty and brutish humanity demands taming. Without control, our wild selves would uncaringly seek to lash out and destroy anything that stands in our way.

In their defense, you get what you wish for.

In any society where power exists, social or political in nature, it is wielded over others. Power is always defined by who holds it as much as it is by who does not; be they individuals, ecosystems, other animals, or any other created groups. Power is the necessary precursor for politicians. And for those with power, the system serves well. Everyone else is left with varying degrees of disempowerment, without a voice or redress.

The demands of the state weigh heavily. Stagnancy fosters unrest. Robbed of the means to mitigate conflict, the disempowered lash out, violating the presumed sanctity of the law. The state calls it violence and uses the digressions as evidence for its own necessity. Criminals are to be punished.

Throughout all of this, violence, like the law, remains a thing: separated from flesh and soul. Violence becomes something we can object to, quarantine, divert, control or reject. It is removed from any and all context. Radicals uphold it. Pacifists reject it. The State arbitrates it.

Violence becomes the *subject*.

In the process, we completely miss the point. The discussions remain in the hands of the domesticators, the programmers: what level of violence is just? What level is unjust? We accept the premise of civility: this is how things are, this is how things must be.

Violence is a reaction to circumstances.

And our circumstances are the problem. Those circumstances are civilization: the domestication of our world and our beings. The pacification of our animality and the passiveness we put upon the world around us. We become spectators instead of agents within our own lives.

Nomadic foragers, the immediate return hunter-gatherers that all of our ancestors were, understood the importance of this. The complexity of being an animal, with a full range of emotions and needs, remained central to their relationship with the world and each other. That dynamic tension didn't cause their lives to be overrun with fear of violence and a need for retaliation, but they accepted the possibility and probability of violence in many forms.

These societies, these egalitarian communities living in primal anarchy, work because they were built upon fluidity, with accepting the complications of our emotional states and giving the space to address and confront them. I didn't open with the story about /Twi's execution to rationalize it away nor to say that this story is exemplary of nomadic forager societies.

The case of /Twi was the exception, not the norm. And it is by understanding how egalitarian societies respond to such exceptional situations that we can shed light on our own circumstances: what does it look like to live without the State? As our society continues to spiral through an epidemic of mass killings, to constantly expanding its killing technology, and to embrace the fractured mentality of eternal war, typified by militarized police systemically targeting non-white communities and individuals, it is not enough to call the organization of violence implicit in the State into question.

We need to understand what life lived on our own terms, on the band level, looks like.

We need to understand what it means to be free.

And that means we need to grapple, with openness and honesty, with how we deal with each other without the State and its infrastructure.

But it also means questioning the perceptions we have of violence.

It means confronting our circumstances. /Twi's violence didn't shake the core of /Kung communities. He attacked them, but they were not terrorized by it to a place where they could no longer return. /Kung society, like all nomadic forager societies, understood violence not to embrace it, but to learn to cope with it: to diffuse it.

Written into books, isolated from time and place, we can extract and imply our fears. That is because our understanding of violence only knows retaliation and punishment. The /Kung, like all other wild beings, know reconciliation and dissolution.

For us, tensions constantly mount. Our violence is born of a brooding hatred.

And it swells.

Short of external force and mediation, our societies know only of peace as toleration. Circumstances aren't changed: policy is mitigated. The fluidity of egalitarian societies is stilled in sedentary lives and the need for stagnancy that fields and storehouses demand.

Our lives, carried out before an audience of strangers, each of us boiling over in our own minds, is steeped in violence that we likely will never see nor experience. And our ability to take part in or resolve our tensions is robbed from us by a system that requires obedience.

It is us who have to confront violence, to understand its circumstances, so that we can learn to live without fear of it. Just like our nomadic forager ancestors and cousins.

For the nomadic forager, violence exists, but it is not a defining trait of society. It is one type of conflict resolution and most often it is the last resort. When it arises, it often passes without escalation. And society moves on.

Like all wild things, the community must move on.

Reconciliation and the Society without Strangers

> *Our bodies and minds are made for social life, and we become hopelessly depressed in its absence. This is why next to death, solitary confinement is our worst punishment.*
> - Frans de Waal, *The Age of Empathy*[7]

It can be disheartening to read biologists' accounts of the importance of community, within human societies or any other. As social beings, we have an innate need and deep fulfillment that comes from simply belonging to something larger than ourselves.

That doesn't typically translate well for scientists. It's simply not logical enough.

And so you have biological and anthropological accounts of why we are social animals that must contest with the overt brutishness granted by Richard Dawkins assertion that "we are born selfish." That we should "understand what our own selfish genes are up to, because we may at least have the chance to upset their designs."[8]

The presumption that biologists, whose field cut its teeth during periods of colonization and war, are working with is exemplified by Dawkins who extrapolated from Charles Darwin: we exist to do what is best for ourselves. We reflect the survivalistic individualism of life within civilization upon the world.

And so biologists feasted upon work like that of Jane Goodall discussing the brutal warfare of chimpanzees.[9] They disregarded the fact that Goodall's encampment at Gombe created unprecedented hierarchy among wild chimps, much like early colonizers amongst uncontacted indigenous societies.[10] This is what the biologists were looking for: evidence that human nature was the "nasty, brutish and short" existence ascribed by Hobbes.

Despite the fact that humans share equal genetic ancestry between violence-prone chimpanzees and the pacifistic bonobos, a new wave of biologists bolstered the notion of innate human warring, partly, as primatologist Frans de Waal observes, "based on a single puncture wound in the fossilized skull of an ancestral infant, known as the Taung Child."[11] That puncture wound, it turns out, was caused by an eagle.[12]

This reinforced a one-sided view of animality: as beings evolving with a machine-like drive towards self-preservation and self-interest. A distraction that kept biologists from seeing an important part of violent outbreaks within animal populations: reconciliation.

For de Waal, that distraction was lost while observing chimpanzees at the Anaheim Zoo. A high-ranking male lashed out and fiercely attacked a female. The chimpanzees reacted loudly to this, other apes coming to the female's defense:

> *Suddenly the entire colony burst out hooting, and one male produced rhythmic noise on metal drums stacked up in the corner of the hall. In the midst of this pandemonium, two chimpanzees kissed and embraced.*[13]

This was more than an act of empathy; it was a sign of momentum. A violent outbreak had occurred, a chimpanzee was injured, but along with coming to her aid, there were acts of reconciliation.

The violence hadn't innately changed the group, it had broken out within it, and then it was over.

This incident happened in captivity, but the observations were then found in the wild. Ethologist Peter Verbeek observed that in both "the wild and in captivity chimpanzees regularly make peace after fights within the community or group" and "console victims of aggression."[14]

Acts of reconciliation were seen not only amongst monkeys and apes, but in wolves, dolphins, hyenas, and elephants.[15]

35 years after de Waal's observation, ethologists had case studies of post-conflict resolution in "close to 40 nonhuman primate species." And then the door was open to observe reconciliation in humans. Ethologists found that "across cultures young children tend to make peace following peer aggression and conflict." These acts of reconciliation decreased only when adults intervened in the situations.[16]

The crude biologist's basis for not being able to see reconciliation following acts of violence is a reiteration of how violence is perceived within civilized societies. It is here that violence, or even the threat of violence, are grounds for mediation or decisive judiciary or military action. There is no de-escalation without force or arbitration.

Within civilization, there is neither incentive nor grounding for de-escalation. There is only punishment.

The problem with civilization is the problem of mass society. There are a lot of people, far more than the band-networks of nomadic foragers. When violence breaks out, it is largely faceless and nameless. With so many people so tightly wound that their unraveling might be imminent, it is not surprising when strangers unleash on each other, but shocking when it doesn't happen.

Anonymity doesn't exist within band societies.

If you do something, you are unquestionably responsible for your actions. There is no technology to buffer accountability or causation. There is no sea of people to fade into, nor is there the ability to flee without leaving a trace.

For the most part, this simply comes down to scale. The average hunter-gatherer band consists of roughly 25 people.[17] That band will consist of men, women and children affiliated with a group of other hunter-gatherers who share languages, customs, and proximity. The average size for that larger group leans around 500 people though that can vary.

Anthropologist John Bodley puts 500 as the number of people an individual can typically sustain relationships with.[18] The number game gets a bit tricky as the "scale differences are so vast that they cannot be comprehended or visualized within our ordinary perception." But to continue putting numbers out for the sake of comparison, 500 is the average number of people within band or tribal level societies, 50,000 for chiefdoms, 50,000,000 for agrarian empires, and 500,000,000 for colonial empires.[19]

Lofty though these numbers may be, they are evidence of the fact that population, as Thomas Malthus famously observed, grows exponentially when left unchecked.[20] But that number, 500, is barely a drop in the bucket of the global society that technology has created where we are quickly approaching a population of 7.5 billion people.

Naturally speaking, numbers are tricky and reductionist. The typical nomadic forager band could look vastly different for ecological or social reasons. Average band size amongst the Penan of Borneo ranged from 32 to 50 and 25 to 40.[21] In 1968, the Hadza living east of Lake Eyasi in Tanzania an average "camp contains about eighteen adults," sometimes that meant a camp of an individual, other times a camp of a hundred.[22]

This variation is far from inconsequential, but we will return to that point. What matters here is that when any camp generally consists of a range of 18-40 people, nothing goes unnoticed. No *one* is going to go unnoticed. There is no need for secrecy here, because for all intents and purposes, there is none. As individuals from that camp intersperse and travel amongst their affiliation of roughly 500 people, the ability to simply fade into the background disappears.

Strangers, as we have come to know most of the people we personally interact with, simply don't exist here.

They simply *can't*.

Affiliations, relationships, friendships, feuds, shared food, communal rituals; all of these things create bonds. It doesn't mean that they always end well, but it means that you know who your neighbors are, often being intimately aware of or exposed to them. That plays a huge role in understanding and interacting with your world. One that we have easily ignored as people living in places like New York City with its population of nearly 24 million people or Tokyo nearing 38 million or Jakarta just over 30 million could potentially cross paths with thousands or hundreds of thousands of *strangers* every day.[23]

My point in juxtaposing these numbers, arbitrary though averages may be, isn't to approximate a sustainable number of people on earth, but to reflect on the kind of scale that we, as humans, as social animals, are psychologically capable of co-existing with. It's a sense of our reach, as individuals, to impact others, typically without negatively harming them.

That is a balance that is impossible within mass society. Be it agrarian kingdoms or hyper-technological, post-industrial consumerist ones, the complexity of social relationships becomes intertwined with the machinery of a society based on extraction and production.

Even as technology infuses the mirage of narcissism as self-worth, we fade into the fabric of the quilt of Ego. Each of us is unique, all of us are special; all of us oblivious to our impacts upon the world.

And all of us unknown to the other Selves we are thrust upon.

When we push beyond that 500 person threshold, when we are born into a world with 5 billion others and see the world hit 7.5 billion people, we have no sense of place or community other than the notion of what we are sold.

Yet civilization ensures that all of our lives are enmeshed.

500 people says nothing about the carrying capacity or thresholds for humanity. It just says: this is an approximation of the number of people I can interact and empathize with. Nomadic forager communities are built on that axiom and they can deal with each of those 500 people, their moods, their attitudes, their joys, and their grief.

None are lost here.

And none of those people live in a way that blindly impacts

everyone outside of that sphere. Within the society without strangers, you are responsible for you own actions, for mending ties or seeking resolution, just as you are expected to be able to provide for yourself and the band. There is no place to hide and no reason to cover up your actions.

This is why band societies value methods of conflict resolution that don't include violence, but also anticipates that violence can and will happen. That's a complicated web for our minds to wrap around: nomadic foragers are peaceful in the sense that warfare does not exist, they seek to avoid escalations of hostilities, but they are also able to move past violent incidents when they inevitably do occur.

To the more liberal of sensibilities, this response to violence or even homicide should be a direct challenge to the notion of nomadic forager societies as the most egalitarian societies to have ever existed. The existence of violence is a trait of social animals: it doesn't make us fascist. Fights can be broken up or avoided entirely, but that isn't always the case.

Egalitarianism is about equality of access to subsistence, the freedom to exist on your own terms. It is the absence of systemic suppression that grants certain segments or individuals within society access to a subsistence base, food, ritual knowledge, shelter, or anything else. Nomadic foragers are notably capable of self-subsistence and they are raised from an early age knowing and accepting this. Band life exists because self-reliance doesn't fulfill our emotional needs as individuals: we are social beings; we want and need community.

And we don't always get along.

Arguments happen, fights may break out, but being fully capable and able to move on, to settle, diffuse, or reconcile disputes on your own terms is a hallmark of egalitarianism, contradictory though it may seem.

It is the absence of overarching political and socio-economic conditions that force people to stay within one society or circumstance. It is the absence of the ability of others to determine what you must do or not do that epitomizes the loss of freedom inherent in non-egalitarian societies.

Outbursts of violence are not a threat to egalitarianism; they are a latent understanding and acceptance of our animality. One that is understood so that it can be curtailed rather than simply controlled as an emotion.

Violence is something that may happen, but for nomadic foragers, it is not a defining trait of society.

Violence within the Society of Strangers

> *Thus the point to make about the Ju/wasi and their murder rate is not that they didn't have one, not that they were peaceful by nature, and not that our species isn't violent or hasn't always been violent since we parted from our sometimes violent relatives, the chimpanzees. The point is that the Ju/wasi knew only too well what the human animal is capable of doing. The point is that they knew how to suppress anger and aggressive impulses, and placed a very high priority on doing so.*
> \- Elizabeth Marshall Thomas, *The Old Way*[24]

Much has been said of the homicide rate of the !Kung.

In nearly every discussion about the role of immediate-return hunter-gatherers, it is not uncommon for the !Kung to take the exemplary center stage. And as a case point in egalitarian societies, rightfully so. Yet their homicide rate, famously comparable to 1970s Detroit, was touted as evidence of a seeming oversight in violence within the "state of nature." Elizabeth Marshall Thomas came under scrutiny from anthropologists for having titled her ethnography on the !Kung of Nyae Nyae as the "Harmless People." A claim she has supported as a translation of how the !Kung of Nyae Nyae saw themselves and also, generally true, as a statement of fact. In her mother, Lorna Marshall's words, "The !Kung are strongly set against violence, and accord it no honor."[25]

Nonetheless, socio-biologists and other engineers of civilization grabbed on to the statistics. Pinker makes it instrumental in his laughable argument for the notion that civilization has resulted in a net decrease in violence. He also touts the Master's Narrative by flattening the violence among the !Kung by listing fights with intruding Bantu neighbors or European colonialists as evidence of their "pre-historic" violence.[26]

This cannot be overlooked.

As much as discussion of the !Kung and other nomadic foragers has been accused of "romanticism," it is absolutely apparent that the opposite is far more widely and insidiously spread: the notion that violence is interchangeable with warfare and that eras of colonization are a reflection of a society's pre-contact behavior.

The 22 cases of homicide that Richard Lee found amongst the !Kung occurred during a period of intensive contact and colonization by Europeans and their neighbors, including the Bantu. This is an important point that we will return to. But before White people actually came into the Kalahari in the 1930s, their path was exacerbated through the previously contacted and embattled Tswana and Herero pastoralists and Bayei and Mbukushu agriculturalists.[27]

To add to the context and give a glimpse of the reality behind intrusions upon the !Kung at this time, the Herero and Nama (Khoisan pastoralists, ethnically and linguistically tied to the !Kung) were subject to militaristic extermination at the hands of German colonizers. Between 1904-1907 alone, the Germans reported killing "more than forty-five per cent, 7,682 of approximately 17,000 Herero and Nama."[28]

It is befitting for us, as the descendants of such genocidalists, to later draw an increase in violence as a justification for berating human nature, just as it had been used to justify the extermination to begin with. I would hope that no one would fault the !Kung for fighting back against intrusion. Brutal oppression came at the hands of Whites and the Bantu then, just as it continues to today. The !Kung were "taken as slaves, hunted down like animals, and, wherever possible, forced from their land."[29]

The violence of colonization increases pressure on even the most intact of communities. And the increased contact with neighboring pastoral and agricultural societies can also influence social behavior. Of the 22 cases of homicide documented by Lee, 15 occurred as parts of feuds, a form of retaliation typically occurring in delayed return societies.[30] That most certainly includes the Bantu.

Not surprisingly, the !Kung had stories of pre-contact times when blood feuds did not exist. As a result of fights, parties would "hang up their quivers", //gau!kurusi, so they could "announce symbolically that the fighting was over for good." The elders would split the group to keep tensions and further violence from mounting.[31]

Again, my point is to contextualize the period of violence in which the famously echoed rate of homicide amongst the egalitarian !Kung occurred. Colonization didn't create violence among the !Kung, but it unquestionably amplified it. Regardless of not placing social value on violence, "the Ju/wasi had violence in them," as Thomas points out.

"We all do."[32]

And so we have stories like the one we opened with: the murders committed by /Twi and his ultimate execution. There are certainly others. Even without colonial pressure, it is likely that they would have existed. With or without a state, with or without external pressure, a society without strangers is forced to confront its own when they become dangerous.

In looking back over the stretch of time Marshall and her family had spent amongst the Ju/Wasi, she was made aware of five homicides, two of which she considered "safety measures." One case was similar to the one already told of /Twi's execution after causing three of the five homicides.

The other was of a man who began hiding in an aardvark burrow, jumping out and startling those that passed by. Clearly, to the group, he had lost his sanity. In their assessment, it became unquestionable that he was too dangerous. A few men went out into the veld and killed him with poisoned arrows.[33]

It can be difficult, coming from our own disconnected society, to see such a response to what is clearly mental illness. In the society without strangers, however, there are no mysteries. These aren't faceless people.

Nor are the potential victims.

Within this society of 550 people, here is an accounting of 5 murders, 3 of which were committed by one person who was subsequently killed as a "safety measure." In our own assessments, executing someone for jumping out of burrows seems overwhelmingly excessive. In light of the situation as the Ju/Wasi saw it, as those who would have ultimately had to lose and bury their own family members and loved ones, as those who could not bring sense back to the man in the burrow, there was no question and no vengeance in their decision making process: they were faced with the likelihood of worse outcomes and chose, collectively, to mitigate the risk.[34]

Life beyond the state requires action. There is no infrastructure to fall back upon. No prison to lock up the excessively violent.
Everyone knows this, just as they know each other.

And for the most part, homicide is the exception, not the rule.

Fighting amongst hunters is largely discouraged and avoided when possible. A hunter is exceptionally skillful at killing. For the !Kung, the use of poison tipped arrows for hunting ensures that the weapons capable of taking lives are widely available within camps. Like all weapons, they can be used indiscriminately.

The use of such weaponry is the most extreme form of violence, the fallback when emotions spiral beyond all social mechanisms, beyond the reproach of others in the encampment to intervene. The !Kung have three levels of fighting; *talk*, *fight*, and *deadly fight*.

> A talk *is an argument that may involve threats and verbal abuse, but no blows. A* fight *is a dispute that includes an exchange of blows but without the use of weapons. A* deadly fight *is one in which the deadly weapons-poisoned arrows, spears, and clubs-are used whether or not someone is killed.*[35]

Of the arguments observed by Lee, less than half involved the use of weapons. It is most likely that many other arguments or talks would have occurred without being reported, as the use of weapons is likely to cause physical harm that is hard to overlook. Verbal arguments, as we shall see, are a more aggressive form of joking that is typical throughout non-state societies, be they immediate-return hunter-gatherers or semi-nomadic horticulturalists. In the case of the !Kung, it "is often punctuated by a joke that breaks the tension and leaves the participants rolling on the ground helpless with laughter."[36]

If the joking only escalates the tension and others haven't been able to step in and break it up, physical fights are likely to break out. Fights without weapons aren't unlike the kind of flaring that de Waal mentions amongst chimpanzees and as anyone who has fought with friends or siblings when joking went too far can attest. Lee explains:

> *Fights are of short duration, usually two to five minutes long, and involve wrestling and hitting at close quarters rather than fisticuffs. Fighters are quickly separated and forcibly held apart; this is followed by an eruption of excited talking and sometimes more blows. Serious as they appear at the time, anger quickly turns to laughter in Jul'hoan fights. We have seen partisans joking with each other when only a few minutes before they were grappling. The joking bursts the bubble of tension and allows tempers to cool off and the healing process to begin.*[37]

We see again this emotional flare leading to an outbreak of violence and then acts of reconciliation. This is an escalation of arguments more than a precursor to the potentially lethal fighting with weapons.

It is worth pointing out that these fights typically involve men, but can involve or be strictly between women as well. The kind of violence inflicted is not the kind of battery typical of one damaged person trying to physically dominate and suppress another; these fights aren't particularly effective in that regard. Even though men are more likely to fight with women than vice versa, there is no presumption that women are innately victims of male violence. Women are much more likely to start fights with men than other women. Since women don't use weapons they are rarely used in fights where women are involved.

Patriarchy has as much to do with the pacification of women as it does the oppression of women as a whole. Even in the far more hierarchical societies of Australia's hunter-gatherers, women are equal in terms of fighting and the expectations of violence as men.[38]

In the case of deadly fights, those involved in the argument are likely to reach immediately for weapons instead of grappling.

In that moment, whether built up or spontaneous, the individuals have crossed that line and are willing to risk, often before the entirety of the band, the probability of lethal violence. The presence of poisoned arrows makes the lethality of !Kung fights far greater. Though the poison used is relatively slow, often taking six hours to kill someone, the person struck with the arrow typically will receive help from the rest of the band. Knowing the likelihood of death as a result of being hit with an arrow, it is rare that the fight goes any further.

Others will cut the wound and try to extract the poison from it. They will talk and begin the *kia* healing trance ritual,[39] attempting to aid the victim and to soothe social tension arising from a fight. Regardless of whether the victim lives or dies, the immediate task is to try to heal all bonds. The attacker will leave the camp.[40]

As a community, whatever the outcome of a fight may be, the immediate goal is reconciliation.

There are no secrets here.

There are no random murders or unknown suspects. Fights typically occur in camps before the rest of the band. They will take part in the arguments, interjecting jokes, trying to break up physical confrontations, or yelling about the "yikkity-yack" of arguments. The goal, for everyone, is resolution, ideally without violence.

But there is always the expectation that violence may arise.

There is the expectation that it may have to be dealt with.

It is because of the seemingly exceptional homicide rate of the !Kung, the self-described *harmless* people, that I chose to open with them. In particular, I chose to focus on some of the more exceptionally violent incidents that we know of. Egalitarianism is, I believe, in our nature. It is written into the primal anarchy of the nomadic foraging lifeway that we have evolved to. It is a part of the social lives that we live as wild animals.

One that is particularly unfit for captivity.

These incidents give a glimpse of what can happen in a society without strangers, a society without a state, when the failsafes don't work. More often than not, they do. But egalitarianism doesn't mean that everything works in angelic form or fluidity. Everyone within a nomadic forager society has the skills, ability and access to choose to remove themselves from tense circumstances.

They also have the choice to stay.

But what is most important, is that they accept, without delusion and without lament, the nature of being a social animal: that arguments may occur and that, as a community, they will have to be able to deal with unpleasant and even potentially lethal situations.

In the !Kung case, the oft-cited example for egalitarian societies also tends to have the record of being the more violent. As such, what we've just looked at, warts and all, is more the exception than the rule.

Among the Hadza of Tanzania, between 1967 and 1997 there were 2 homicides by Hadza against other Hadza.[41] Among the South Indian foragers and the Batek, no homicides were recorded within these societies. For the Batek, the *talks* of the !Kung involve the whole of the group "in a direct discussion between the person involved or in the form of loud complaints made to anyone who was willing to listen, sometimes done during the evening hours in cross-camp arguments, discussions, or simultaneous monologues."

And if resolution cannot be reached, then movement is the response.[42]

The Orang Asli of Peninsular Malaysia are openly hostile towards violence, a stance that has bolstered their refusal to succumb to attempted conversions to Islam and to domesticate animals. As one individual states,

> *I don't know how it feels to hit someone or be hit by someone. ... I never felt angry or knew how to get angry enough to want to fight with others. When I was angry before, I always felt, it's all right if that person wants it his way, I will let it go.*[43]

The Hill Pandaram of Southern India espouse a particularly non-competitive nature which instills a virtue of avoiding violence through movement.[44] The Rautes of Nepal see individual disputes as a threat to the entirety of band integrity and seek to resolve tensions through camp-wide nightly discussions.[45]

Within the Mbuti, the arguments taking place within camp are considered *noise* by the band elders who step in and "demand silence, on the grounds that the noise is offending the forest." It is then the elders who mediate the arguments and determine a resolution, typically, again, consisting of movement either of the band or of individuals.[46]

What becomes obvious from running down this list is one thing: violence is one form of conflict resolution, but hardly the only one.

In being aware of and sometimes accepting the probability of violence, it becomes equally essential to hunter-gatherer communities to learn how *not* to resort to violence. Granted, as we've seen, that doesn't always work, but that's because we've gotten all too used to seeing and accepting homicide statistics.

The problem is that this goes beyond numbers.

As Frank Marlowe observes about the Hadza statistics; "The murder rate among the Hadza is roughly the same as that in the United States. The U.S. murder rate in 1997 was 5.5 for every 100,000 people."[47] To famously meet the *per capita* murder rate of Detroit in the 1970s, it took 30 years of monitoring !Kung society to make the statistics work. And that while active colonization was happening.

It is unquestionably and undeniably true that homicide can and does happen in nomadic forager societies. Clearly far more in some than others, though the reality of forced settlements have taken their toll. As Thomas noted:

> Although the Ju/wasi dealt with anger and violence very successfully as long as they lived in the Old Way, their mechanisms for doing this broke down after the 1970s, when change came and Western civilization overtook Nyae Nyae. Then, when there really were police and government officials, when the Ju/wa population become concentrated at a government post where they lost their ancient lifestyle, when hunger, alcohol, drugs, disease, and poverty overtook them, they began killing one another like madmen.[48]

There are cases like the Orang Asli settlement Air Bah, where the non-violent virtue has given rise to active resistance to alcohol consumption as it breeds violence.[49] This is also seen amongst the Paliyan of Southern India.[50]

But as Douglas Fry points out, "as alcohol becomes available to nomadic forager societies violence goes up. Often the traditional mechanisms of social control and conflict management are not effective in dealing with drunken aggression."[51] The reality of this is just another part of the colonization process: a finalization of the ethnocide that results from attacking indigenous communities spiritually, physically and ecologically.

The infusion of intoxicants only feeds the perpetuated mythos of the violent savage in need of civilization. This morbid view of humanity, and the animality it arises from, spews from the mouth of the domesticator's pulpit. From Hobbes to Pinker, the intent is clear: violence is violence, and it is the duty of the state to protect you from it.

And yet here we have hundreds of thousands, if not millions, of years of evidence to the contrary. The nomadic forager lifeway is peaceful in the sense that there is no war. But it is peaceful in its acceptance of violence and refusal to allow hierarchical institutions to arise to mitigate it.

Instead, they default on the egalitarian version: amongst free people, disputes will arise. It is a testament to the enduring strength of their society that they neither hide from it nor let the potential of violence dictate their existence.

This is our open and willing acceptance of the human condition.

And it is our ability to cope with the presence of violence through understanding that there are other forms of conflict resolution without the state.

How to Cope with Violence: Conflict Resolution and Dissolution

> *Conflict is an inevitable feature of social life, but clearly* physical aggression is not the only option for dealing with conflict.
> - Douglas Fry, *The Human Potential for Peace*[52]

Of the various forms of conflict resolution amongst nomadic foragers, none is more pervasive than mobility.

On the ecological level, movement keeps bands from over-harvesting areas; it can follow the movement of hunted animals, it can follow the shifting seasonality of foraged foods, it can lead to streams seasonally overrun with fish. It lets the ecosystem recover while the refuse composts. It ensures that the people living within a living landscape are aware of the population flux of flora and fauna within the region.

On the biological level, the movement of camps, like the movements latent within foraging, it pushes back the onset of menses in young women and helps reinforce birth spacing for children: both of which greatly check the band population.

On the social level, mobility is the epitome of freedom.

The movement from camp to camp, the fluidity of moving between groups, the chance to bring the camps together for periods; all of these things reinforce not only the ties between individuals, they ensure that people who don't get along with each other have their options open.[53] As arguments arise, the offending individuals will split apart. If fights or homicides occur, the perpetrators will split off. If whole camps are feeling ecological pressure from outsiders, they will even "typically move apart or settle in unpopulated areas, even if these are less desirable, or avoid or reduce conflict."[54]

To a certain degree, sometimes ecology becomes an excuse for mobility.

There are two types of Mbuti groups; the net-hunters and archers. Net hunting is a communal activity based around driving game towards a net where hunters then take them. Archers, by comparison, are more solitary when on the hunt. By virtue of methodology, net hunting bands have more people, which carries more potential for possible conflicts. Their typical group size and potential for conflicts play into how each group views honey season: the ecology of honey plays into their justification for banding together or splitting up. The net hunters claim it "is a time of such plenty that the game can easily be caught by hand, and so there is no need for the large cooperative net-hunt." Conversely, the archers *only* hunt in larger bands during the honey season, which they claim is "a time of poor hunting, and thus, maximum cooperation is demanded."[55]

Logically, both can't be true, but it's an ecological justification for social actions. The want is to break up how bands and camps exist most of the year, get a bit of variation. It is to have a reason to come together if it's not what they typically do or to split up for a bit for those with higher population densities.

They get the chance to dissolve tension through flux.

As James Woodburn observes, it is always possible that

> *members of a camp all move, they may go together to a new site; they may split up and form camps at two or more new sites; they may go as a body to join some existing camp, or they may divide, some joining an existing camp at a particular site, the composition of the camp changes: some people move in and some move out.*[56]

This is the ingenuity of nomadic forager, immediate-return hunter-gatherer, communities. This is what strangers can simply ignore: we can't and won't always get along *and* we all get along better when we can move and cycle through areas, camps, and gatherings.

Proximity is not an argument for mutual aid. That is an innate problem that sedentary societies are forced to deal with and none have nor will be able to cope with appropriately. It is a part of the domestication process stripping down our innate needs as social beings and redirecting that into a notion that any people are good to be around.

That is, so long as you have the right attitude about it. Can't we all get along, right?

The answer is no. We can't.

But the beauty of the primal anarchy of nomadic forager life, the way of existence that literally wrote into us how we see, feel and interact with the world and all its inhabitants, is that we don't have to. Ecologically, biologically, socially, and spiritually, we're better off being nomadic.

We're better off when we embrace our fluidity.

This is a lesson so vital to nomadic forager life that it is consistently the most profoundly iterated virtues taught to children.

This is a point I want to focus on: for us to be able to isolate violence requires that we ignore the causation. Violence, as we have abstracted it, within domesticated societies is always to be avoided, unless it is coming from the hands of the state or hidden through the day-to-day violence inherent in civilized living. It is always *un-*

civilized.

Hunter-gatherers, trained and equipped to kill by livelihood, know that violence is something they'll have to deal with, to respond to, and that it likely can become lethal. This is a practical concern. This is a practical reason to instill and uphold other forms of conflict resolution that bring the society closer together rather than to draw it apart. Violence, in this context, is not something abstract: it is the result of other forms of conflict resolution failing to mitigate an individual dispute. In so far as there can be a "goal" asserted onto their approach to avoiding violence, it would be that the intent is to resolve conflict rather than to penalize its outbursts.

Even in incidents where a homicide does occur, the killer is either chastised or resolves to relocate to another camp until the tensions soothe over and the healing has occurred. Other members of the group may choose to shun them. Life is flowing, fluid. A society that choses stagnancy, as we all know, is stuck in an endless cycle of self-perpetuated escalations on one hand and punishment on the other.

If we're being honest about it, I think that's something we all can recognize as horribly unhealthy.

But let's get back to the children.

Anthropologist Tim Ingold observed that "hunter-gatherers act as self-conscious agents endowed with subjective intentionality."[57] From a civilized perspective, that sounds counter-intuitive as a foundation for functioning and egalitarian communities. We simply take everything to its furthest extent: buying into the narcissistic cult of the individual or a religiously dogmatic refusal of any personhood.

It should be a given that both aspects are pushed into overdrive as technology becomes smaller and more pervasive in our own lives.

For stateless indigenous societies, this kind of identity crisis is dealt with between childhood and adolescence. You learn who you are in the world with other children, mimicking parents, slowly taking over your own subsistence, playing and exploring the wild, as a group, as individuals.

It is telling that coming from a society such as ours, where survival is such a flaunted virtue, that we make much of the skills that hunter-gatherers learn instead of understanding the context in which they learn them. Seeing children hunt or catch shell fish, to start a fire and cook them, is certainly impressive, but only noticeable if you lacked that context in your own upbringing, as I'm sure is the case for many of us.

The skillset of nomadic foragers or any self-sufficient person or group, is absolutely fascinating, but within their own context they can easily be taken for granted. There is no specialization here, there is no industry: this is about exploration, child's play. It is about replicating relationships with each other and with the larger community of wildness that surrounds them, the materials are just tools.

Within this context, they are a given.

Self-sufficiency, learning the ins and outs of these lifeways is a comfortable expectation. You should be able to provide for yourself. There are no lifeguards on duty. None are necessary, children learn by watching their parents, getting guidance where needed and then interpreted through play with other children in a mixed age group.

So what lessons do the parents spend time upholding? Passing on the importance of mobility and conflict resolution. Namely, mobility *as* conflict resolution.

"Teaching," amongst the nomadic forager Nayaka of Malaysia, "is done in a very subtle way." As anthropologist Nurit Bird-David writes, "Knowledge is inseparable from social life."

> *I believe knowledge in this context has to do with learning how to behave within relations, in order to keep these relations going, rather than with knowing things for their own sake, as a known detached from the knower. Young people learn their skills from direct experience, in the company of other children or other adults, in the course of everyday life.*[58]

Infants within nomadic forager societies are cared for greatly by parents and surrounding groups. Affection is openly displayed, fathers and mothers take to tending children instinctually and without hesitation.[59] As an infant becomes a toddler and young child, that affection remains as they increasingly turn towards their peers in their social life.

Amongst the Nayaka, "a person becomes a child when he or she starts socially engaging with others, independently, responsively, and responsibly."[60] To a certain degree, the case has been made by Paul Shepard that domestication stunts this process of becoming independent, leaving most of civilized individuals stuck within a childhood level of development and awareness.[61]

Within the Nayaka, the role of the parent "connotes an emotional sort of caring." This is the same kind of relationship that their society expresses between themselves and the forest. When they refer to themselves as *children of the forest*, it is a statement of "an emotional attachment, a shared living, a shared sense of identity and mutual responsibility."[62]

Amongst the !Kung, toddlers typically start integrating into play groups of mixed ages and sexes by the second half of their second year.[63] For the Agta of the Philippines, communal coddling and care begins at birth. Parents lead by example, allowing the children their own group:

> *When a child learns to walk he turns more and more toward the companionship of peers, who are not only playmates, but also teachers. They teach games of skill and dexterity which prepare a child for his adult economic roles. They instruct each other in how to swim, fish, and gather vegetables and shellfish and generously share their treasures, food, secrets, and knowledge.*[64]

It is reiterated again and again through the accounts of children's play groups that the interventions of adults typically revolve around one central aspect: fostering cooperation and resolution. Within the Hill Pandaram, "Children are treated as autonomous individuals, and are not taught, or expected to obey their elders."[65] The play group of the Mbuti children have their own camp, the *bopi*, where "they are learning the fun and beauty of working and playing *with* not *against* other, they are in a positive way learning by prescription rather than proscription." The "children will find that mobility is one of their prime techniques for avoiding or for resolving a dispute, for once they move elsewhere their spheres move with them and the dispute is discarded."[66]

The games played within the *bopi* are meant to manifest situations of conflict so that they can learn to resolve them. And if resolution fails, they simply walk away.[67] But the bonding that occurs strengthens their resolve. Those limits of resolution, tested within the safety of the *bopi* and instilled into their interactions with the world at large, brings the circumstances which foster violence directly into the light. They learn to identify and respond before they boil over.

Violence isn't something external or looming within context, it is simply an emotional reaction.

And, more to the point, one that can be avoided.

This circumstance, this primal approach to parenting, reaffirms the lived primal anarchy of nomadic forager bands. It breeds egalitarian societies based upon mutual aid and respect. By embracing the facets of life that cause tension, it frees the individuals from becoming paralyzed by them.

So while the homicide rate of the !Kung was famously and unjustly being compared to that of 1970s Detroit, it's easy to see why the comparisons fail: violence, within egalitarian societies, is largely mitigated through resolution, but its existence is not forgotten. Outside of external pressures, random and horrific acts of faceless violence do not occur, so there is no need to live in fear of them. When violence does occur, there are ways of healing and reconciling it.

For the most part, the means of mitigation work. But what is most important is that in the confrontation with these unpleasant aspects of social existence, they give those within a given band and society a lot of room to freely be themselves, to uphold laughter and joy as a given in life. These are societies that dance and sing to bring themselves together. They aren't locking themselves away at night.

It comes back to childhood. It comes back to being affectionately and lovingly held by the camp as infants. Kin or not, there is acknowledgement, care and interaction. There is comfort and acceptance.

And these are the circumstances we have evolved into, as *Homo sapiens*. This is what is written into us: a world where we are given the space to exist and therefore actively create our own lives, with others.

This is freedom.

This is what egalitarianism comes down to: we come together not because we need to, but because we want to. As stated about childhood among the Batek of Malaysia:

> *Despite occasional parental worries, as long as children remained within earshot they were allowed to do almost anything they pleased. They chopped down trees. They built fires and cooked food. They pretended to smoke porcupines out of holes. They carried sticks on their shoulders like bundles of rattan or firewood. Many children enjoyed pretending they were moving camp.*[68]

And just in case anyone wants to stand in the way of that, they also learn to laugh.

The Anarchist's Laughter: Sharing Jokes and Meat

> *It is difficult to be dangerous or violent if you are laughing so hard you cannot stand.*
> — Colin Turnbull, *The Human Cycle*[69]

For the Inuit, anger is something that was expected with children, but unacceptable for adults. Hugh Brody found the question, *"Ningngarpit?"*, or "Are you angry?" to lie somewhere between "a tease and reproach."

Anger, simply put, was for children.

There are many aspects of life, be it that of an immediate-return hunter-gatherer or a hyper-technological, post-industrial consumer, that are difficult. There are aspects of being alive that can bring euphoria and aspects that can result in endemic depression if they aren't resolved. Social life, for all its joys and comforts, also creates tension and can allow an individual to bring out all of their unresolved conflicts into this situation.

As we have seen, that can be lethal.

The question *Ningngarpit?* is a gut check. This simple question, half jest and half ridicule, is a reminder: the purpose of community is to help resolve those tensions, not to amplify them. As Brody puts it:

> *To laugh, to be happy, to feel welcome or welcoming, to experience shyness, to be nervous about dangers in the world or society, and to feel ilira, the mix of apprehension and fear that causes a suppression of opinion and voice: all these states of mind are spoken of and exhibited with real freedom. They have helped to shape the stereotype of the Inuit as a people with unfailing goodwill, good humor, and generosity. Yet the intensity of feeling that can exist within this restraint and dignified self-control, breaking through at times of extreme difficulty, is also remarkable.*[70]

Laughter and humility are virtues taught through childhood. Nearly every violent situation that has been mentioned among nomadic foragers already is precipitated by attempts of either the individuals involved in fights or those around them to try and keep the "yikkity yak," as the !Kung call it, on the lighter side. That the ridicule leads to more laughter and less anger.

This doesn't always work, but more often than not, it does.

Returning to the *bopi* of the Mbuti children, arguments quickly "revert to ridicule which they play out until they are all rolling on the ground in near-hysteria." Which echoes into their adult life as a primary form of resolution. "Chortles quickly become laughter, and this laughter becomes the Mbuti's prime weapon against conflict, aggression, and violence."[71]

Band life, in nearly all non-state societies, consists as much of joking around as it does singing and dancing. Communities elicit joy and comfort; otherwise they wouldn't exist at all. This is an aspect that is easy to miss when revolutionary perspectives become so dogmatic about what the ideal society might be and how it might deal with unpleasant circumstances that it strips the life from situations which may potentially arise. The tension of the struggle often overshadows the coercive aspects demanded of many intentional communities: again, based in the liberal notions that we can all get along and the agrarian squalor of sedentary life.

Removed from those constraints, it's easy to see more about the organic nature of life without the state, freed from the tension and presence of its infrastructures. As anarchist and anthropologist Pierre Clastres observed amongst the Yanomami, they enjoyed a good dick-joke or waking the lulled sleepers with a sneaky fart in the face.[72]

Having spent over two decades attending anarchist conferences and gatherings, it's obvious that people living in anarchy, less preoccupied than anarchists, seem like a lot more fun to be around.

Jokes aside, ridicule is often seen as a means of social leveling.

To an extent it's true, certainly as societies become more stratified, but there have been arguments made that the presence of such mechanisms is an indication of the fragility of egalitarianism.[73] However, the idea of keeping individuals from getting a big head about what they've done is a far cry from a big head resulting in non-egalitarian situations and the presence of social power. Without property, being capable of packing up and leaving while being fully self-sufficient, it's hard to imagine the ability to create a structure for power being that simple.

In other words, "social leveling" in this case is really just about checking, habitually and hilariously, any time someone thinks their contributions to the group are greater than any others. It is a testament to the degree to which egalitarian societies value the contributions of everyone. Early ethnographers sought out the "big hunter" as they presumed, with patriarchal zeal, that in a hunter-gatherer society, the hunter rules the roost. Among complex hunter-gatherers, those who were sedentary or had domesticated animals to store or carry a surplus (respectively), they were able to find a semblance of that.

Among nomadic, immediate-return hunter-gatherers, however, not so much.

To the extent that ridicule is used to check the potential narcissist, it quite often seems to go to young men as they become successful at hunting larger game. For the Orang Asli, "it appears that 'leveling mechanisms' designed to challenge self-aggrandizers, such as joking, shunning, meddling, demanding, and mocking, only apply when the perceived 'self-aggrandizer' is a younger man."[74] Outside of this, heckling is just a way of airing out irritations as jokes instead of attacks.

And it becomes habitual.

A famous case for habitual heckling as a means of reducing potential areas of tension or, simply, socially irritating people has been made by Richard Lee, who learned about it first hand amongst the Ju/Hoansi. At the end of a lengthy stay among them, Lee wanted to share his gratitude from their generosity and hospitality, choosing Christmas as a time to celebrate them: to give back to the community that had hosted and tolerated his presence.

He ended up purchasing a large cattle from a neighboring Herero pastoralist. An "ox of astonishing size and mass," for a feast at the /ai/ai camp for roughly 150 !Kung. He had hoped telling his hosts about his purchase and plans would be graciously received.

It didn't play out as he had anticipated it. The following conversation occurs right after he confirms his plans and which ox he had chosen:

> *"I have purchased Yebave's black ox, and I am going to slaughter and cook it."*
> *"That's what we were told at the well but refused to believe it until we heard it from yourself."*
> *"Well, it's the black one." I replied expansively, although wondering what she was driving at.*
> *"Oh, no!" Ben!a groaned, turning to her group. "They were right." Turning back to me she asked, "Do you expect us to eat that bag of bones?"*
> *"Bag of bones! It's the biggest ox at /ailai."*
> *"Big, yes, but old. And thin. Everybody knows there's no meat on that old ox. What did you expect us to eat off it, the horns?"*[75]

Having spent years studying the social life of the !Kung, Lee still missed an essential feature: the degree to which egalitarianism was innate within their society. He hadn't been prepared for it even though he was effectively seeing it in action daily.

Unprepared for this kind of response, he was devastated. Coming from the apex of civilized society within America, the structure of power along with the tyranny of the gift is so ingrained that it can be an unshakeable core of how someone relates with the world. Like the problem of thinking we can always get along, the nomadic foragers, those living in a state of primal anarchy, thought of that too.

Upon discovering the core of meat insults from those at /ai/ai, Lee asked one of its residents, Tomazo, to clarify its universality:

> *"We refuse one who boasts, for someday his pride will make him kill somebody. So we always speak of his meat as worthless. This way we cool his heart and make him gentle."*
> *"But why didn't you tell me this before?" I asked Tomazo with some heat.*
> *"Because you never asked me," said Tomazo, echoing the refrain that has come to haunt every field ethnographer.*[76]

For nomadic foragers, heckling, like joking, is as latent as it is lacking in our society where hierarchy is constantly reinforced.

Along with heckling the hunter are intentional complexities around meat "ownership," built to obscure the relationship between the hunted animal and the hunter who fired the arrow which itself may "belong" to someone else.

As the Inuit saying goes, "Gifts make slaves like whips make dogs."[77] Gifts are refused because sharing is expected. "Ownership" is, by and large, a façade. Paired with the lack of stored or storable meats, it's equally impractical. Children's demands for meat are respected which feeds the ongoing and self-perpetuating role of sharing: the essence of the communality within communities.[78]

This is the aspect of the society without strangers that Tim Ingold reiterates is the "central attribute" of "face-to-face relationships":

> *Far from being an index of the submission of the particular man or woman to the authority of the social collectivity, sharing underwrites the autonomy of the person, who thus remains wholly accountable for his or her actions. In short it is not in spite of their mutual involvement, but because of it, that people in hunting and*

gathering societies enjoy a fundamental autonomy of intention and action.[79]

Just as egalitarianism centers on equal access to a subsistence base and society, egalitarian societies are "underwritten by a principle of collective access": "The band is conceived as one big household, whose members enjoy unrestricted use of the resources of its country and who labor in common to draw a subsistence from them."[80]

It is property that complicates this ecology of social relationships, not the tendencies of self-aggrandizing young men.

Without property, they have nothing to harvest but an ego.

As Tomazo reminds us, the fostering of egos is exactly the kind of circumstance that can lead to the violence that nomadic foragers uphold avoiding.

Society Against the State and Mitigating Tensions

Faithless, lawless, and kingless: these terms used by the sixteenth-century West to describe the Indians can easily be extended to cover all primitive societies. They can serve as the distinguishing criteria: a society is primitive if it is without a king, as the legitimate source of the law, that is, the State machine.
  - Pierre Clastres, *Society Against the State*[81]

Property, namely in the form of stored foods or domesticated plants and animals, among non-state societies does in fact create tension. But this isn't an on/off switch. The changes, in many ways, are subtle.

Sedentary life further creates a more malicious form of property: territory.

It is the very functionality of conflict resolution: the ability to move, to laugh, to splinter after a fight and cool down, that keeps nomadic forager life fluid and flowing. Horticultural societies, that is, typically speaking, gardener-hunters rather than small-scale farmers, don't completely break with these methods, but they are forced to adopt them to new circumstances. As they lose the ecological benefits of nomadic life, they start to feel the pressure of an increasing population.

As anthropologist Marvin Harris noted:

> *Were it not for the severe costs involved in controlling reproduction, our species might have remained forever organized into small, relatively peaceful, egalitarian bands of hunter-collectors. But the lack of effective and benign methods of population control rendered this mode of life unstable.*[82]

The problem is that the ecological balance of the nomadic forager band is no coincidence. This is the lifeway that has been written into us going back, potentially, millions of years. This primal anarchy is etched into our mind, body and spirit.

It is no surprise that this is the society where we thrive the best and are defined by egalitarianism.

That primal anarchy isn't easily shaken. The domestication process, the ongoing attempt to subjugate our innate egalitarian, nomadic spirit, is a constant reiteration of a totality. It is a retelling of the world as it is through the mouths of specialists and segmented into the mirrored world of production and division of labor.

But none of this comes quickly or universally.

Martin Fried identifies four levels of what becomes "political society." The primary level is the "simple egalitarian society" of nomadic foragers. Then there are "rank societies" noted by limited "positions of prestige without affecting the access of its entire membership to the basic resources upon which life depends." Notably these are largely slash-and-burn horticultural societies.

There are "stratified societies" where members of the same sex and equivalent age status do not have equal access to the basic resources that sustain life. By and large, this type of society is harder to pin down, though it seemingly exists in the build up among sedentary hunter-collector, mounted hunter-gatherer, or early agrarian societies.

They become hard to pin down because these are societies in flux, typically towards the next type of society, "the state". In Fried's words: "Once stratification exists, the cause of stateship is implicit and the actual formation of the state is begun, its formal appearance occurring within a relatively brief time." Rarely in human history is the notion of "Progress" or "social evolu[...] does it follow the prescribed paths offered by ea[...] social thinkers, but in terms of John Bodley's po[...] state is itself a response to Harris's dilemma of p[...] sion and its required intensification. The state is [...] the complex of institutions by means of which [...] society is organized on a basis superior to kinship."[83]

The path from egalitarian nomadic foragers to hyper-modernized consumers is hardly a straight one, but there are clear distinctions in the rise and nature of political society here. Simple egalitarian societies deal with conflict on the band-level because it's realistically the only "level" of society that exists. Rank societies, and some stratified ones, typically have both property and territory. These are tribal societies and chiefdoms that we're speaking of.

Through the production of surplus, either in the form of stored grains and proteins or in the form of domesticated plants and animals, the flux of group identity and residence is largely losing out to affiliation based on kinship, place, and locality.

Or, as Harris puts it, "Permanent houses, food-processing equipment, and crops growing in the field sharpened the sense of territorial identity."[84]

This leads to increasing social and ecological pressure on the group and the primary means of conflict resolution succumb to the need for reliability upon static groups. If fights break out, splitting up the camp or group is increasingly less of an option. It becomes the role of individuals to mitigate conflict and to offset its rise.

In practice, this looks like the rise of Big Men or Headmen, individuals who wield influence, but lack the leverage of the state. In Marshall Sahlin's assessment, "A big-man is one who can create and use social relations which give him leverage on other's production and the ability to siphon off an excess product."[85]

Unlike chiefs or kings, the Big Man is a position of respect, not power. They are a leader without authority and without permanence. As Fried states: "In rank society leaders can lead, but followers may not follow. Commands are given, but sometimes they may not be obeyed."[86]

This is where egalitarianism is hard to shake loose.

The Big Man, and to some degrees, a Chief, are still rooted in a society where the essential power of the state: the ability to organize and coerce individuals to work or to war does not exist. These roles of leadership exist because the position offers a talker, someone who is willing to insert themselves into disputes and areas of contention because the society, as a whole, needs to find resolution to tense situations otherwise it would dissolve into roaming bands again.

It is in that laughter, the heckling implicit in egalitarian societies, once used against self-aggrandizing young hunters that could be used to put a leader back in their place. In Pierre Clastres' words, this is the essence of the "society against the state", one that refuses an economy, refuses political power and the power of coercion:

> *This mode of constituting the political sphere can be understood, therefore, as a veritable defense mechanism for Indian societies. The culture asserts the predominance of what it is based on – exchange – precisely by treating power as the negation of that foundation.*[87]

While the social mechanisms of egalitarianism may remain intact to some degree, the ecological consequences of settled life remain. The Big Man and Chief may not be able to coerce individuals to work, but in their influence, through their giving back to society and mitigation of disputes, they become the instigators of war.

Like all sedentary and domesticated societies that follow, the inability to mitigate tension through movement, laughter, dancing, and even outbursts of internal violence, means that the source of tension must be externalized.

Removed from the ecological contraceptives and diverse food stores that come with nomadic life, societies grow and intensify. It becomes inevitable that other societies, whether they are nomadic foragers, slash-and-burn horticulturalists, totemic kingdoms of hunter-collectors, or the technologically infused drive of twenty-first century corporate-colonizers, the *others* become an intrusion.

It is arguable that the tribal identity is only created as "a consequence of external force," perceived or real.[88] In a stateless rank society, warfare becomes the way to bring the group back together: there is no greater unifier than a common enemy. In Harris's words, "Having external enemies creates a sense of group identity and enhances espirt de corps. The group that fights together stays together."[89]

And as we are emerged into an era of rampant nationalism and xenophobia in response to economic and political turmoil, this is a concept that we ought to be familiar with.

It is the nature of domesticated societies to externalize, to *otherize*, the sources of our tension.

This process might only be seen in minutiae within slash-and-burn horticultural societies, but the innate loss of the means of primal conflict resolution is central to the function of all societies. Relatively egalitarian though many of these societies may be, their palatability is another issue.

I don't say any of this to judge the supposed morality or lack thereof in stateless societies, but my own preference to avoid war comes from living in a society where constant war is a prerequisite. The scale is greatly different, but in all regards, warfare is a long shot from the way disputes are handled and resolved within nomadic forager societies.

The insurmountable feeling of tension felt within the society of strangers is a historical creation.

It is one that we have been born into, but it has a beginning and it will have an end.

The society without strangers is not a sudden or immediate loss, but, as we are sadly all too aware, situations arose that allowed it to continue growing. Through the organization of violence, the externalization of aggressions, empires can become created and boundaries pushed. Left unchecked, we enter a social and ecological downfall into the political economy: the State.

We lose sight of each other and, in turn, lose sight of who we are. Of where we belong.

We lose each other at the moment that we desperately need each other the most. Entering into untold new places and roles that we were never adapted for. We cling to created identities. We create *Others*.

And we lose sight of our own causation. We no longer assume the responsibilities of our own actions. Community succumbs to tribe. Tribe falls to country.

We kill, but we no longer are held to our own actions.

All of this is most prevalent in the organization of violence through the origins of war.

The Organization of Violence and the Origins of War

> *War does not go forever backwards in time. It had a beginning. We are not hard-wired for war. We learn it.*
> — R. Brian Ferguson, 'Pinker's List'[90]

Arguments among nomadic foragers, with or without violent outcomes, center on individuals, not groups.

These are personal grievances, "not fighting over land, for political power, or material wealth, and they are not raiding to abduct women from other groups or attempting to kill cultural outsiders should opportune situations for killing present themselves."[91] Furthermore,

> The targets of homicide attempts are rarely randomly chosen members of other groups. They are offenders who have committed specific misdeeds or acts of abuse.[92]

Lacking property and territory, group identity is a complicated notion. "Due to the cultural flexibility and contextual identity," Orang Asli foragers do "not perceive any more commonality with Orang Asli than within members of majority groups."[93] When societies settle down, this changes drastically. Among the sedentary hunter-collector Tlingit, there "was no such thing as a crime against the individual, only against his clan."[94]

It becomes the job of the Big Man and the Chief to foster that sense of group identity.

As populations grow, as gardens expand and shift, as fish and mammals become scarcer, a new ecological reality creates the need for a new social order. And so we get tribes. We get a firmer sense of group identity.

And in response to these mounting pressures, we get warfare.

War, as stated by anthropologist R Brian Ferguson, "by any definition, is a *social* activity, carried out by groups of people."

Beyond combat, war is about group mobilization. It is "organized, purposeful group action, directed against another group that may or may not be organized for similar action, involving the actual or potential application of lethal force."[95] As societies intensify socially and economically, "the deflection of aggressive behavior onto neighboring bands or villages would certainly be preferable to letting it fester within the community."[96]

In social and ecological terms, warfare serves as a means to spread out human populations, through deaths, slavery, or forced relocation which can ease pressure on the land. It leads to the redistribution of territories. It can be "preventative" to punish transgressions from the moral code of a tribe. And it can be cathartic in the sense of giving the release of anxiety, tension, and hostility that arise from sedentary life so that "domestic frustrations and other in-group tensions can be kept within tolerable limits."[97]

War requires a cohesive tribal entity and circumstances that permit the "internalization of a group identity." It requires planning, division of labor, and the sustained collective will to attack.[98] This is a far cry from the potentially, though not typically, fatal arguments that can break out amongst nomadic foragers.

Anthropologist Andrew Vayda has pointed out that it's best to understand warfare as a process: there are stages, phases, and varying levels of intensity.[99] Without the coercive power of the State and using the volunteer army of kin, warfare amongst horticulturalists can easily disintegrate if social and ecological tensions fade. Among the Yanomami, members of raiding groups have been known to simply drop off the raiding party complaining of sore feet or stomachaches. Easy enough to do when there is no system for reprimand.

As Douglas Fry put it: "Command structure and authority are very weakly developed within tribal society."[100]

Conversely, they don't exist among egalitarian bands of nomadic foragers.

To get a closer look at what warfare looks like among horticulturalists, let's look at the Maring of eastern New Guinea. Upon contact in the 1960s and 70s, there were roughly 7,000 Maring spread over roughly 190 square miles. The Maring had gardens and, most notably, they had pigs.

And they had lots of them.

The pigs and gardens go hand-in-hand. Aside from being a source of food, the pigs left in fallow gardens would dig out the scraps their human counterparts missed or didn't find worth it to dig up, their rooting kept the ground soft for replanting, eliminated weeds and seedlings, but the pigs also ate the human refuse that piles up from sedentary life.[101]

Self-contained though this may seem, the population of both the people and, even more so, the pigs created a perpetual socio-ecological conflict: they would run out of room and the efforts to maintain the hogs became too much work. The result: a perpetual cycle of warfare that centered on the ritual slaughtering and feasting of pigs. In Marvin Harris's words:

> *Every part of this cycle is integrated within a complex, self-regulating ecosystem, that effectively adjusts the size and distribution of the Tsembaga's human and animal population to conform to available resources and production opportunities.*[102]

The Maring follow a very common form of horticultural warfare: there is a period of truce and as escalations arise internally, they expand externally, resulting in less intensive battlefield warfare with low mortality rates and intensive battlefield warfare with high mortality rates. The underlying cause of warfare is population pressure, but it is the social consequences of that population pressure that lead to warfare.

Materialist and ecological analysis tells us a lot about why we do the things that we do, across all cultures. But rarely, if ever, do we speak in these crude terms. As social animals, we create a mythos to justify what it is we do and what we don't do. Just as the Mbuti archers and net hunters have varying ideas about the ecological bounty of hunting during honey season based on their camp compositions, the circumstances for war amongst horticulturalists are typically the same, but the social justification may vary.

For the Maring, the initiation of war can be set off by any of the following; taking women, rape, shooting pigs that have invaded gardens, stealing crops, poaching game or stealing wild resources, and sorcery accusations.[103]

The last cause is an essential one in non-state sedentary societies, chiefly states and kingdoms: witchcraft and sorcery. Effectively speaking, the witch or the sorcerer is the ultimate means of externalizing internal drama and tragedy. It's a harsh form of internal conflict resolution. And while those of us in the First World might shrug at these notions as antiquated and primeval, it's just because we've substituted witches and sorcerers with terrorists, immigrants and rogue states as Others.

"Witchcraft," writes Peter Wilson, "especially welds these elusive and diffuse effects people have on one another with the dramatic and tangible effects the natural world has on them in the form of illness, death, and misfortune."[104] The witch and sorcerer are the ultimate scapegoat; they are also the most typical cause of war and raiding cycles.

Not surprisingly, there is an intimate link between disease and warfare. Anthropologist Alexander Alland notes, "Disease may be linked to transgression of the moral code, to social enmity, or to super-natural power, with consequent treatment of these "causes" rather than of the disease-producing organism." This is something that is verifiable throughout our entire recorded history.[105]

Most of Maring life is lived during periods of prolonged truces.

The follow up to the battle cycle is a truce ritual, carried out by each tribe amongst itself, where *rumbim*, a small tree, is ritualistically planted at the borders of the territory. Part of the ritual is that all adult men of the group grasp the *rumbim* as it is planted, "symbolizing both his connection to the land and his membership in the group that claims the land."[106] This is the material representation of the tie that binds the sedentary together. It's how focus is kept on externalizing internal disputes and tensions.

It is the externalization of conflict resolution through killing as a group.

Maring warfare takes two forms: *nothing fights* and *true fights*.

Nothing fights have gotten a larger reputation. Fatalities do happen, but they are rare. Men from two groups will get within range of each other, bringing a bow-and-arrow and large wooden shield. Close enough that they can hear each other voices, but far enough that the arrows are largely ineffective.

More than launching arrows, they are throwing insults. The opponents are not complete strangers, but they are also not kin. They are neighbors with just enough distance to be Others, but also the kind of neighbors capable of maintaining decade long truces.

At this stage of battle, which can last days or months, it is possible to deescalate the disputes: to talk them out, to use mediators to settle arguments, or that a fatality might lead to an end of hostilities without revenge killings. The men go home at nights and come back in the morning until the fight ends or it grows into a *true fight*.

The true fight is close combat. The bows-and-arrows return alongside spears and axes. When the nothing fight escalates, the men retreat from the battlefield for days to prepare for the axe fight. The *rumbim*, planted to signal a truce and now grown, is symbolically uprooted. Pigs are slaughtered and roasted, the salted bellies consumed prior to going out to war. When fatalities occur the individual is mourned and more pigs are slaughtered for a funeral feast.

This too can last for weeks or months: a warrior is killed and pigs are slaughtered. Until the population of people and pigs have waned to sustainable levels. It lasts until the *rumbim* is once again planted.[107]

Brute though warfare may be, this is what non-state societies engage in to keep their numbers low enough to support otherwise relatively egalitarian situations. This isn't the primal anarchy lived by nomadic foragers, but it's also not the ordered hierarchy of the state: a place where this level of warfare can easily become an everyday reality rather than a ritualistic necessity.

Regardless, this kind of warfare is a cultural establishment. It changes the relationships within the bands and their relationship to the world at large. The dynamic tension of the wild and of life becomes something to fear and to fight.

And this is reflected in their social relationships.

Power Goes to the Head(Man)

> *Violence can never be understood solely in terms of its physicality – force, assault, or the infliction of pain – alone. Violence also includes assaults on the personhood, dignity, sense of worth or value of the victim. The social and cultural dimensions of violence are what gives violence its power and meaning.*
> - Nancy Scheper-Hughes and Philippe Bourgois[108]

The Jívaro are horticulturalists that live in the Amazonian basin of Ecuador. At roughly 100,000 people, they're solidly fitting in the chiefdom category that Bodley offers.

And the Jívaro are also notably violent.

Their reputation as headhunters put them on the global stage early in the colonization of South America for all the wrong reasons. In some regards, their warring nature nearly worked for them. By 1589, the Jívaro had been nearly wiped out by the smallpox and measles that the Spanish colonizers had brought with them. But ten years later, in 1599, the remaining Jívaro banded together and successfully threw the Spanish out.[109]

Unfortunately, they would come back, but this is a rare moment of decisive victory in a history of colonization far more deadly than the warfare the Jívaro practiced.

The Jívaro are a warrior culture of raiding parties. Being sedentary horticulturalists with such a high population leaves far less room for times of peace when compared with the Maring. And like the Maring, the social and ecological build up for warfare is never the stated reason for war. It is again the fear of malicious spirits and the want for social and political power that drives the men to war.

And they are out for trophies: the nefarious shrunken heads.

In this society, the chiefs and the shamans are intrinsically tied. Most men vie for both positions and they are allotted to the most outstanding killers.[110] And outstanding killers they are. Warfare is so pervasive and effective at curbing population here that the

Jívaro practice polygyny, where men have multiple wives. Because so many men die in raids, the adult population is 2:1, female to male.[111]

That number is high, but not necessarily beyond characteristic of horticultural warfare:

> *29 percent of Dani men die as a result of injuries sustained during raids and ambushes. Among the Yanomamo village horticulturalists along the Brazil-Venezuela border, raids and ambushes account for 33 percent of adult male deaths from all causes.*[112]

So who is the target of Jívaro warfare? They are after *arutam* souls.

Men are not born with them, but they possess them by killing other *arutam* men, who gain them both through hallucinogenic vision quests and killing. There are only so many *arutam* in existence, but "The Jívaro believe that the possessor of a single *arutam* soul cannot be killed by any form of physical violence, poison, or by sorcery." Perhaps a nod back to the unfortunate reality of 1589 however, "he is not immune to death from contagious diseases such as measles and small pox."[113]

An individual can possess no more than two *arutam* souls at one time, but they have a work around on this. The spirits will cycle out, the newest taking over for the older ones. But the warriors are capable of continually compounding the accumulated *power* from their bounty.[114]

Effectively speaking, in a society this large and entrenched in the warrior ethos, there is no need or reason to cap the amount of murder. This is the sheer externalization of the need for the kind of conflict resolution that nomadic societies are capable of.

When an *arutam* man is killed, the *muisak*, or "avenging soul" is unleashed. The *muisak* is thwarted only by the process of properly creating *tsantsa* by removing the head and hair from the skull, shrinking them through boiling, sealing the eyes and mouth to create a shrunken head trophy. This is all done within the *tsantsa* ritual ceremony. And if not done timely, the *muisak* will come for the head taker.[115]

Brute though it may be, the trophy carries its own powers. It is "believed to make it possible for them to work harder and to be more successful in crop production and in the raising of domesticated animals, both of which are primarily the responsibilities of women in Jívaro society."[116]

In contrast to the crude materialist or ecological reasons for why a sedentary chiefdom might seek outside assistance for "successful crop production" and the "raising of domesticated animals," we have a mythical one. As social animals, we prefer the better story. The *tsantsa* heads aren't unlike the flags of nations: a physical source of symbolic pride for their cultural values.

It becomes easy to judge this, as early colonizers surely had, as a form of savagery, a primeval act. We say that to feel better about our own forms of decimation. But as Modernity continues to turn the world into a singular, global culture it is important to remember that the beheadings of ISIS, made for social media, represent the same technological imperatives of the military drones.

We can excuse ourselves from the ecological consequences of lives lived out of the balance achieved by our nomadic forager cousins, ancestors and relatives because we can distance ourselves from the violence and tension our society is capable of externalizing. We ignore the causation of mounting tension and then watch the aftermath on TV or online in disgust.

I don't uphold the warring life of the Jívaro as an ideal, but I don't doubt for a single second that the Jívaro warrior and his victim, even though they may likely be strangers, both know exactly what they are responsible for at the moment when they meet in battle.

The same most definitely can't be said for us.

One problem that we run into when trying to understand, from a social and ecological perspective, about why societies do what they do, is that none of these societies exist within a vacuum.

I don't point out the warfare of horticulturalists to judge them, but to emphasize that these are the stakes that come with yearning for a non-state society, but denying the primal anarchy implicit in nomadic forager lifeways. As we have seen, they have violence and they have created and fostered means of conflict resolution to generally avoid it.

We see amongst warring horticulturalists, or among settled hunter-collector societies and agrarian kingdoms, an attempt to slow the scaling of society through curbing growth. While violence was once the result of options breaking down, we see the situation shift to where violence, namely homicide, becomes necessary for the future of society.

It is this situation that becomes the hallmark of domestication.

It has been argued that the basis for arising patriarchy is the social power granted to *man the hunter*. But this is a complete fabrication, one granted by a patriarchal society that sought to find a glimpse of itself in less complex societies.

That basis is found in *man the warrior*. The scale may vary greatly, but we know this is a historically created and self-reinforcing feedback loop that arises with sedentism and surplus. In some regards, these responses may work. Compared with the hyper-technological, fossil fuel dependent civilization we are a part of, these even appear relatively sustainable. We'll have to leave aside for now whether or not individuals would find them desirable.

The question of their sustainability faces an external threat. And in this regard warring societies have not fared well: if the infrastructure for externalizing the cause of social tensions is in place, what happens when new intruders come?

In this case, those intruders are a whole other level of strangers: militarized colonizers and their technology. As I have argued is the case amongst the Ju/'Hoansi, their uncharacteristically high levels of homicide coincide with the intrusion of colonizers, both directly and indirectly. Alcohol, steel tools and guns create the perfect trifecta of toxic social substances.

History is a living example of this.

In the case of the Ju/'Hoansi, their influx caused the override of potential conflict resolution through traditional means. But without a social infrastructure in place for warfare, they still largely did not escalate beyond personal grievances. Just as they always had.

In the case of the Jívaro, that warring and warrior culture did exist. And just as it always had, the influx of civilized tools and vices led to catastrophic escalation of what was meant to be a curbing mechanism and safety valve for social tension and ecological balances.

The ability to accumulate power from *arutam* while not retaining the spirits likely goes back to the demand upon intrigued Westerners for the *tsantsa* heads. Going back to 1870, the heads became a source of currency with Ecuadorians. The trade began of giving heads for steel tools, but by the early 1900s, they were trading heads for guns.[117]

Similar patterns of outside trade escalating hostilities resulted in genocidal loss among the Yanomami[118] and the complete annihilation of societies, as it had when the Haudenosaunee expanded their territory and networks for the European fur trade.[119]

For the Jívaro, chiefs and shamans became trade partners. Feeding into the role of the chief as one of social stature created a "trend to the desire of individuals to acquire 'white men's valuables,' especially machetes and firearms, and to distribute these goods in order to win friendship."[120] The role of the shaman was available for purchase; their services could be compensated for in trade goods.[121]

The outlawing of the head trade was paired with missionary intervention to pacify the Jívaro.

True to form, the old trade heads can still be found for sale on the internet.[122]

This is tragic and toxic history, but it is important to point out that warfare as a mechanism scales with freakish ease. Once the social and cultural norms are established, they don't typically scale down.

The spread of these cultures looks like a distorted reflection of the way children are raised in nomadic forager societies. Jívaro childhood is almost the exact opposite of the *bopi* that the Mbuti child inhabits. Children are discouraged from play as "such behavior leads to a disinclination to work." Embracing the fears implicit in sedentary life, children do not interact with the children of other households. Which adds "to the child's sense of insecurity vis-à-vis the rest of the population" as "the frequent attribution of illness within the household to the bewitching activities of hostile shamans."[123]

Both mothers and fathers regularly strike children. Wrestling among boys is encouraged and approved of. Young boys may even begin to follow their fathers on raids as early as the age of six, but typically no later than when the sons are nine. And if the boys disrespect the authority of their fathers, they will make them drink the "the juice of the *maikua*," otherwise known as the powerful hallucinogen *Datura*.

If a child is being particularly bad, the parents may indulge a particularly harsh form of punishment: "This consists of dropping a large quantity of hot peppers into a small fire and forcing the child to remain over the fire under a large cloth until he becomes unconscious."[124]

There is no question that this is the domestication process.

Children are broken much like domesticated pack animals, but they are inversely instilled with the identity of the group and drawn into the allure of social power that is created. From a distance, it may be hard to see the correlation, but this is how we are raised in domesticated societies: refused the rite to self-subsistence, we are fed subservience and find our merit in the ideology of the tribe or the nation as our case may be.

The purpose of this upbringing is to uphold social power. It allows us to remain disconnected from ecology, even if we are reluctantly shaped by it. The will to power is the will to control the sustained stagnancy of sedentary life. And it is an uphill battle.

Warfare confirms this.

Fearing Others is the ultimate introduction to the world of strangers. It is the necessary step to assure that responsibility for your actions can be shouldered by the culturally constructed sense of justice and necessity.

Like the Jívaro, the Mundurucú are headhunting horticulturalists living in Brazil. Despite their equally perpetual state of war, it has been observed that:

> *The seemingly tranquil life of the Mundurucú is fraught with fears of the unseen and unknown. There is little violence, or even aggressiveness, among them, but violence and aggression are indeed present in repressed and residual form.*[125]

This insulating relationship with the world and the ability to push all internal conflict onto others made it possible for the

Mundurucú to consider all other tribes as enemies while being seemingly peaceful with each other. That externalized sense of us-versus-them just kept pushing them farther and more mercilessly out into the forest:

> *After perhaps months of travel through the forests, they would surround an enemy village by night and launch an attack at dawn. Burning arrows were shot into thatched roofs, driving the bewildered occupants outside—to the lances and arrows of the Mundurucú warriors. Enemy men and women alike were slaughtered and decapitated, and the trophy heads thrown into carrying baskets.*[126]

Once the cultural infrastructure is there, these societies scale in one direction: growth, expansion; conquest. That is until they can no longer sustain themselves and they fragment. Or they collapse.

The same happens among sedentary hunter-collector societies, where "we see, as a pattern, an increase in the severity of fighting." Along the Pacific Northwest of North America, the Haida were considered the "Vikings of the coast," warring relentlessly with all neighboring tribes. To the south of them, the Klamath "warred for revenge, booty, and slaves."[127]

It is the nature of settled societies that their surplus makes them as likely to war with neighbors as they are to become targets themselves: "When food is stockpiled, it inevitably becomes a key military objective of raiding parties."[128]

It is the direct immersion in these acts that keep the communities intact. We are social animals. We are drawn towards each other. As we have all seen, we're willing to endure pretty horrible things to stay closer to other people, even if our relationships are just a fragment of what it is we are looking for.

We yearn for the fluid sense of belonging that comes with nomadic forager life. And we will grasp onto anything that bares it semblance.

So perhaps the question left to ask is: why?

The Society of Strangers: the Trauma of Isolation

> *The play goes on, more or less imperfectly. The person, so deprived, bears the consequences as unregenerate elements of immaturity, glossed by repression and compensation, distorted by unconscious yearnings for overdue fulfillment and resentments against the nurturers.*
>
> — Paul Shepard, *Nature and Madness*[129]

So why are we drawn to community? What pulls us closer to each other?

There are many possible answers to these kinds of questions. We tend to focus on biological ones: stripping away the emotion and wants of our social animality. There are truths to the biological explanations, but those approaches don't really get at the heart of the matter.

I believe we enjoy the solace that we offer each other. We find joy in the company, care and companionship that we have to offer each other. In healthy communities, we can air our frustrations, we can sing and dance them away: we can ritualize the conflicts that arise from the reality of life and death.

We can rely on each other to help cope with the difficulties that can come with living.

And there are many things about living that can be complicated. There are many reasons why we might end up snapping, much like the aardvark burrow dwelling !Kung man. Or like the 18.2% of Americans who suffer from mental disorders.[130]

One of those reasons is a high rate of infant mortality among nomadic forager societies.

Stillbirths, miscarriages, and other sources of infant loss are suffered silently within Modernized societies. In terms of industrialized, First World nations, the United States is actually fairly high with an average of 6.1 infant deaths per 1,000. No doubt, the advancements of technology in terms of prolonging life play a huge role in this, but, like all things civilized, the U.S. stands out in terms of a massive gap in access to that kind of technological health care. Children of poor families are nearly five times more likely to lose a child within the first year compared to wealthy families.[131]

This is stark in contrast to the Batek where about 25% of

Society Without Strangers

infants died within their first two years. It is worth noting that during that same period, malaria was the prime killer and one that arose from contact with civilization.[132]

This kind of number is one that is hard to hear.

That is due, in large part, to the fact that within civilized societies, we don't speak about things like infant mortality. Statistically it is far less significant than in nomadic forager societies under active colonization, but 6.1 deaths per 1,000 births are not none. We carry these losses personally and, as a culture, refuse to acknowledge them.

In refusing to acknowledge tragedy, we create trauma.

It becomes easy to look at the society without strangers through the same kind of potential for punishment that we have been instilled with. Living without strangers shouldn't be seen that way. Losing anonymity means that mourning and loss become communally understood, felt and accepted. We care for each other, empathize with each other, and help deal with bad things that can happen.

We help with the bad things that do happen.

And within nomadic forager societies, infant mortality is one of those things.

As mentioned earlier, toddlers become children when they begin to have signs of autonomy: when they begin to interact with others within the community on their own. This is a coping mechanism. Once a nomadic forager child passes the test of the first couple years, their chances of living to old age increase greatly. "Young babies are," within nomadic forager societies, "an extension of the mothers' self, until they start to communicate and interact with others, independently."

There are cultural acknowledgements and beliefs to contextualize the potential for loss. The "Aka believe that dead young babies come back again reborn as other babies." Seen as an extension of the mother, the loss of infants "registers with the community as a failed birth, rather than as the death of a person."[133]

This recognition and acknowledgement of a potentially demolishing experience of losing a child doesn't take away how infants and toddlers are treated. As stated earlier, they are loved, coddled, held close, and engaged with passionately by the community at large.

The interests of the child to be are always upheld. It is part of the ecological awareness that comes with mobility that nomadic foragers will make decisions based on ensuring that children within the group are loved and never neglected. Infanticide, when it does occur amongst the !Kung, occurs "with the stated goal of enhancing the quality of care and survival of existing children and to avoid caring for seriously defective children, almost certain to fail."[134] Among the Batek, infanticide only occurred in cases of babies born with severe physical deformities.[135]

It is equally unfair to talk about the rates of infant mortality within nomadic forager societies, which seemingly are far greater than those within countries like the United States, without acknowledging some caveats: of the recorded instances of pregnancy in the US in 2012, 15% ended in abortions.[136] A fate that is arguably far less sufferable than being born unwanted by uncaring parents who feel the moral and social obligation to maintain the pregnancy.

If you include those statistics and consider the rate of unwanted children within civilized societies, it's hard to believe that we really have it better off.

From the perspective of the nomadic forager, there is an acceptance that not all children who are born will live and they have adapted for it. It may be impossible to say how much the realities of contact and colonization have increased rates of infant mortality, but considering scum like Pinker have included the killing of children among foragers by colonizing agents such as loggers and miners, it's impossible to think that both the direct killing and stress it carries haven't increased that number.

But the point remains, it is the understanding of what can happen and the readiness of the community to help heal, foster and move on, ushered with a cultural acceptance that the spirit of the child will likely return, that it wasn't ready, all turn a potentially traumatizing situation, one that I think every living being wishes to avoid, into something that isn't emotionally endemic.

The processes of mourning and healing are made public.

These losses, unthinkable as they may be, are not settled in isolation.

The care of children is tantamount to the survival of the group.

Alongside adultery, the primary cause of arguments among the Agta is "careless or irresponsible use of a bush knife or bow and arrow within a campsite where onlookers, particularly children might be injured."[137] Mothers have been known to even go to blows with other women for verbally reprimanding their children.[138]

Everything is out in the open. There are no personal problems that escape the empathy of the group. The community exists to nurture each other.

In our own society, we bury that pain, that conflict. We ironically live in fear of what may happen to us as a result of external forces while we blind ourselves to the things that are likely to happen.

Within the United States, the top ten leading causes of death have almost no reflection in the fear mongering politics of control. Almost all of those causes of death are preventable illness (cardiovascular, certain cancers, and diet related). "Accidents" are the fourth leading cause of death, which includes drug overdose, medical mistakes, and automotive collisions. But while suicide is barely trailing influenza and pneumonia, homicide (including terrorism) doesn't make the list.[139]

We return to the Others.

We focus on the common enemy so we can foster an artificial sense of group identity as we stumble through the motions of a social animal living in a sore replacement for community.

We suffer, alone. Together.

This is the society of strangers. Individuals, wound up, lost, and hurting, who are willing to externalize their own inner turmoil. A place where once healthy individuals seeking comfort through fluid movement and affiliation are left without recourse for a shattered process of personal growth and cognitive development.

This is the scourge of domestication.

Neoteny, as Paul Shepard explains, is the process of stunting our development into fully aware and active beings. That is into individuals capable of maintaining communities. This process of severing the competency of a capable adult is no accident; this is a need for agrarian societies:

> *Politically, agriculture required a society composed of members with the acumen of children. Empirically, it set about amputating and replacing certain signals and experiences central to early epigenesis. Agriculture not only infantilized animals by domestication, but exploited the infantile human traits of the normal individual neoteny.*[140]

Post Traumatic Stress Disorder, PTSD, is said to impact 7.8% of adults in the United States. It is two times more prevalent among women than men.[141] Because of technology, we can suffer historically unique forms of brutality. As we suffer alone, without a cultural preemption or recognition of that probability, it is not surprising that one of the wealthiest nations has such a high rate of PTSD. Considering our refusal to acknowledge the possibility of infant mortality and the silencing of women's voices through patriarchy, the disparity between men and women having PTSD should also not be surprising.

Surely as nomadic foragers our brains are built to withstand stressful situations.

Life in the wild may not be "nasty, brutish, and short," but that doesn't make it stress-free either. Infant mortality is a looming tragedy, but it's not alone. There are a lot of harsh ways to die living in the wild outside of homicide; falling from trees while collecting honey, being bitten by snakes, being attacked by predators, facing periods of hunger, and weather extremes. Most of the situations are not necessarily lethal, but, by and large, nomadic foragers aren't suffering from PTSD even though they may likely have dealt with a number of those situations.

I believe the difference comes down to the acceptance and acknowledgement of things that can happen. If the community is aware and capable of mitigating those tensions and possible sources of stress, then they need not become traumatic. No one suffers alone.

But the civilized do.

We become lost in our trials and tribulations, left to reiterate them or to refuse to cope with them in a dance of neoteny. We become strangers, mere neighbors: a concept that, prior to domestication "had no significance, no social meaning."[142]

And this permits us to both perpetuate and permit systemic violence. This allows us to remove our sense of responsibility from the world and each other. It keeps us from giving children the space to explore boundaries and find themselves among friends.

It keeps us from seeing and believing the violence of the state.

With 7.5 billion people, we have created 7.5 billion variations of how the domestication process has fucked with our minds. We all create our uniqueness through how we have endured as individuals. Dependent upon the law to control and mitigate our unresolved conflicts, we give away our ability to become self-sufficient, both physically and cognitively.

As Stanley Diamond stated, "schizophrenia is the process through which the inadequacy of the culture is concretized in the consciousness of individuals."[143] We become fractured. Our punishment becomes self-propagating. Diamond continues, the "development of the early civilizations as instruments of oppression was the result, not of some environmental or technical imperative, but of the new possibilities of power which men in certain positions found it necessary to cultivate and legitimate."[144]

Domestication is about dependency. And that is what we are: dependents of the custodial State.

Each of us is born to be a *child of the forest* and becomes a *child of the machine* through indoctrination. Our own pain becomes a justification for pushing further and further into the depths of the mechanisms of the State.

And as the power to respond and resolve is taken from our hands, it is given directly to the State.

The unresolved, unreconciled tension of existence tightens the shackles.

The Violence of the State

> *The hallmarks of civilization may be as much the conquering warrior, the armed guard, the city wall, the whipping post, the prison, and the gallows as they are the high arts, religious monu-*

ments, and writing.
> — Timothy Earle, *How Chiefs Come to Power*[145]

I can't breathe. I can't breathe. I can't breathe. I can't breathe. I can't breathe. I can't breathe. I can't breathe. I can't breathe. I can't breathe. I can't breathe. I can't breathe.
> — Eric Garner, as he was suffocated by a NYPD cop on July 17, 2014[146]

Till this point, my focus has been on non-state societies. I've made it my goal to focus on violence, particularly violence within a society, because neither egalitarian nomadic foragers nor warring horticulturalists see violence as an ideal way to deal with kin, with family, with anyone where a personal relationship exists.

Nomadic foragers are not shaken by acts of violence, but they have instilled numerous coping mechanisms to try to stem off tension before it is overflowing.

Horticulturalists, by and large, uphold violence as an institution. Their means of internal conflict resolution are to ritualistically and habitually externalize the sources of social and ecological pressures. And they do this so that they don't turn on each other because they need to all get along; to tend gardens, to keep their domesticated animals, and to fill raiding parties.

Though these societies may be polar opposites in many ways, they are tied by a refusal of *social power*. The members of these societies are willing participants in their cultures. They celebrate them without the cognitive dissonance afforded to state-dwelling nationalists who may never see the inside of a mine or have to stand armed on a battlefield.

As populations grow unchecked, as societies grow in number, as territory must continue to expand: the effective function of mobility or influential, yet powerless, leaders crumble. As the scale expands, "the number of decisions required by any node increases until it exceeds an individual's personal capacity to make decisions and requires an expansion in the hierarchy of decision makers."[147]

As horticultural societies grow, they take on the infrastructure of sedentary hunter-collectors and the technology of agrarian society. The role of the Chief becomes a specialization. And as the position grows into an occupation with subordinates, the growth "creates certain dynamics of competition, management, and control that underlie the eventual evolution of the state."[148]

War in societies without a state is waged for revenge, defense, land, plunder, and/or prestige. Within states, war is waged for political control, economic gain, social status, and defense.[149] War becomes an essential part of the ideology of the state: a self-justifying conquest of the world. "The form of political organization which we call the state," explains Marvin Harris, "came into existence precisely because it was able to carry out wars of territorial conquest and economic plunder."[150]

It is worth noting that there is nothing inevitable about this entire situation.

Our lineage is evidence of this. The hundreds of thousands, if not millions, of years of our combined ancestry is virtually all the lived primal anarchy of nomadic foragers. The problem is that when societies do settle, when they do domesticate plants and animals, they *must* grow. The speed and path may vary, but the results, left to their own devices, in time may all look the same.

And when the state does arise; it doesn't exist quietly.

The state arises when the coevolution of war and society merge. The segmentation of the world into an ordered hierarchy is the necessary precondition for the cornerstone of states: the law.[151]

The law stands in defiance of the conflict resolution implicit in nomadic forager life. Not content to merely externalize tension into warfare, as stateless horticulturalists do, the state absorbs the function of the war machine while it refuses the legitimacy of internal group tension. The group is given an outlet for aggression to build identity, but it is a lesson in subservience: a lesson in absolute domestication.

"The latent purpose of the law," as seen by Stanley Diamond, "was punishment in the service and profit of the state, not prevention or the protection of persons, not the healing of the breach."[152] The ambiguous influence of Headmen and Chiefs is now increasingly ineffective: power becomes absolute.

Hierarchy is cemented into the foundation of bureaucracy and production. The religious sanctions granted by shamans and priests lay the groundwork for the legal sanctions of kings. Within the stratification of the state are the roles and duties of its officiators. To take matters into your own hands is now a crime and a punishable one. The goal of the law is to punish and to make an example of the perpetrators.

The judge replaces the mediator.[153]

The law is the social construct of the society without strangers. It exists solely in the place where all other forms of conflict resolution fall into the pit of anonymity. True to the schizophrenic nature of civilized life as it seeks to dissociate circumstance and action, action and consequence. We continue to externalize our aggressions, but we are forced to fear our internal tensions. The law is order. And a violation of the law is personal failure.

And we are accountable only to the law.

This is where the true terror of the state becomes apparent: in the absolute refusal to grant us our own means of resolving and reconciling tensions, we become statistics. We become a broken record of violations of the stagnant and impersonal nature of legislated morality. Our subservience upon the state grants it the ability to exist by bending the moral code as it declares the justice of its own necessary evils.

Witihin this realm, homicide becomes the crème-de-la-crème of crime. To kill another person, to violate the sanctity of "thou shall not kill." We take this for granted, but it's because we deny all the circumstances where killing another person *just may be* the most peaceful form of conflict resolution.

Rare though those cases may be, they do exist.

The !Kung, for example, have no need for moral or legal codes because they have no distance between action and consequence. They mostly avoid violence, but if they were to impose anything resembling legal or religious sanctions against murder, then what would they have done with /Twi after he violated it? The society without strangers doesn't need law because if the law is to be enforced, the people who kept /Twi from killing more would be seen the same as /Twi: murderers.

The law is black and white to all who can't afford to bend it: the very people who governments pretend to protect and serve.

The state is the gold-bearer of double standards. Above all else, "the state and government are organizations for war." As anthropologist and anarchist Harold Barclay puts it, "No more efficient organization for war has been developed."[154] That double standard works because of our dissociation: first in production, then in warfare.

"War," writes Paul Shepard, "is the state's expression of social pathology."[155]

We simply follow orders. We don't connect the dots.

Resolved to refuse the rite of resolution, absolved from the flux of circumstances; we become the consumers of nationalized ideologies spread from pulpits and talking heads. We become the audience for programmers like Steven Pinker applauding our civility and restraint against our "savage" impulses.

And so we end up in a nation where the president evokes the notion of "a just war" while he receives a Nobel Peace Prize, simultaneously carrying out indiscriminate drone strikes and military operations globally.[156] We are absolved of our responsibility, our consequence.

This is how we become monsters, when we are so removed from the reality of our world that we can look at it with indifference. It is when we become the efficient cogs of the globalized machine that we can compare homicide rates, without circumstance or attentiveness, to feel good about our own notions of social progress.

As Stanley Diamond points out, it is here that we become the threat:

> *Dissociated, not good, persons can do impersonal evil. Persons who have become* personae, *masks; persons who have permitted themselves to be reduced to social functions, alienated, bureaucratized; persons who can kill out of abstract strategy, but who are out of touch with their own capacities to express and transcend hostility, persons who obey orders in societies where the civilizing process has become hyper-rationalized. ... It is dissociated persons doing impersonal, and therefore potentially boundless, evil who are the threat in modern civilization—they are the irresponsible.*[157]

The violence of our society includes the breakdown of our universalized schizophrenic reality. It includes the mass murderers, the killing sprees, gang violence, workplace shootings, domestic violence, racist and xenophobic attacks, parents killing their children, cops killing unarmed individuals, and acts of "homegrown" terrorism. It includes crimes that spread from endemic poverty and as an outcome of addictions. It includes those who kill to reclaim their social power and those who must kill in self-defense.

To compare the murder rate of Detroit and nomadic foragers in the Kalahari, our programmers will readily pat themselves on the back for achieving stasis, so any improvement on the numbers looks good.

There is no replication; there is no equation for the weight of egalitarianism within this. There is no weight put on circumstance, no need for further reflection beyond the sheer numbers of dead bodies. There is no thought put into the prospects for resolution and reconciliation, for the ability to have a dispute end in ritualistic celebration rather than funerals.

There is no responsibility in any of this.

But there is deception.

The state creates an entire form of violence that has no precedent in a society without strangers: structuralized, systemic violence.

A life mired in unending, and often unseen, war.

Economic power, a historical creation upon which all social power is built, "is based on the ability to restrict access to key productive resources or consumptive goods."[158] This is the production that begins when gardens or fields are planted, when animals are bred in captivity, and when storehouses are filled.

The economy originates when the self-reliant nomadic forager is forced into social dependence rather than choosing social life.

Like all change, things happen slowly. Perhaps even imperceptibly.

Yet by the time the state appears, there is no question: social hierarchy and stratification are implicit. The side effect of authority is poverty. And "the world's poor are the chief victims of structural violence – a violence which has thus far defied the analysis of many seeking to understand the nature and distribution of extreme suffering."[159]

The supposed benefits of civilization, the triumphs of Progress, have never been even handed. Not even close.

And despite the stories spun by domesticators, priests and programmers, it can't be. If domestication requires conquest, civilization is the epitome of it. Literally everything that we touch within civilization is soaked in blood. Down to the finest details; the sugar in your cup, the rare earth metals in your cellphone battery, your "sustainably sourced" organic palm shortening; everything that we touch in the civilized world is produced on a global scale and distributed through the technological infrastructure that consumes resources at an unprecedented rate.

The reason that nomadic foragers and horticulturalists are being imposed upon is because of us. Because of our civilization and its unrelenting need for perpetual growth. Nothing is sacred. Nothing is left untouched.

So when we begin to proselytize about the supposed virtues of our "improving conditions," it is a continued act of colonization to disregard that the rising homicide rates that accompany contact with stateless societies are a part of our own homicide rates. At this point, we are no longer disconnected, we just perceive ourselves to be because that is the lie that we are told.

It is the definition of irony that this globalized civilization is the most violent force in the history of this planet, one that if left unchecked could result in the extinction of humanity itself in less than a hundred years,[160] while promoting itself as the bastion of peace and prosperity.

This bravado is the malicious internalization of the Otherization that arises with sedentism and domestication: we remove ourselves from responsibility and consequence. We raise flags over the mass graves of the conquered and massacred. There is no shortage of examples of the level of brutality implicit in the building of Modernity. We can dissociate from the death tolls, the destroyed forests, the displaced populations, the slavery, the power of coercion and domination, the diseased and polluted habitats, dead rivers, dying oceans, and, everywhere, the crude spills, the toxic leaching, the carcinogenic spraying, and the looming unknown present of abrupt climate change with increasingly violent weather patterns.

As our social and ecological circumstances worsen, we too turn towards our own variations of witchcraft and sorcery accusations. The refugees of war-torn Syria, a result of the intersection of climate change and fragile geo-politics, become targets themselves as they are suspected of perpetuating the very terrorism that they are risking their lives to flee. One murdering religion turns on the others. We have caliphates and drone strikes. We have the pathologically fragmented perpetuators of military occupations emboldened with the power of a badge in increasingly militarized police forces.

As the semblance of climate stability withers, we turn further and further inwards. We get lost within the narcissistic sea of the Self, enshrined in social media and technology. We increasingly fragment our world, looking for outcasts to blame for our worsening condition so that we don't have to face the insurmountable whole of our condition: so that we don't have to face the reality of a globalized civilization that has far surpassed its peak.

We are harvesting our diminishing returns at the cost of each other's lives, our own future, and any sense of ecological sanity or hope. Technology allows us to get hyper-focused on singular events long enough to feed the overwhelming sense of mutually assured destruction.

But the thoughts don't stay. Eyes on our devices, we refresh daily with a new tragedy.

As the Jívaro can only retain two *arutam* souls, but can accumulate their power infinitely, we become cumulative rage.

As cell phones increase the ability to quickly record and disperse videos documenting the way that police systemically target black men, we become the filters for seeing the reality of brute force in real time. In true form, the reaction to these increasingly visible displays of brute force is met with a further raising of flags, restating allegiance to the ideology of the state: *they* must have done something wrong. Force, meted out by the state, is always justified. For those buying the merits of civilization, they can be presented with counter-evidence to the false confidence eschewed by Pinker and his kind, but they can't recognize it.

This comes back to the domestication process: that internalization of both the group identity and the need to counter the ecological imbalance of sedentary life. Headmen can call upon the group to band together to fight an externalized source of tension. Chiefs can pull together an army.

But kings, like presidents, can coerce them.

And with the Law at their hands, they can use them against anyone who tries to stand in their way.

Perhaps those who seek authority are not unlike /Twi. The ability to kill on mass scale, to order the death of thousands, if not millions, from afar takes a certain kind of psychotic personality. The very person that most likely was never checked by parents and other children in a *bopi* kind of environment.

Perhaps those individuals would kill in any society, regardless of their upbringing and any attempt to resolve or dissolve conflicts before they mounted. It's nearly impossible for us to say, as nearly every person alive, even within recent memory, has not been a stranger to civilization and its systemic violence in one form or another. But we have unquestionable evidence that even if those personalities had existed, a society without strangers created coping mechanisms for dealing with them when they get out of hand.

Civilization, on the other hand, has found ways to empower them.

You have this constant current throughout the history of civilization of patterns of behavior that are unusually vicious, even for societies with militaries; that is societies where there are not only specialists in killing, but specialists in strategizing mass killing and technocrats dedicating their life to increasing the ability to kill more efficiently.

At the outposts of civilization, you have systemic empowerment of unhinged psychotics like King Leopold II of Belgium who built an empire of terror in the Congo on the fortunes of rubber.[161] A man who took hands and feet of slaves for not meeting his imposed rubber quotas and killed with absolute indifference to foster his own power. He became the influence for the character of Kurtz, an ivory trader, in Joseph Conrad's *Hearts of Darkness*. His source of power became interchangeable because this bloodthirsty king of the frontier story arises again and again throughout the history of civilization.

We have child sacrificing Mayan kings and the decapitating soldiers of the Caliphate, like the Old World crusaders or New World colonials. And they are all a part of the ongoing expansion of the civilization that we inhabit.

Technology scales carnage. Though some acts might be more brutal than others, it is only because they can be. Warfare, within Modernity, can "be waged by technicians." While politicians are quick to rile up public support for their killing, the needs of civilization are of a more rational sort: to protect resources, to maintain order, to advance territory, and to eliminate potential threats.

As Stanley Diamond points out, this kind of violence may be even more frightening by its inhuman and methodical nature:

absolutely modern, up-to-date war, lacking in ritual, lead by technicians, in a kind of rationalized madness, does not require hate, or rather, I should say, the open and direct expression of hostility. Such a war between antagonists at more or less equivalent levels of civilized development, would be, of course, obliterating, but if there were survivors, it would leave, I believe a heritage of hate at the commission of dissociated evil *that staggers the emotional imagination.*[162]

Drone strikes may typify this kind of behavior, but warfare, as purely the realm of technicians, has not come. Soldiers are embedded within the pride of nationalism and tasked with its defense. But like the rest of us, they are stuck within the consequences of insurmountable tensions and the feeling of subjugation implicit in the state.

All of us, as we have clearly all seen, are equally capable of breaking. "Caged creatures show much aberrant behavior," Paul Shepard writes, "including psychopathic fits of bloody carnage, and many of the same psychotic symptoms as humans in our developed nations."[163] And with the technology of civilization, the death count increases. Exponentially.

So while the kind of psychotic murderer that we've empowered with technology and given authority through politics may have existed at any point in our nomadic forager past, there were social mechanisms to cope with them. They risked being shunned or exiled. They had to know their potential victims and face their kin.

They weren't given more authority.

They weren't given justifications.

They weren't rewarded with more efficient killing technology.

And if all else failed, they faced the unrelenting spears and arrows of an egalitarian society capable of handling them.

Cultures of Resistance

> *All the movements of the left and right are functionally the same inasmuch as they all participate in a larger, more general movement toward the destruction of the human species. Whether people stay confined within certain obsolete strategies and forms, or whether they submit to the mechanisms of technology—either way the result is the same.*
>
> - Jacques Camatte, *This World We Must Leave*[164]

So what do we do about this? How do we respond to a globalized civilization and its implicit violence?

This is no simple question and there are no simple answers. But we have plenty to work with.

For me, the question of conflict resolution is both empowering in terms of how societies can function without the law and in exposing the fragility of domestication. The state is built upon technology, and that is neither a small feat nor a minor footnote in the history of civilization and systemic violence. As we see every day, when people stand up to power, they face the blunt force of its physical brutality. The law serves it well to lock away potential threats.

But it is fragile in the sense that it works because we are trained to ignore even the potential to deal with each other without the inclusion of state infrastructures; that is, without prisons and without police.

The state is strong if we continue to see resistance only on civilization's terms: limited by the law and by the ownership of violence. If you focus on the source of that power, technology, or to be more specific for our current world, electricity, then things look very different.

In order to understand and undermine civilization on that level, we have to go back to the beginning: why do primal anarchistic societies function? The answer is community. Namely egalitarian communities built on the foundation of flux and fluidity.

For us, I'm talking about building *communities of resistance*.

As I have argued elsewhere and repeatedly, the success of indigenous resistance, in contrast to revolutionary movements, lie within the strength of communities.[165] Revolutions are fought for ideologies; they are fought to correct the wrongs of the State and the want to reshape the enlightened future society upon the failures of the existing empires.

Needless to say, even when they are successful, it's hard to argue that they're more appealing.

Radicals and extremists, in many ways, simply mimic the form of religious death cults, most notably, in our times, ISIS. The vision of the Caliphate and the righteousness of the martyr need no real world actualization. In offering the promise of life after living, the martyr is the ultimate ideologue. By the time they are able to be disappointed about the future that wasn't awaiting them, it's too late to matter.

Being untethered by the existing world, the relentless nihilism of indiscriminate murder sadly draws a new kind of allure. Terrorism grants an escape from the consequences of being dispossessed by the domestication process. It gives vindication to ending an unfulfilling life. A justification that serves as the only difference between the two technologically infused archetypes of Modernity: the suicide bomber and the mass shooter.

We get to this point because we believe the domesticator's innate lie: authority lies within the law and the power of authority lies in its monopolization of violence. So long as violence remains reified, so long as violence becomes and remains a *thing*, it has allure. It becomes the tool of liberation just as much as the functional force of conquest.

If the end goal of revolution, true to its innately political nature, is the conquest of authority, then time is always working against it. The Soviets who fought in the Russian Revolution might have had the numbers to take on tanks and cannons. I suspect they wouldn't have fared quite as well against drones.

Nor would we.

But it is the *demystification of violence* that creates the potential to erode the sanctity of authority and to understand, much like egalitarian nomadic foragers, that there are ways to mitigate and dissolve tension without violence. In a world of billions of people, it is vital to recognize that it is not the lives of individuals that seal our fate, but the technology that grants individuals the power to wield authority and coerce systemic violence. It is the domestication process that keeps us in line and keeps us from viewing civilization as a failed attempt at creating a biological organism and acting upon it.

In the words of John Bodley, "Civilizations are artificial cultural constructions, not biological organisms, and they would be poor biological performers if we insisted on considering them as organisms."[166] Civilizations are not alive, but they are parasitic. They demand the wholesale consumption of entire ecosystems, of the devouring of their wild hosts.

Civilizations may not be biological organisms, but their existence demands that they act like one.

So they can die like them.

So they have died like biological organisms.

Like its forbearers, this civilization too will die.

The decaying infrastructure of its technological reign crosses the span of nations and oceans. The precision of its war machine and logistics both lie in the precision of satellites and cell phone towers, neither of which is impervious to destruction, intentional or not. The earth decimating ability of power stations can be undone by storms as well as sabotage. The perpetuation of its growth is dependent upon agricultural production as its primary crops continue to be threatened and tainted by climate instability. Its need for an unrelenting stream of finite resources remains undeterred.

Its bloated and overwhelmed rendition of a biological organism, unlike its ever-growing harness of militaristic force, is exceptionally fragile and vulnerable.

Humanity has survived millions of years of evolution by embracing fluidity and flexibility.

There is no reason to believe that our biology can't outlast the synthetic one of the state.

Our resistance, like our potential to survive the collapse of this civilization, lies in grounding.

It lies in reclaiming the refusal of authority that was innate in societies without a state. It lies within the heart of primal anarchy: by returning to the world of face-to-face existence. It lies in connecting with the resistance against civilization that the communities of wildness have always taken part in. It lies in viewing the world in terms of ecosystems rather than the separated and programmed world of the state.

Domestication is a process. It needs to constantly adapt to the channeling of our needs as social animals into the authority of domesticated societies, but it can never be complete. We are captives, caged animals in a cell comprised of technological gadgetry on one end and the blunt force of the police on the other.

We may be unfit to match their force, but we may not need to.

When we resist authority in our own lives by handling our own conflicts without outside intrusion, we can get a glimpse of what we are capable of. In fostering self-sufficiency, we undermine the state's hegemony of dependence upon stagnancy. In fighting against the circumstances that make inequality possible, as opposed to fighting for equality in the eyes of the law, we embolden ourselves within community.

Considering the ways that civilization has bastardized any notion of what "community" might mean, it is easy for my intents to be overlooked here. Community, as I use the term, carries no reflection of the pacifist, hippie want for communal living. Like the horticulturalists, liberals seek to create situations where "we all must get along"—only they've removed the internalized "safety valves" of external warfare.

Such delusions can lead to the other extreme of mystified violence: ideological pacifism. The epitome of violence externalized. A false sense of security in believing that if you don't respond to the violence of the state in kind, that your rights under the law will be respected.

This stems from the notion of community as a thing of ease: supplanting the dynamic tension of the wild with the well-massaged sense of arrogant removal implicit in a placid view of *nature*. That center of communal life amongst nomadic foragers revolves around singing, dancing, playing and, overall, joy, comes at the recognition and confrontation with the potential and likely unpleasant aspects of being a living creature.

As we've seen, this can be far from traumatic. But it requires openness, honesty, and, above all else, an ability to handle circumstances as they arise: as individuals, as a community.

That means dealing with internal tensions and external ones.

That means being able to take on civilization directly.

There have been individuals and groups that have sought to co-opt the fury of indigenous resistance while refusing the connectivity implicit within them. They have sought to adopt the rage of grounded peoples without the grounding and pair it with the displaced, reified violence that we have been impregnated with.

To understand indigenous resistance, you have to understand that it is inseparable from the world of native peoples. It is when their communities are assaulted that they can respond in kind.

It is here that it is almost tragic that more indigenous societies weren't as warring as they were made out to be. The Huaorani were able to keep Westerners at bay by spearing the first missionaries that attempted to contact them to death. Having been subjected to the attempts to raid for slaves by the Malays and Burmese, "shipwrecked mariners and the members of landing parties seeking to replenish water supplies were often killed by the Andamanese."[167]

It is telling that most nomadic foragers lacked the experience to be openly hostile to colonizers. The result of which has been nothing short of tragic. And that tragedy is still on going.

It is possible that the act of rebuilding communities, which, much like rewilding, will take place over generations, will be able to incorporate this reality into their mythos. The resistance to and refusal of civilization may become the central stories told around the hunting campfires of our descendants.

Against all odds, this has happened before.

James Kaywaykla lived from 1877 to 1963. He was a part of the Warm Springs Apache and grew up during the most violent period of their history. In his words, "Until I was about ten years old I did not know that people died except by violence."[168]

As horticulturalists who reintegrated with the horse to become mounted hunter-gatherers, the Apache were no strangers to warfare. They had an established pattern of raiding and warfare prior to colonization and a reputation for being particularly effective warriors.[169] However, they weren't prepared for the wholesale onslaught of the Europeans who intentionally sought to decimate the entire ecosystem to destroy the inhabitants of this New World. This led to a familiar rise of inter-tribal warfare, but quickly escalated.

A series of back-and-forth battles between the Chiricahua Apache and the intruding whites peaked in 1863. Mangas Colorado, among the most respected of chiefs and father-in-law to Cochise, came to a colonizer's encampment under a truce agreement that, to his surprise resulted in his arrest upon arrival. Considered an instigator of hostilities, the officers didn't respond in kind. After torturing him alive,

> *they shot him six times through the head and torso. His body was rifled for souvenirs, while his corpse was later scalped and dismembered, the massive head being cut off and boiled down to a skull in a big pot.*

This incident shook the Chiricahua and led to a decade of war with whites.

And it didn't fare particularly well for the whites. Between 1862 and 1871, the US Army spent $38 million on a campaign of elimination that resulted in 100 Apache men, women and children being killed. But in that time, the Apache killed 5,000 whites.[170]

Having the knowledge, skill, and grounding of a hunter-gatherer paid off. Proficiency and skill with a bow-and-arrow certainly were crucial, but ecological knowledge is helpful. The whites, they knew, never learned to dig for water in the dry desert. They would drink "a spring dry, leaving only mud for the soldiers" who would often die of thirst. Or they would poison aboveground pools of water for the soldiers to drink.[171]

Kaywaykla was born during this war. He saw all of it and his story tells about Nana, Victorio, Lozen, Juh, and Geronimo; their battles, victories and executions. But what is most inspiring about his retelling of this period of exceptional violence and forced settlement is not the warfare, but the importance of what Chiricahua life, even amidst genocidal conquest, means.

It is our dissociation that allows us to split the violence, to uphold the heroism of violence against civilization, from the essence of Apache identity and culture. It is by understanding and respecting the essential nature of that identity and community, to know its place and how it tied them to the land giving unflinching purpose to their resistance that we stand to learn the real lessons here.

Against all odds of survival, the Apache fought.

And while many died, others survived and continued that struggle.

Against all odds, this is happening now.

As I write this, the most diverse gathering of Native Americans in the history of the occupied Americas is taking place at Standing Rock where the Hunkpapa Lakota and Yanktonai Dakota stand their ground against pipelines carrying hydraulically-fractured natural gas seeking to destroy the remnants of their home.

This is the latest among a series of indigenous resistances to energy extraction in North America that includes the Unist'ot'en, the Madii Lii and Lax U'u'la among others.[172] The strength of these camps is their communal nature: the establishment of camp, the invigoration of traditional cultures, and the indisputable tie to the resistance of their parents and ancestors.

This is not about politics: in contrast to the efforts to confront the law on its own terms I have to borrow a phrase from Iyuskin American Horse of Standing Rock: "We are protectors, not protestors."[173]

Communities integrated to the wild, integrated with the vast web of ecosystems, cannot dissociate from their actions and responsibilities. The ability to become anonymous or to escape consequence is something they have the fortune of not knowing.

And in their grounding, idleness ceases to be an option. Resistance becomes reality.
Fate ceases to be an ideological or moral abstract.
Strangers fade from existence.

Trained from an early age to understand the dynamic tension of life, these communities and the individuals that they are comprised of are capable of confrontation.

In embracing the complexity and complications of life, in being prepared and ready to take on its challenges, the wild communities can also dance and sing in its joy.

They can find peace within its potential violence and not live in fear of it.

And in embracing that tension, in creating and fostering our own wildness and self-reliance, in refusing the authority of the state and the myths of domestication, we may one day dance and sing upon the rusting remains of this empire.

Endnotes

1. Richard B Lee, *The !Kung San*. London: Cambridge UP, 1979. Pg 399.
2. This story was told to Richard Lee and printed in Lee, 1979. Pgs 394-395.
3. Nancy Scheper-Hughes and Philippe Bourgois, 'Introduction: Making Sense of Violence' in Scheper-Hughes & Bourgois (eds), *Violence in War and Peace*. Malden, MA: Blackwell, 2004. Pg 2.
4. For more on this topic, see my essay 'To Speak of Wildness' in *Black and Green Review* no 2.
5. Tamarack Song, *Becoming Nature*. Bear & Co, 2016.
6. Steven Pinker, *The Better Angels of our Nature*. New York: Penguin, 2011. Pg 1.
7. Frans de Waal, *The Age of Empathy*. New York: Three Rivers Press, 2009. Pg 10.
8. Richard Dawkins, *The Selfish Gene*. Oxford: Oxford UP, 1979. Pg 3.
9. Jane Goodall, *The Chimpanzees at Gombe*. Belknap Press, 1986.
10. R Brian Ferguson, 'Ten Points on War' in Alisse Waterston, *An Anthropology of War*. New York: Berghahn, 2008.
11. Frans de Waal, 'Foreword' in Fry (ed) *War, Peace and Human Nature*. Oxford: Oxford UP, 2013. Pg xi.
12. Smithsonian Museum of Natural History, 'Taung Child': http://humanorigins.si.edu/evidence/human-fossils/fossils/taung-child
13. Ibid. Pg xii.
14. Peter Verbeek, 'An Ethological Perspective on War and Peace' in Fry, 2013. Pg 56.
15. Ibid. Pg xiii. See also Marc Bekoff and Jessica Pierce, *Wild Justice*. Chicago: University of Chicago Press, 2009.
16. Verbeek, 2013. Pgs 66 & 67.
17. Joseph Birdsell, 'Some Predictions for the Pliestocene Based on Equilibrium Systems among Recent Hunter-Gatherers' in Lee and DeVore (eds), *Man the Hunter*. New York: Aldine de Gruyter, 1968. Pg 235.
18. John Bodley, *The Power of Scale*. Armonk, NY: ME Sharpe, 2003. Pgs 87-91.
19. Ibid, pg 55.
20. Thomas Malthus, *An Essay on the Principle of Population*. New York: Penguin, 1983 [Orig. 1798].
21. Bernard Sellato, *Nomads of the Borneo Rainforest*. Honolulu: University of Hawai'i Press, 1994. Pg 143.
22. James Woodburn, 'Stability and Flexibility in Hadza Residential Groupings' in Lee and DeVore, 1968. Pg 105.
23. https://en.wikipedia.org/wiki/List_of_urban_areas_by_population
24. Elizabeth Marshall Thomas, *The Old Way*. New York: Sarah Crichton Books, 2006. Pg 230
25. Ibid, Pgs 225-227.
26. Pinker 2011, Pg 54.
27. Lee, 1979. Pg 401.
28. Mark Cocker, *Rivers of Blood, Rivers of Gold*. New York: Grove, 1998. Pg 344.

29. Thomas, 2006, Pg 227.
30. Lee, 1979. Pg 389.
31. Ibid, pg 395.
32. Thomas, 2006. Pg 228.
33. Ibid, pg 229.
34. Ibid.
35. Lee, 1979. Pg 371.
36. Ibid, pg 372.
37. Richard Lee, *The Dobe Ju/'hoansi: third edition*. St Davis, CA: Wadsworth, 2003. Pg 114.
38. Victoria Katherine Burbank, *Fighting Women*. Berkeley: University of California Press, 1994.
39. For more on this, see my essay, 'Hooked on a Feeling' in *Black and Green Review* no 3. Spring 2016.
40. Carleton Coon, *The Hunting Peoples*. New York: Lyons, 1971. Pg 238.
41. Frank Marlowe, *The Hadza: Hunter-Gatherers of Tanzania*. Berkeley: University of California Press, 2010. Pg 141.
42. Kirk Endicott & Karen Endicott, *The Headman was a Woman: The Gender Egalitarian Batek of Malaysia*. Long Grove, IL: Waveland, 2008. Pg 66.
43. Csilla Dallos, *From Equality to Inequality*. Toronto: University of Toronto Press, 2011. Pg 132.
44. Brian Morris, *Forest Traders: A Socio-Economic Study of the Hill Pandaram*. New Jersey: Athlone Press, 1982. Pgs 160-161.
45. Jana Fortier, *Kings of the Forest*. Honolulu: University of Hawai'i Press, 2009. Pg 97.
46. Coon, 1971. Pg 240.
47. Marlowe, 2010. Pg 141.
48. Thomas, 2006. Pg 230. For more of this, see 'Hooked on a Feeling'.
49. Dallos, 2011. Pg 135.
50. Fry, 2013. Pg 11.
51. Ibid.
52. Douglas Fry, *The Human Potential for* Peace. New York: Oxford University Press, 2006, Pg 22.
53. David Dye, 'Trends in Cooperation and Conflict in Native Eastern North America' in Fry, 2013. Pgs 133-134.
54. Ibid, pg 136.
55. Turnbull, ' The Importance of Flux in Two Hunting Societies' in Lee and Devore, 1968. Pg 135.
56. Woodburn, 1968. Pg 105.
57. Tim Ingold, 'Notes on the Foraging Mode of Production' in Ingold, Riches and Woodburn (eds), *Hunters and Gatherers: Volume 1*. Oxford: Berg, 1988. Pg 278.
58. Nurit Bird-David, 'Studying Children in "Hunter-Gatherer" Societies" in Hewlett & Lamb (eds), *Hunter-Gatherer Childhoods*. New Brunswick, NJ: Transaction, 2005. Pg 96.
59. This is a huge topic that I will be following up in later works. For more see Hewlett & Lamb, 2005, Barry Hewlett, *Intimate Fathers: The Nature and Context*

of Aka Pygmy Paternal Infant Care. Ann Arbor, MI: University of Michigan Press, 1993, Barry Hewlett (ed), *Father-Child Relations*. New Brunswick, NJ: Transaction, 1992, and Jean Liedloff, *The Continuum Concept*. Cambridge, MA: Perseus, 1985.

60. Bird-David, 2005. Pg 97.

61. Paul Shepard, *Nature and Madness*. San Francisco: Sierra Club, 1982.

62. Bird-David, 2005. Pg 101.

63. Melvin Konner, 'Hunter-Gatherer Infancy and Childhood: The !Kung and Others' in Hewlett & Lamb, 2005. Pg 29.

64. Jean Peterson, *The Ecology of Social Boundaries: Agta Foragers of the Philippines*. Urbana, IL: University of Illinois Press, 1978. Pg 16.

65. Morris, 1982. Pg 147.

66. Colin Turnbull, *The Human Cycle*. Simon and Schuster: New York, 1983. Pgs 42-45.

67. Colin Turnbull, 'The Ritualization of Potential Conflict Among the Mbuti' in Leacock and Lee, *Politics and History in Band Society*. Cambridge UP: London, 1982. Pg 142.

68. Endicott & Endicott, 2008. Pg 117.

69. Turnbull, 1983. Pg 47.

70. Hugh Brody, *The Other Side of Eden*. Pgs 57-58.

71. Turnbull, 1983. Pgs 47 & 45.

72. 'What Makes Indians Laugh' in Pierre Clastres, *Society Against the State*. Brooklyn: Zone, 1989.

73. O. Yu. Artemova, 'Monopolisation of knowledge, social inequality and egalitarianism'. *Hunter Gatherer Research*. Volume 2, Issue 1. 2016.

74. Dallos, 2011. Pg 168.

75. Richard Lee, 'Eating Christmas in the Kalahari.' *Natural History*. December 1969: 60-64.

76. Ibid.

77. Michele Ruth Gamburd, *The Kitchen Spoon's Handle*. Ithaca: Cornell University Press, 2000. Pg 111.

78. An example of this is Koji Sonoda, 'Give me the Meat, the Child Said.' *Hunter Gatherer Research*. Volume 2, Issue 1. 2016.

79. Ingold, 1988. Pg 283.

80. Tim Ingold, 'On the Social Relations of the Hunter-Gatherer Band' in Lee and Daly, *The Cambridge Encyclopedia of Hunters and Gatherers*. Cambridge UP: Cambridge, 1999. Pg 401.

81. Clastres, 1989. Pg 205.

82. Marvin Harris, *Cannibals and Kings*. New York: Vintage, 1977. Pg 7.

83. Martin Fried, *Evolution of Political Society*. New York: McGraw-Hill, 1967. Pgs 109, 186, 185, & 229.

84. Harris, 1977. Pg 50.

85. Marshall Sahlins, *Culture in Practice*. New York: Zone Books, 2000. Pg 78.

86. Fried, 1967. Pg 133.

87. Clastres, 1989. Pg 46

88. Neil Whitehead, 'Tribes Make States and States Make Tribes' in R. Brian Ferguson and Neil Whitehead, *War in the Tribal Zone*. Santa Fe: School of American

Research Press, 1992. Pg. 129.
89. Harris, 1977. Pg 51.
90. R Brian Ferguson, 'Pinker's List: Exaggerating Prehistoric War Mortality' in Douglas Fry (ed), *War, Peace, and Human Nature*. Oxford: Oxford UP, 2013. Pg 126.
91. Fry, 2013. Pg 7.
92. Ibid. Pg 11.
93. Dallos, 2011. Pg 97.
94. Coon, 1971. Pg 262.
95. R Brian Ferguson, 'Introduction: Studying War' in Ferguson (ed), *Warfare, Culture, and Environment*. Orlando: Academic Press, Inc, 1984. Pg 5.
96. Harris, 1977. Pgs 51-52.
97. Andrew Vayda, 'Hypotheses About Functions of War' in Fried, Harris and Murphy (eds), *War: The Anthropology of Armed Conflict and Aggression*. Garden City, NY: The Natural History Press, 1968. Pgs 88-89.
98. Raymond Kelly, *Warless Societies and the Origins of War*. Ann Arbor, MI: University of Michigan Press, 2000. Pgs 3-6.
99. Andrew Vayda, *Warfare in Ecological Perspective*. New York: Plenum Press, 1976. Pg 2.
100. Douglas Fry, *Beyond War: The Human Potential for Peace*. New York: Oxford University Press, 2007. Pg 73.
101. Roy Rappaport, *Pigs for the Ancestors: Ritual in the Ecology of a New Guinea People*. Prospect Heights, IL: Waveland, 2000 [1984]. Pgs 57-58.
102. Marvin Harris, *Cows, Pigs, Wars, and Witches*. New York: Vintage, 1989 [1974]. Pg 48.
103. Rappaport, 2000. Pg 110.
104. Peter Wilson, *The Domestication of the Human Species*. New Haven, CT: Yale University Press, 1988. Pg 146.
105. Alexander Alland, 'War and Disease: An Anthropological Perspective' in Fried, Harris and Murphy, 1968. Pg 65.
106. Rappaport, 2000. Pg 19.
107. This process is detailed in Rappaport, 2000 and Vayda, 1976.
108. Scheper-Hughes and Bourgois, 2004, Pg 1.
109. Sylvia Fisher Carrasco, *Peru: A Chronicle of Deception*. Copenhagen: IWGIA, 2010. Pg 15.
110. Michael Harner, *The Jívaro: People of the Sacred Waterfalls*. Garden City, NY: Anchor Books, 1973. Pg 111.
111. Ibid. Pg 80.
112. Harris, 1977. Pgs 50-51.
113. Harner, 1973. Pg 135.
114. Ibid. Pg 141.
115. Ibid. Pgs 143-147.
116. Ibid. Pg 147.
117. Daniel Steel, 'Trade Goods and Jívaro Warfare: The Shuar 1850–1957, and the Achuar, 1940–1978.' *Ethnohistory*, Volume 46, Number 4. Fall 1999 and Jane Bennett Ross, 'Effects of Contact on Revenge Hostilities among the Achuarä Jívaro' in Ferguson, 1984.

118. See R Brian Ferguson, 'A Savage Encounter: Western Contact and the Yanomami War Complex' in Ferguson and Whitehead, 1992; R Brian Ferguson, *Yanomami Warfare*. Santa Fe: SAR Press, 1995; and Patrick Tierney, *Darkness in El Dorado*. New York: WW Norton, 2000.

119. See Eric Wolf, *Europe and the People Without History*. University of California Press, 1997 and Francis Jennings, *The Ambiguous Iroquois Empire*. New York: WW Norton, 1990.

120. Harner, 1973. Pg 201.

121. Ibid. Pg 118.

122. Sadly, I'm not kidding: http://www.realshrunkenheads.com/

123. Harner, 1973. Pg 88.

124. Ibid. Pgs 89-93.

125. Yolanda Murphy and Robert Murphy, *Women of the Forest*. New York: Columbia University Press, 2004 [1984]. Pg 111.

126. Ibid. Pg 106.

127. Fry, 2007. Pg 80.

128. Kelly, 2000. Pg 68.

129. Shepard, 1982. Pg 113.

130. Victoria Bekiempis, 'Nearly 1 in 5 Americans Suffer Mental Illness'. *Newsweek*. 2/28/14. Accessed on September 26, 2016: http://www.newsweek.com/nearly-1-5-americans-suffer-mental-illness-each-year-230608

131. Christopher Ingraham, 'Our Infant Mortality Rate is a National Embarrassment'. *Washington Post*, 9/29/14. Accessed on September 26, 2016: https://www.washingtonpost.com/news/wonk/wp/2014/09/29/our-infant-mortality-rate-is-a-national-embarrassment/

132. Endicott and Endicott, 2008. Pg 114.

133. Bird-David, 2005. Pg 97.

134. Konner, 2005. Pg 20.

135. Endicott and Endicott, 2008. Pg 114.

136. Percentage figured using the following data: 'A Visual Guide: Abortion in America' CNN

http://www.cnn.com/2016/06/27/health/abortion-in-america-charts-and-graphs-trnd/

2012 Abortions: 699,202 and 'Births: Final Data for 2012' National Vital Statistics Report

http://www.cdc.gov/nchs/data/nvsr/nvsr62/nvsr62_09.pdf. A total of 3,952,841 births were registered in the United States in 2012. 15.03% of total pregnancies (births plus abortions).

137. Peterson, 1978. Pg 10.

138. Kelly, 2000. Pg 37.

139. Center for Disease Control, 'Leading Causes of Death'. 2015. Accessed on September 26, 2016: http://www.cdc.gov/nchs/fastats/leading-causes-of-death.htm

140. Shepard, 1982. Pg 113.

141. 'Facts about PTSD' Accessed on September 26, 2016: http://psychcentral.com/lib/facts-about-ptsd/

142. Peter Wilson, 1988. Pg 183.

143. Stanley Diamond, *In Search of the Primitive*. New Brunswick, NJ: Transaction, 1987. Pg 229.
144. Ibid. Pg 17.
145. Timothy Earle, *How Chiefs Come to Power*. Stanford, CA: Stanford University Press, 1997. Pg 106.
146. 'I can't breathe': Eric Garner put in Chokehold by NYPD officer – video, *The Guardian*. https://www.theguardian.com/us-news/video/2014/dec/04/i-cant-breathe-eric-garner-chokehold-death-video
147. Timothy Earle, *Bronze Age Economics*. Boulder, CO: Westview Press, 2002. Pg 55.
148. Ibid. Pgs 43-44.
149. Kelly, 2000. Pg 101.
150. Harris, 1977. Pg 55.
151. Kelly, 2000. Pgs 7, 44-45.
152. Diamond, 1974. Pg 270.
153. Harold Barclay, *People Without Government: An Anthropology of Anarchy*. London: Kahn & Averill, 1990. Pgs 24-25.
154. Ibid. Pg 32.
155. Paul Shepard, *The Tender Carnivore and the Sacred Game*. Athens, GA: University of Georgia Press, 1998. Pg 123.
156. Jeff Zeleny, 'Accepting Peace Prize, Obama Offers 'Hard Truth''. *New York Times*, 12/10/2009. http://www.nytimes.com/2009/12/11/world/europe/11prexy.html
157. Stanley Diamond, 'War and the Dissociated Personality' in Harris, Fried and Murphy, 1968. Pgs 187-188.
158. Earle, 1997. Pg 7.
159. Paul Farmer, 'On Suffering and Structural Violence' in Scheper-Hughes and Bourgois, 2004. Pg 288.
160. Jonathan O'Callaghan, 'Will Your Child Witness the End of Humanity?' Daily Mail, June 19, 2015: http://www.dailymail.co.uk/sciencetech/article-3131160/Will-child-witness-end-humanity-Mankind-extinct-100-years-climate-change-warns-expert.html
161. See Adam Hochschild, *King Leopold's Ghost*. Boston: Mariner, 1999 and Sven Lindqvist, *Exterminate all the Brutes*. New Society, 1996.
162. Diamond, 1968. Pg 187.
163. Shepard, 1998. Pgs 215-216.
164. Jacques Camatte, *This World We Must Leave and Other Essays*. Brooklyn: Autonomedia, 1995. Pg 95.
165. See 'Revolt of the Savages' and 'The Failure of Revolution' in Tucker, 2010.
166. Bodley, 2003. Pg 65.
167. Kelly, 2000. Pg 81.
168. Eve Ball, *In the Days of Victorio*. Tucson: University of Arizona Press, 2003 [1970]. Pg xiii.
169. Keith Basso, *Western Apache Raiding & Warfare*. Tucson: University of Arizona Press, 1998 [1971].
170. Cocker, 1998. Pg 216.
171. David Roberts, *Once They Moved Like the Wind*. New York: Touchstone,

1994. Pg 180.
172. See 'Wild Resistance, Insurgent Subsistence' in *Black and Green Review* no 3.
173. Iyuskin American Horse, 'We are Protectors, Not Protestors.' *The Guardian*. 8/18/2016. Accessed at https://www.theguardian.com/us-news/2016/aug/18/north-dakota-pipeline-activists-bakken-oil-fields

To Speak of Wildness

He says that woman speaks with nature. That she hears voices from under the earth. That wind blows in her ears and trees whisper to her. That the dead sing through her mouth and the cries of infants are clear to her. But for him this dialogue is over. He says he is not part of this world, that he was set on this world as a stranger.

— Susan Griffin, *Woman and Nature*[1]

It is not inherently in the nature of the world that it should consist of things that may or may not be appropriated by people.

— Tim Ingold[2]

The memory is vivid.

It was nighttime and the sky had been dark for hours. My wife and I were driving on a stretch of road, cars were clustered, but it was neither busy nor desolate. There was some space between the cars ahead of us, but a good number of cars following. And then there was a sudden, unmistakable flash of white dotted with brown. It moved quickly and it was gone. Had we blinked, we could have easily missed it entirely.

Neither of us blinked. We knew immediately that what had flown feet in front of our windshield was a Great Horned Owl. There was a stillness to it, as if it all happened in slow motion. Even with a decent amount of traffic, that owl had flown in front of our car only.

And this wasn't the only time. It wasn't the first and it certainly wouldn't be the last, yet this time there was no question: the owl wanted to be seen.

Owls are often solitary animals. As someone who has dedicated a fair amount of time to tracking them, I can assure you of this. There are some variations to that. Barred Owls can be downright social. We have had them swoop in over fires just to inspect.

This, however, is far from the norm.

Owls are as excellent at camouflage as they are hunting carried out with a nearly imperceptible hush to their flight. Even expert owl trackers who literally wrote the book on the subject, Patricia and Clay Sutton, observed that "it is amazing how [owls] can seem to simply not exist until the perfect angle makes one visible." This doesn't change the fact that despite their invisibility, owls "are all around us."[3]

When an owl wants to be seen, it is awe-inspiring. An extremely different feeling than the joy of finding Great Horned Nestlings or catching the flash of Screech Owl eyes as light crosses thickets at night. For us, that flood of feeling is always eclipsed by one thought in particular: confirmation. The Great Horned Owl is our messenger of death.

When death comes for a relative, a friend, an acquaintance of those close to us, there can be heaviness in the air that is inexplicable otherwise. Things feel off. My wife and I have regrettably become accustomed to it over the years. We start doing a mental inventory of whom we know that might be going through some turmoil or difficulty. But when the Great Horned Owl shows themself, little doubt remains: something has happened.

The night that stood out so clearly in my memory stands out because it was the time when the rational, domesticated part of my brain broke down. When the probability of coincidence was worn too thin and the veneer cracked. There is something here. Sure enough, we found out fairly quickly that there had been an accident. A family member had been involved in a fatal collision. While he was revived on the scene, the driver was not. That happened nearly 1,000 miles away and at the same time the owl came.

This was nearly 12 years ago now. Circumstances changed, but the Great Horned has come numerous times. As grandparents passed, as relatives took their own lives or succumb to cancer or diabetes, as family and their acquaintances overdosed; every time, we get the news from this majestic winged hunter.

The silent flier speaks up.

That night opened a door of perception that I had only casually noticed before. The Great Horned was a messenger of death, but there were many others. There was a distinct air of familiarity and comfort in the Mockingbird that sat on my grandfather's casket during his funeral and watched silently. A Rattlesnake made themselves known to indicate that a family member had died from heroin overdose, a fitting messenger for having injected too much venom. A calming White Tailed Deer that stood before me as I nervously wondered about my as-yet-unborn daughter. And there was a Flycatcher screeching outside of our home to warn us about an instigator amongst us.

These messengers were there all along; I just hadn't put the pieces together. I still feel discomfort even speaking of them openly, but I cannot deny them. And I am only scratching at the surface here.

Seeking council from the wild isn't a matter of being fully integrated into the world around you. These messengers don't come because you seek them; it is not their purpose to serve you. They are simply doing what they do: responding with empathy to impulses that are more apparent to them than to us. That we are continually missing such messages is on us, our own aloof non-presence in the world.

This isn't meant to downplay the breach of any civilized social contract that is happening when wild beings are bringing news, warnings and offering direction. Considering our sanitized sense of intellectual superiority and deadening of senses, it's not surprising to know that something like Laurens van der Post's account of a hunter-gatherer of the Kalahari telling him: "We Bushman have a wire here,' he tapped his chest, 'that brings us news'"[4] is interpreted as evidence of telepathy. Anything other than pure supernatural power is unthinkable.

That the world speaks to us shouldn't be news. The Lakota-Sioux Lame Deer echoes the word of indigenous peoples the world over with statements like this: "You have to listen to all these creatures, listen with your mind. They have secrets to tell. Even a kind of cricket, called *ptewoyake*, a wingless hopper, is used to tell us where to find buffalo."[5]

The writing is in the thickets and the cracks in the wall, yet this isn't the headline. To get messages from wild beings is tantamount to pleading insanity in this society. But those messages are always there. What keeps us from receiving them is our own ability to perceive that they exist.

Perception and the Better Angles of our (Human) Nature

> *In spite of our precious rational process and in spite of our cherished scientific objectivity, we continue to maintain an absolute and unchallengeable distinction between man and the nonhuman. It has occurred that the firmness of this insistence may be one measure of the need we may perceive for justification of our overwhelmingly antibiotic actions.*
> — John Livingston, *The Fallacy of Wildlife Conservation*[6]

And here lies the root of our problem: the process of domestication, the taming of our wild souls through constant programming, can only exist in a dead world. The world that makes our existence possible is flattened, dissected and reassembled as a sum of all parts.

Our compliance is built upon an uprooted lack of place. We are aliens in our own home. Our virtues and pride are built around artificial replacements for community, for a sense of being, for a sense of belonging, and an amplified sense of self. Domestication is the process of stunting the growth and relationships that our hunter-gatherer minds and bodies require and redirecting those impulses to productivity. Our entire sense of identity is built upon *neotony*, an incomplete process of personal development within the greater community against a backdrop of living remembrance and myth.[7] Psychologically speaking, we are runts.

Our senses are dulled, the instincts that we possess as children are subdued. Our world is flattened. As the anthropologist Colin Turnbull observed in comparing the stages of "the human cycle" between hunter-gatherers and Modernized consumers: "if in our childhood and adolescence we have not learned other modes of awareness, if we have not become fully integrated beings, and if we persist in dissociating reason from these other faculties, these other modes of knowing and understanding, then we remain fettered by the limitations of reason and cease to grow."[8]

We absorb the fears of the farmer, politician, priest, and industrialist. We regurgitate them so that we can find some solace in their hollow promises. We build cities, countrysides, nuclear power plants, and open pit mines upon that foundation. We volunteer in the war against our own animality.

And all the while, these wild beings are constantly reminding, warning and telling us what our bodies and hearts know: we are connected. There is something here. A message lost as owl carcasses pile up on the sides of highways: we are born wild. And to our would-be messengers, we still are. We just aren't recognizing it.

This is wildness. Yearning. Reaching. Crying out and carrying on.

And the blood of the messengers is on our hands.

Our perception of the world is fickle. Our subjective experiences can turn into self-sustaining feedback loops that only serve our own ideological biases. Biases crafted and sold to us by programmers, priests, and salespersons. But the world is more than that.

The world, to put it simply, exists.

Wildness exists.

It exists in its own right, comprised of billions upon billions of living beings. Physical separation may be real, but the stoic independence that the domesticated uphold is a fragment of our own fractured minds. A blinder: a limitation.

We look into a mirror of the isolated soul of a civilized being, a consumer of life, and subject the world to the distortions that we carry. We unload our burdens onto that barren soil, onto "nature". It too must feel our loneliness, our isolation. Our wanting.

There is much to be said about the importance of critique. My short sell on anarcho-primitivism (AP) is that it is a critique with implications. And those implications are things that I don't take lightly.

The AP critique is a short hand way of saying that civilization is killing the earth and that the domestication process is perpetually taking its toll on our lives in every sense of the word. Most importantly, the AP critique is saying that civilization, the culture of cities, doesn't arrive out of thin air. There are roots here. To understand how we've gotten to this point, we must dig.

And so we dig.

The crisis we face is an old crisis, going back in some places nearly 12,000 years. That is literally to the beginning of History. In ecological time, that's a drop in the bucket. Fortunately, as wild beings, our roots lie in ecological cycles, not linear time. Our roots go deep. Infinitely deep. We, human beings, are the slow outgrowth of millions of years of wild existence. It would be easy to regurgitate the narrative of Progress that our presence indicates a tooth-and-nail conquest of a world that is both Social Darwinian and Hobbesian in nature.

But we know this isn't the case. Our development as a species has been relatively slow and stable. Our timeline for the antiquity of stone tools pushes back continually and is largely fogged by the inability to admire the ingenuity of our grounded ancestors and cousins. We *want* to believe that things have gotten better, that *we* have improved. Yet this isn't true. All of the psychological and physical breakdowns of the human body and mind are an indicator that as adaptive as humans are, we can't tolerate the domestication process and the reality it has created. This only becomes more increasingly apparent.

In short, the implication here is that we are not starting from scratch.

We are not born with the *Tabula Rasa*, the "clean slate," that Plato and his predecessors had described. Philosophy, an indicator of our trained disconnect with the world around us, has always been a crucial tool of programmers and specialists alike. We are wild beings: each and every one of us. The AP critique is about understanding how changes in circumstance (specialization, surplus orientation, agriculture and pastoralism, sedentism; to name the primary culprits) created the vestiges of social power that have ultimately held our world, the wild community, hostage. Our mythos is cracking.

Human nature may historically have a lot of baggage, but from an ecological and biological perspective, it's pretty impossible to dismiss. We are born hunter-gatherers, everything that domesticators have sought to impose is working against that basis. And they are failing as much now as they always have. "Wildness," ecologist Paul Shepard was known to remind us, "is a genetic state."[9]

Wildness is *our* genetic state.

The Nature of Language and Language of Nature

> *Reification, the tendency to take the conceptual as the perceived and to treat concepts as tangible, is as basic to language as it is to ideology. Language represents the mind's reification of its experience, that is, an analysis into parts which, as concepts, can be manipulated as if they were objects.*
>
> — John Zerzan, *Elements of Refusal*[10]

Wildness is a complicated concept.

Its critics have conflated *wildness* with *Nature*, a move that obscures intentionality with conventional shorthand. From the very start, proponents of wildness have made a decisive choice in this language. What is being lost in the shuffle is that if you hold an ecological perspective, that the presence of wildness is hardly a means to supplant god/s, but indicative of the connections that we, as wild beings, share with the world. It's an exploration of empathy, not an apathetic move to remain enthusiastic by-standers like conservationists.

The purpose isn't to evoke wildness as an aesthetic, but as continuity, as our baseline: this is the ground that we are standing upon and it is worth defending. That the word is indefinable speaks to its complexity, it demands engagement.

So why use it?

There are many reasons not to use a word or to avoid naming altogether. Wildness, at least how I experience and conceptualize it, is sacred: that word is an indicator, not an encapsulation. That would be a good argument for leaving it even more obscure. But the problem then comes down to intentions. If I want to discuss civilization with anyone, this is my baseline, my reference point: wildness is the attainable and lurking reminder that we were not meant to live civilized lives.

Wildness, as the term is often used, transcends space and time: unlike *wilderness* it is not a place and unlike *nature* it is not external. Wildness is reflective of a continuum. Sure enough, hippies and New Agers may have tried touching on it and self-help gurus might delve into the term,[11] but there's a degree of inescapability to that. Words travel. As recent attempts to completely own and market *rewilding* have highlighted, you can't control the usage, but you can contribute to the context.

That is not a minor point. Anthropologist Hugh Brody saw it as a more practical observation in terms of the age old question as to whether language shapes the mind or mind shapes language: "a person can explain how a word is used and what it refers to, but the word's *meaning* depends on knowing a web of contexts and concealed related meanings."[12]

That the term *wildness* can be written off isn't an indication of how the word itself is reification, our abstract representation, because all words are arguably reifications. The difference is in the *context*. Should wildness be defined and corralled into a trap of stagnancy, then the context, that flowing, organic, struggling and ever-presence that defies reflection, would be another matter altogether.

Like domestication, it's easier to know it when you see it.

The problem is that we aren't seeing it.

Ecologist David Abram in his landmark book on perception, *The Spell of the Sensuous*, echoes a trajectory of philosophy in pointing out that: "the perceptual style of any community is both reflected in, and profoundly shaped by, the common language of the community." For our rooted hunting and gathering relatives, that language includes "the speech of birds, of wolves, and even of the wind." Contrast that against the world of the civilized, the world we've all been raised in, where "we now experience language as an exclusively human property or possession."[13]

For all of our narcissistic obsessions with technological development, we have completely disregarded that the counterpoint to the self-applied badge of Progress is our increased our dependency upon stimulation overload on one side and complete sensory depravation on the rest.[14] Building upon civilization's foundation of hierarchy and complacency, we externalize our frustrations to (and often beyond) the point of self-destruction. I'll allow an anthropologist to state it lightly:

> *if our species really did evolve in the context of social relationships approximating those in current immediate-return societies, then our current delayed-return societies may be requiring us to behave in ways that are discordant with our natural tendencies*[15]

Put bluntly: removed of our own wild context, we are out of balance.

Nature, the bandage we apply on the externalized wild world that we are actively destroying, is our counterpoint. It is our Other.[16] "Nature" as sociologist Peter Dwyer aptly points out, "is an invention, an artifact."[17] Not one to mince words, anthropologist Tim Ingold gets down to it: "the world can only be 'nature' for a being that does not belong there."[18] As we will elaborate, this is yet another civilized disease which hunter-gatherers have not suffered:

> *[Hunter-gatherers] do not see themselves as mindful subjects having to contend with an alien world of physical objects; indeed, the separation of mind and nature has no place in their thought and practice.*[19]

The obedience required by the domesticated demands a world of binary dualisms: of innately oppositional forces. In turn, it created those dichotomies. Nature versus civilization, wild versus domesticated, developed versus undeveloped: there are many iterations of an increasingly antagonized division between the individual and the world that surrounds them. We can say this is a problem of linguistics, we can use philosophy and theory to try to perfect the language and have an asterisk on every word we utter, but none of this escapes the fact that the *reality* domestication has created is one of binary opposition.

Civilization doesn't just oppose nature; it created it so that it could stand against it. This is what we have conquered. This is what we have crawled out from to stand on our feet with pride.

To Speak of Wildness

Wildness vs Wilderness

The idea of wilderness, both as a realm of purification outside civilization and as a special place with beneficial qualities, has strong antecedents in the High Culture of the Western world. The ideas that wilderness offers us solace, naturalness, nearness to a kind of literary, spiritual esthetic, or to unspecified metaphysical forces, escape from urban stench, access to ruminative solitude, and locus of test, trial, and special visions—all of these extend prior traditions. True, wilderness is something we can escape to, a departure into a kind of therapeutic land or sea, release from our crowded and overbuilt environment, healing to those who sense the presence of the disease of tameness. We think of wilderness as a place, a vast uninhabited home of wild things. It is also another kind of place. It is that genetic aspect of ourselves that spatially occupies every body and every cell.

  - Paul Shepard, *Coming Home to the Pleistocene.*[20]

This realization about the limitations of nature can stupefy any attempt to use that history as a foundation. It can be easy and, at times, soothing to get lost in a metaphysical escape and quandary. But to look back to the observations brought up by Brody, language isn't our problem, context is. And our context is a frightening one.

We live in an era of great disruption and unprecedented change: weather patterns have destabilized, blind desperation and a complete lack of foresight allows us to drill deeper and clear-cut mountains, economies respond, those who have the least to gain from this hyper-Modernized global economy stand to suffer the most impact of ecological consequence.

Our problem ends in catastrophe if a change in perception doesn't turn into action on its behalf. And this is why we speak of wildness. It is not the externalized passive matter that may constitute *nature*.

It surges. It pulses.
It is your heart beating.
It is your lungs taking in air and your throat exhaling breath.

Wildness is beyond matter. It ties and connects. In moments of growth and destruction, beauty and carnage, wildness is the functioning whole: in a sum-of-all-parts scientific approach, it is the unsolvable equation. Reiterated through the worldview of rooted hunter-gatherer and horticultural communities, what has been called traditional ecological knowledge "goes well beyond noting the interrelatedness of specific organisms; it embraces an all-encompassing world-view of total relationship."[21] Furthermore, this enacted knowledge "is generally holistic, and not easily subject to fragmentation. To deconstruct it and arrange its features in analytic categories, and then to discuss them cross-culturally, is to Westernize them."[22]

Much of what can be said of wildness in defiance of nature echoes into the discussion about *wilderness*.

Following up on his observations about wildness as a "genetic state," Paul Shepard contrasts wilderness as the place we have dedicated for wildness to exist. An extolling of demons, a soothing of lingering desires: the playground and museum to engage our senses through voyeurism. But the cost of entry here isn't just complacency, it's far more malicious. The narrative offered is a reiteration of our distancing, but the trip is courtesy of your local tour agent: our leisure is another purchase.

In Shepard's words: "Wilderness sanctuaries presuppose our acceptance of the corporate takeover of everything else. Privatizing is celebrated as part of the ideal of the politics of the state, masked as individualism and freedom."[23] The experience of wilderness is far from an expression of wildness. The terms may only differ by a mere two letters, but the implications couldn't be greater.

That adventures in wilderness have become a basis for actual dispossession and displacement for those hunter-gatherers, who lacked a context for *nature* as a removed place, is no coincidence. Exemplifying the point, the Hadza of Tanzania were threatened with forced removal from ancestral lands by a hunting safari company based out of the United Arab Emirates.[24] A fate that resonates amongst the !Kung of Botswana and Namibia who are arrested for poaching and trespass within reserves that bear their names.[25]

These are stories that repeat and play out constantly throughout history, which is since civilized people began recording time instead of living within it. These are the footnotes to the autobiographical legacy of colonizers and conquerors. While we have been ingrained with their perceptions and narratives, they still must constantly be positioned to work against our own wild state: the hunter-gatherer inside your mind, your being.

To awaken those senses, it is helpful to understand how those rooted peoples see their world. *Our* world.

Perception and the Living Earth

> *I was born in the forest. My forefathers came from here. We are the Wanniyala-aetto and I want to live and die here. Even if I were to be reborn as only a fly or as an ant, I would still be happy as long as I knew I would come back to live here in the forest.*
> - Kotabakinne (Veddah) chief, Uru Warige Tissahamy.[26]

The abolition of *nature* is not an uncommon theme amongst post-modern philosophers. Their impulse is born of Modernity and interacts with the world as they have been trained to see it. They are correct in their assessments that the world is constantly in flux and that stagnancy stands in the way, but they continue on the legacy of the ungrounded, the uprooted. Their sense of entitlement to a present without bounds neglects the consequence of the world as we know it: the world where our actions impact life across the planet and beyond our generation.

They carry on without context.

To see the past, present and future as evident in all life is an ability that we should have, but that perception comes only with living in a way that is not detrimental towards the past, present and future. Rooted indigenous societies have notoriously lacked any sense of linear time. Like *nature*, they lack the separation necessary to create it.

In living with the hunter-gatherer Pirahã of Brazil, missionary turned agnostic Daniel Everett observed that the inability to "spread the word" was attributed in part to the fact that Pirahã "only make statements that are anchored to the moment when they are speaking, rather than to any other point in time."[27] Their world lacked a need to speak in historic terms and, subsequently, their language lacks anything beyond a simple form of tense.

A world without presence was unthinkable.

That is the world in which wildness runs rampant. It is the place where language has never been solely attributed to humans. This is the place where the messages of animals, plants, and weather are taken at face value and understood. The ability to read the language of birds is a given. The ability to read bodies and movement are not separated from the definitiveness that we attribute only to speech. This isn't the world beyond nature; it is the world where it is unnecessary.

The connectivity that New Agers and their ilk have sought to be proponents of is a by-product of our own limits to perception. Our glass is fogged over. Those connections are within reach, but we have to be prepared for the humility of breaking down the domesticator in our minds.

For the hunter-gatherer, no such obstructions exist until they have been forced upon them. Their perception minces no words on the matter of matter. In the words of Ilarion Merculieff, an Aluet native, speaking of the world of the hunter-gatherer;

> *Theirs is a world in which the interdependence of humans, animals, plants, water, and earth – the total picture – is always immediate, always present. And the total picture – every day, every season, every year – is seen as a circle. Everything is connected: the marshlands to the beaver, the beaver dams to altered conditions, the new conditions to the moose herd, the moose herd to the marshlands. Each affects the other, and it is in this intimate knowledge of the environment (all the curves in the circle) that has allowed these people to survive for hundreds of generations.*[28]

The ability to externalize "the Other" is demolished through proximity and familiarity. Anthropologist William Laughlin observes a common theme amongst the development of children in hunter-gatherer societies: the passing on of the world of the hunter as a trade in and of itself. The wholeness of climate, growth patterns, migration movements, the knowledge of track, sign and bird language, the detailed knowledge of anatomy that comes from butchering and stalking; all of these elements are integral to life in the wild.

This is not particular to humans, but in using language to reflect upon it, Laughlin observes: "Their conversations often sound like a classroom discussion of ecology, of food chains, and trophic levels."[29] This is not lost on the children, whose growing knowledge of animals is "prominently based upon familiarity with animal behavior and includes ways of living peacefully with animals, of maintaining a discourse with them."[30]

Philosophy is not an adequate replacement for proximity without separation. Wildness here needs no interpretation, but is often subject to exaltation. "I suggest," observes Mathias Guenther of the timeless rock art of the !Kung, "that animals are beguiling and interesting to man prima facie, in and of themselves, without any mediation through social structure."[31]

The relationships in question bare more resemblance to symbiosis than the symbolic. The case of the Honey Guide bird in the Kalahari is one oft-cited example. The Honey Guide leads a more physically able being towards beehives to harvest honey. It matters not if that being is a human or a honey badger so long as the harvester sets honeycomb aside for the willing and patient guide.[32]

And yet the language of wildness here maintains a circumstantial definition. Little more is needed.

The participants in this world need no terminology and, in light of solid context, the terms may be translated into a placeless language like English, but without having relative experiences, the meaning is lost. I feel the weight of the words used by the Mbuti, whom Colin Turnbull lived amongst, as they spoke of *ndura* or "forestness" represented by the symbols of fire, water, air and earth, which they "cannot move, eat, or breathe without being conscious of one or all of these symbols, and all are treated with respect, consciously recognized as integral parts of the ultimate giver of life, the forest."[33] What resonates further within me is that the wind is upheld as *pepo nde ndura*, or, "the breath of the forest itself."[34] Amongst the Nayaka of southern India, the forest is similarly referred to as "the giving environment".[35]

It is important to note that while my emphasis so far has been on animals, the same notions and connections extend to plants themselves. They too can serve both as messengers and healers. Herbalist and natural veterinarian Dr. Randy Kidd shares a story of having attempted to grow mullein in his own rock garden to no avail. He decided to ask his neighbor about the beautiful stalks of it growing in their yard. The neighbors had paid little to no attention to the sage-like green stalks and their tiny yellow flowers protruding amongst the rocks, but they happened to mention that one of the residents was currently hospitalized for asthma – a disease which mullein is known to treat.[36]

Our ability to forget that our connections extend beyond other animals has led equally to the facilitation and "the loss of plant species, the loss of health in ecosystems and our bodies, and the loss of the sense of who we ourselves, are."[37]

The tragedy that we face arises both from our distancing from that timeless world and the ways in which our rooted hunter-gatherer minds are physically incapable of thinking on a global scale.[38]

We are trapped by circumstance.

Our escape demands a realization of the world as it has been and will be, but remains hindered by the obstructions, the sheer physicality and devastation that civilization has created. The urge is there to delve completely into the world of the hunter-gatherer, a place both rooted and unbound. It is the place where we belong and it lurks within us and struggles to stand its ground on the periphery. But ignorance is not our path there.

Empathy is.

By seeking to immerse ourselves in the wildness that surrounds us, we can't expect the spiritual salvation offered by Gurus on weekend retreats. This place is sacred, but it is not a safe place. It is under assault. As are we. As are all living beings.

It is through connection, through grounding, that we understand what is at stake, what is lost and forgotten, buried and removed. When we begin to prod our constant process of pains inflicted upon our being, when the Self and Other fade, when we identify that source of agony: only then will we fight with passion and meaning for what is *known*.

To Speak of Wildness

Wild Existence, Passionate Resistance

> *An-archic and pantheistic dancers no longer sense the artifice and its linear His-Story as All, but merely one cycle, one long night, a stormy night that left Earth wounded, but a night that ends, as all nights end, when the sun rises.*
> — Fredy Perlman, *Against His-Story, Against Leviathan.*[39]

The term *rewilding* has had its share of false Gurus and snake oil salespersons attempting to derail the process and turn it into consumable fodder.[40] False hopes and rewilding "Ninja Camps"[41] aside, the rewilding process, like the anarcho-primitivist critique, carries with it an innate understanding of human nature as rooted in nomadic hunter-gatherer life. To *re*-wild is to acknowledge that wildness is our baseline.

Rewilding, to put it simply, is about stopping and *un*doing the separation created through the domestication process. As programs may try to sway towards a singular emphasis on primal skills or may tiptoe around with the voyeuristic tourism of a hiker, this underlying principle remains. As the consequences of domestication continue to unfold and assault the world we live in, the radicalism of that sentiment stands.

What separates rewilding from any other form of naturalist and ecophilosophical inquiry is that the end point is integration. The path overlaps in terms of observation, but the "leave only footprints" Nature fan has no interest in undoing the dichotomy that civilization requires. Their quest is one of indulgence, not subsistence and substance. It is akin to meditation.

To embrace the wild, we have to undergo the process of allowing wildness to help us evaluate our baggage. To remove our separation requires a transformation of thought that erodes the scientific taxonomy that seeks to understand the world through a microscope. As naturalist Jon Young points out, native knowledge and scientific knowledge are "two ways of paying supremely close attention."[42] Native knowledge, or "science without all of the trappings," is riddled with empathy, itself "a dangerous word in science" as it stands in complete opposition to the necessary removal implicit in the intent cloak of objectivity.[43] Young argues that his primary focuses, bird language/communication and tracking, rooted at first in observation inevitably lead those who take the time to "not just show up, but really tune in," to build relationships and experience the community of wildness on its own terms will experience what can only be called a primal awakening.[44]

That is a spiritual awakening.

Echoed by tracking instructor Paul Rezendes, what I call the "radical humility" of having your ass handed to you by the wild in terms of thought and physicality is no easy process. As having been raised with the redirected impulses of a wild being towards consumable traits, we have much work to do. It is only "when the self becomes tired and weak and pride languishes can the awareness that is wildness step in."[45]

The salvaging of scientifically understood connections through biology, ecology, psychology, as well as anthropology and sociology, requires a difference in perception. That the methods used to gain knowledge are flawed doesn't change that they can still glean elements of reality; they just took the long way there. The pride of achievement domestication awards us can quickly fade in light of, as Young states, "what the robin already knows."

The teachings of the robin are not far off from those of our hunter-gatherer relatives. They remind us of the timeless place where history is lived rather than charted. "Both humans and non-humans, in short," Tim Ingold observes, "figure as fellow-participants in an ongoing process of remembering."[46] Wildness is within us. Wildness surrounds us. It suffers alongside and through us, its wounds still being inflicted.

Yet it does not give up.

No amount of concrete, steel, ideology, or distancing has succeeded in its conquest. None will. Civilization measures its victories in temporal measures that within a historic timeline appear significant. Removed of linear time, removed of our forgetting, our disconnect, their significance wanes into collections of dusty books and obsolete technology.

Civilization is both a complex and volatile target. Its ideology and mechanics are built upon regurgitated narratives built upon the false belief that our future, as humans, will take us from the dreaded earth. That our history will show a gruesome conquest of animality, ours included, moving from the reflection of gods to a god status.

And yet each of us, every single one of us, is falling apart along the way.

We are testaments to the failures of domestication. Our bodies, built to withstand the extremes of climate, movement, famine and feast, succumb to diseases of the sedentary, the undernourished, the overfed, the toxins, and the meaningless wanderings. Blind to the catastrophe unfolding through us, we miss the connectivity hiding in plain sight: the wildness creeping through the cracks. Turnbull, contrasting the emptiness of civilization against the grounded life exhibited amongst the Mbuti, noted that having "never learned to employ our whole being as a tool of awareness" has kept us from "that essence of life which cannot be learned except through direct awareness, which is total, not merely rational." Encounters with the Spirit, the wildness, in "our form of social organization merely allows it to happen as an accident, if at all, whereas the Mbuti writes it into the charter from the outset, at conception."[47]

The structure of Mbuti life embraces the *pepo nde ndura*, the breath of the forest, whereas the structure of our world is built around avoiding or diverting it at all costs. If another way of being were seen as possible, the sanctity of the Freedom to Consume would fade. The burden of work would collapse.

And it is through the reconnection with the wild, through the erosion of our stagnant sense of removal, that the weaknesses of civilization become apparent. The struggle of the wild becomes real. The impact of climate instability and ecological devastation become our battle cry. The exacerbated feedback loops of drought and flood, the fires of thirsty and embattled forests ignite our animalistic urges.

When we remove the distance between the destruction of the earth and bear the scars of wildness, we will know not only what the robin has told us, but what our indigenous and lost relatives and ancestors have told us: when you know what it means to be wild, you will know what it means to fight.

To struggle.

To resist.

Around the time that I began to acknowledge the messages I had been getting from wild messengers, I began to push myself further into the woods. I tried to escape the sounds of the designed world. But valleys carried the echo of distant engines. Power lines and radio towers carried the news of conquest.

There was much to be found in those forests, but perhaps what I found the most was within myself. I had much to learn. I have much to learn. As my love and empathy grew, my rage burned deeper. The sheer simplicity of symbiosis tears at my soul. How many messages had I missed? Why, in light of my own complicity with ecocide, were the wild ones willing to recognize me, a descendent of colonizers walking on stolen land?

But it wasn't me they were after.

Just as hunter-gatherers lack a conceptual basis for nature or wilderness, the wild lacks the framework for vengeance. The language of birds will immediately ring the alarm over our indifferent, yet aloof demeanor whether we chose to recognize that or not. Their communication has nothing to hide and they share their trepidations widely. Hunter-gatherers and anyone willing to acknowledge this can act accordingly. Strange though our behaviors might be, the birds recognize what we have been trained not to see: the wildness that we carry in our being.

We belong here.

Their songs, their alarms, these messages; all of these are an unquestioned part of their world. Of our world.

And they await our return.

I often wish that Nature was real. That vengeance was within her. That she would undo civilization. No doubt she possesses the might. But it doesn't work that way: the sheer weight of inevitability errs on her side, yet I am left with nothing to transpose my own helplessness onto. There is no escape.

Wild beings under attack simply respond. They bite. They claw. They tear. It is instinctual and instant, not prolonged and devoid of responsibility. Our playing field is not level. Planners and programmers play chess with our fates. The potential of our own demise is the footnote to blueprints for a Future that will never

To Speak of Wildness

come on a planet that was never meant to support it.

There is no easy salvation here. Wildness is not a retreat.

When we overcome our rational minds and embrace it in our souls, we will do as our wild relatives, human and nonhuman, have done: stand our ground.

Bite, claw, and tear.

And we will fight until the wound is no longer inflicted.

The power of the known, the meaning of context, the power of wildness lies in their ambiguity. The inability to define wildness attests to its enduring strength. It refuses constraint.

You will simply know it when you feel it.

And I can think of no greater end to aspire to.

Endnotes

1. Susan Griffin, *Woman and Nature*. Harper and Row: New York, 1978. Pg 1
2. Tim Ingold, "Time, Memory, and Property" in Widlok and Tadesse, *Property and Equality Volume 1: Ritualisation, Sharing, Egalitarianism*. Berghahn: New York, 2007. Pg 165.
3. Patricia and Clay Sutton, *How to Spot an Owl*. Chapters Publishing: Shelburne, VT, 1994. Pg. 18.
4. Laurens van der Post, *The Lost World of the Kalahari*. Harvest: San Diego, 1958. Pg 260.
5. John (Fire) Lame Deer and Richard Erodes, *Lame Deer: Seeker of Visions*. Washington Square Press: New York, 1994. Pg. 136.
6. John Livingston, *The Fallacy of Wildlife Conservation* in *The John A. Livingston Reader*. McClelland and Stewart: Toronto, 2007. Pg 89.
7. This is a point Paul Shepard did not miss. It is a common theme amongst his work, but most notable in *Nature and Madness*. Sierra Club Books: San Francisco, 1982.
8. Colin Turnbull, *The Human Cycle*. Simon and Schuster: New York, 1983. Pg 129.
9. Paul Shepard, *Coming Home to the Pleistocene*. Island Press: Washington DC, 1998. Pg 138.
10. John Zerzan, *Elements of Refusal* (2nd Edition). CAL Press: Columbia, MO, 1999. Pg 34.
11. Radicals are not to be dismissed from this as well. The prime example being Derrick Jensen who tried appropriating the "language older than words" as he believed indigenous peoples have reiterated it. This, however, ends tragically after he began calling himself Tecumseh, talking about domestic animals offering their bodies to his axe, having his dogs eat feces from his source, or having sex with trees. Needless to say, his "conversations" with nature, lacking in any and all humility, bare little resemblance to those reiterated otherwise here.
12. Hugh Brody, *The Other Side of Eden*. North Point Press: New York, 2000. Pg 47.
13. David Abram, *Spell of the Sensuous*. Vintage: New York, 1997. Pg 91.
14. For more on this see my essay 'The Suffocating Void' in *Black and Green Review number 1*. Black and Green Press: Ephrata, PA, 2015.
15. Leonard Martin and Steven Shirk, "Immediate-Return Societies: What Can They Tell Us About the Self and Social Relationships in Our Society" in Wood, Tesser, and Holmes (eds), *The Self and Social Relationships*. Psychology Press: New York, 2008. *Pg* 178.
16. For more on this subject, see my essay "Egocide" in Kevin Tucker, *For Wildness and Anarchy*. Black and Green Press: Greensburg, PA, 2009. Also pretty widely available online.
17. Peter Dwyer, "The Invention of Nature" in Ellen and Fukui (eds), *Redefining Nature: Ecology, Culture and Domestication*. Berg: Oxford, 1996. Pg 157.

18. Tim Ingold, "Hunting and Gathering as Ways of Perceiving the Environment" in Ellen and Fukui, 1996. Pg 117.
19. Ibid, pg 120.
20. Shepard, 1998. Pg 132.
21. Catherine Fowler and Nancy Turner, "Ecological/cosmological knowledge and land management among hunter-gatherers" in Lee and Daly, *The Cambridge Encyclopedia of Hunters and Gatherers*. Cambridge UP: Cambridge, 1999. Pg 421.
22. Ibid, 419.
23. Shepard, 1998. Pg 138.
24. Survival International, "Safari concession threatens Hadza tribe", June 28, 2007. Online: http://www.survivalinternational.org/news/2467. Accessed July 8, 2015.
25. See Rupert Isaacson, *The Healing Land*. Grove Press: New York, 2001.
26. Cited in Lee and Daly, *The Cambridge Encyclopedia of Hunters and Gatherers*. Cambridge UP: Cambridge, 1999. Pg 271.
27. Daniel Everett, *Don't Sleep, There are Snakes*. Pantheon Books: New York, 2008. Pg 132.
28. Ilarion Merculieff, "Weston Society's Linear Systems and Aboriginal Cultures: The Need for Two-Way Exchanges for the Sake of Survival" in Burch and Ellanna, *Key Issues in Hunter-Gatherer Research*. Berg: Oxford, 1994. Pg 409.
29. William Laughlin "Hunting: An Integrating Biobehavior System and Its Evolutionary Importance" in Lee and Devore (eds), *Man the Hunter*. Aldine De Gruyter: New York, 1968. Pg 314.
30. Ibid, pg 305.
31. Mathias Guenther, "Animals in Bushman Thought, Myth and Art" in Ingold, Riches, and Woodburn, *Hunters and Gatherers Volume 2: Property, Power and Ideology*. Berg: Oxford, 1988. Pg 202.
32. Just one great reason to look into Elizabeth Marshall Thomas, *The Old Way*. Sarah Crichton Books: New York, 2006. Pg 167.
33. Colin Turnbull, *The Human Cycle*. Simon and Schuster: New York, 1983. Pgs 50-51.
34. Colin Turnbull, *Wayward Servants*. Natural History Press: New York, 1965. Pg 249.
35. Nurit Bird-David, "The Giving Environment: Another Perspective on the Economic System of Gatherer-Hunters". *Current Anthropology*, Vol. 31, No. 2 (Apr., 1990), pgs 189-196.
36. Randy Kidd, DVM, *Dr. Kidd's Guide to Herbal Dog Care*. Storey: Pownal, VT, 2000. Pg 32.
37. Stephen Harrod Buhner, *The Lost Language of Plants*. Chelsea Green: White River Junction, VT, 2002. Pg 229.
38. For more discussion of this, see "Everywhere and Nowhere" in Tucker, 2009.
39. Fredy Perlman, *Against His-Story, Against Leviathan*. Detroit: Black and Red, 1983. Pg 302.
40. See Four Legged Human, "The Commodification of Wildness and Its Consequences" in *Black and Green Review* no 1, spring 2015.
41. This joke is sadly true. Brought to you by the douche bags of "ReWild University" at rewildu.com.

42. Jon Young, *What the Robin Knows*. Mariner Books: Boston, 2012. Pg xxi.
43. Ibid, Pg xxvi.
44. Ibid, Pg xxviii. This point is really driven home in his excellent 8 CD set with the underwhelming title of *Advanced Bird Language*. I can't recommend it enough to reiterate and elaborate points I've made throughout this essay.
45. Paul Rezendes, *The Wild Within*. Berkeley Books: New York, 1999. Pg 204.
46. Tim Ingold, 'Time, Memory, and Property' in Widlok and Tadesse, *Property and Equality Volume 1: Ritualisation, Sharing, Egalitarianism*. Berghahn: New York, 2007. Pg 166.
47. Turnbull, 1983. Pg 77.

Subjects Object!
Thoughts on Symbolic Thought

"Language," writes John Zerzan, "like ideology, mediates the here and now, attacking direct, spontaneous connections."[1] That essay, 'Language: Origin and Meaning,' sought to raise questions about the depths of domestication. Yet since it's publication in 1984, that sentiment has been considered as a declaration of the anarcho-primitivist critique of civilization.

The line of questioning that Zerzan set upon lied in an upheaval of biological and philosophical assertions about something that has plagued domesticated humans since we started removing ourselves from the community of the wild: what does it mean to be human? Scientists and philosophers, like all historians, seek to write the autobiography of the conquerors. If we are to take pride in our so-called achievements, then there must be purpose.

The Ideology of Progress takes many forms, but it has a strong lineage. The world of the nomadic hunter-gatherer, engaged and a part of the world around them, is etched into our bones. This way of life changed the way that our brains take in information, the way our eyes see and ears hear. The sensations of foliage brushing against our limbs or the feeling of running a hand through the fur of a deceased animal connect us. They make us aware. They make us a part of this unending whole. They ground us within our wider context.

As some hunter-gatherers settled around a surplus of wild grains or proteins, or as they began to spend longer times at camps built around early gardens, that relationship changed. This happened very slowly, likely to the point of being imperceptible unless viewed in terms of generations. One of the first indicators of this shift was the emergence of shamans;[2] interpreters of a creeping delayed return economy of reliance upon stored grains or proteins. It is this interpretation that led to symbolic culture: the point at which humans began interacting with the world as a separate entity.

I want to emphasize a distinction that is seemingly unique to the anarcho-primitivist critique: to draw out that difference between symbolic thought and symbolic culture.[3] Often amongst anthropologists, philosophers and the like, the terms are used almost interchangeably. For the purposes of understanding where abstraction ends and alienation begins, it's important to make that separation. As such, *symbolic thought* may refer to specific means of communication and interaction, like language and art, but I use *symbolic culture* to refer to cultures that are driven by symbolic mediation: where life itself is interpreted and experienced through a culturally defined lens. That is seeing the world through the lens of the symbolic, a steadily increasing mediation between life and the living. In the extreme, you have the nomadic hunter-gatherer taking in stimuli of all forms of life and partaking in them on one hand and you have a social networked First World inhabitant engaged through hand held machines on the other. We outsource our perception.

Furthermore, it is worth pointing out that in terms of the symbolic, a caveat is in order. I personally use the terms *representation*, *symbol* and *abstraction* fairly interchangeably. Other writers have used mediation loosely along the lines of a fill-in for any of those words, which I strongly reject. Abstraction, for example, represents something that is not immediately present: a placeholder of sorts, but it does not require objectification in and of itself. *Mediation*, as it is widely used in terms of social relationships, implies a moderated relationship that creates a psychological distance. Mediation is the necessary precursor of *alienation*, or the ability to be completely removed from a situation, physically and psychologically.

These distinctions become far clearer throughout the increasing complexity of symbolic life. As such, they might come off as unnecessary nuance, but coming from an incredibly alienated society where almost all interactions are carried through hyper-mediating technologies, we need a reminder that our much lauded intellect and capacity for language is only one sensory input amongst many.

The Problem of Searching for Uniqueness

Symbolic thought is often a topic that has nagged at me. In terms of understanding the origins of civilization and the depths of domestication, I've found the speculation behind the critique of the symbolic to be less definitive than mounds of evidence about the consequences of domestication.

As a cultural materialist it is clear to me that modes of procurement and interactions with other societies do more to shape our relationships with each other and the world around us. Sedentism, the settling of nomadic societies, is definitive. Surplus, the storage of wild or cultivated grains and proteins, is definitive. Horticulture, the use of forest gardens, and pastoralism, controlling herd migrations of domesticated animals, are definitive.

We have untold examples of these societies and how they respond to the innate needs of the human-animal in terms of domestication. We can see how numerous examples of symbolic thought; time, number, history, industry, and capital, for example, arise in a historic sense. Accounting comes with storage. Politics come with the distribution of culminated food.

The quest to understand human origins tends to focus on two other forms of symbolic thought: language and art. The reason is obvious: the traditions that emerge and the means to relay them are spoken, danced, preached, built, drawn and carved. Language and art appear to be the means by which civilization, something that has no precedent in the wild world, are carried by.

There is a gaping hole here that both the fans and enemies of civilization have filled: language (and to a lesser degree, art) is what makes us human. Language is what we believe makes us unique.

But there's a big problem here. Unlike other forms of symbolic thought, language didn't make us unique. From my experience, language isn't unique to humans (that includes all ancestors and relatives of *Homo sapiens*) *at all.*

Likewise, one undeniable thread that ties our grounded nomadic hunter-gatherer ancestors and relatives to our civilized existence is that we all communicate using language. Language, in and of itself, is clearly not the source of our mediation. That language becomes the carrier of disconnected worlds is not a reason to condemn it. Language equally takes part in connecting individuals with the world. Art and ritual, to use very broad terms, do the same.

Cultures create language and languages shape and perpetuate cultures. The degree to which language limits our interactions with the world is driven more by the disregard for all other senses and awareness. More to the point: English isn't what is keeping you from having a relationship with the wild, the alienation inherent in this culture is.

Our understanding of what constitutes language comes from the primacy of conquest. The more civilized we are, the more we are reliant upon this singular sensory input. Reinforced by the written word and quantified world, our perceptions and interactions with the world at large are flattened. English, a great example of a removed and lifeless language, has extremely developed laws and principles of application. I'm using it as an example here, but it is just one language coming from a long line of colonizer's tongues. When we are talking about language, we are extrapolating from our own perceptions and extending them into the past. We use our own experience as the yard stick to gauge human-ness and look for reflections of our own systems to draw out how language is used by other societies, mediated or not.

To do so, we must remove the crucial context that separates how 21st century Americans use language from that of nomadic hunter-gatherers. In this backwards glance, we presume that language, the use of symbolic thought, requires mediation. From that point we kind of free fall through a number of other assumptions about our universalized "uniqueness."

The Blue Jay at the Bird Feeder

Noam Chomsky is widely considered a father of modern linguistics. The work that he and his colleagues have undertaken has been crucial in the development of Artificial Intelligence. It is based in a notion of human uniqueness that lends itself easily to a god complex. The irony of pointing and decoding our uniqueness so that we might program and replicate it is often lost.

For Chomsky, language is what makes humans unique. What separates language from the communication of other animals is grammar. Grammar, in the linguistic sense, is the innate rules of language. It is the form that determines the function of language. It makes it so we can discuss in abstracts, to talk about things that are not currently present. By this definition, *Homo sapiens* are the sole users of grammar.

Or at least that is what we think.

The problem with grammar is that it implies a structure that reflects our own perceptions. Animal communication, when granted at all, is permissible so long as it is within context. Experts on bird language, like naturalist Jon Young, seemingly disagree.

"In bird language," Young writes, "the songs are not enough."[4] The reduction of language, of complex communication, is based off of our own perceptions about how it differs from our own unique methods. We don't call it language solely because we don't understand it on the levels that hunter-gatherers and indigenous societies do. As we will see, Young's "Cacophony of Harmony," or the songs of the forest, created human language just as it has shaped the language of all beings.

There are numerous examples that I think counter assertions that language is uniquely human. If I have learned anything through rewilding it is that our uniqueness is greatly overstated and our understanding of the world around us and, most importantly, its interconnectedness through a civilized lens is slim to none. We transpose our perceptions and biases.

We know, for example, that the songs of whales are constantly changing and growing in complexity. We know that bird language, much like our own, is inseparable from other senses and behaviors. What Young has shown repeatedly is that the ways in which bird language communicates extremely detailed information: what is going on, who is coming, who is going, where they're headed. They carry the mood of strangers and prowlers in the forest. Typically that is information that has been understood as relying on an abstract conceptualization. The distance of predators, the presence of potential threats, and the relative sense of danger that they might convey are all things that birds pass on. And all other beings rely on them for that spread of news. This is piled on top of the far more elaborate world of each bird's own songs, including regional dialects and inclusion of external sounds. Elaborate rituals, including dance and ornate displays, are also common, if not universal.

Chomsky very well might indicate that this is not language. That the rules of grammar are imperceptible to us, therefore they don't exist. I don't believe this to be true. And there's one experience that immediately comes to mind: hearing the repeated and imperfect cry of a Red Tailed Hawk. The call of the Red Tail is an iconic sound, even hilariously misapplied by Hollywood to most birds of prey. But in this particular instance, it's not quite right. The reason: this isn't a Red Tailed Hawk at all, it's a young Blue Jay.

Blue Jays are able to mimic sounds; this includes the call of the Red Tail. The reason why they would is clear: upon hearing that tell tale cry, songbirds flee. As regular prey for these hawks, that's a pretty understandable move. Bird feeders draw those songbirds in and predators aren't unaware of this. Being fairly out in the open keeps them on their toes. Blue Jays, having observed the panic that a Red Tail induces, have also observed how this results in clearing out the feeder.

All of this can be explained in terms of non-symbolic communication so far. I believe more is at play here, but regardless, there's one point that is sticking: the sound of a Blue Jay *practicing* the call. This single instance requires layers of abstraction: knowing that the call of the Red Tail clears the feeder, that the Blue Jay can mimic it, and, that away from both the initiated exchange and the final result, this process needs perfection to work.

Chomsky's argument is that grammar, that ability to think and communicate in abstraction, is the underlying principle of language. So if all language is symbolic thought, then we have to accept that this Blue Jay is exhibiting the usage of symbolic thought.

I don't make this point lightly. But my goal here isn't to prove that all animals are human, but to reiterate that all humans are animals. Uniqueness is a delusion of grandeur, a fairy tale that we tell ourselves so that our mediation comes as a gift rather than a burden. This is the basis of civilized thought, the central message of domestication. By emphasizing one means of communication, we atrophy our senses; we disregard our place within the grounded world.

As Paul Shepard observes:

A million species constantly 'make assumptions' in their body language, indicating a common ground and the validity of their responses. A thousand million pairs of eyes, antennae, and other sense organs are fixed on something beyond themselves that sustains their being, in a relationship that works. To argue that because we interpose talk or pictures between us and this shared immanence, and that it therefore is meaningless, contradicts the testimony of life itself. The nonhuman realm, acting as if in common knowledge of a shared quiddity, of unlike but congruent representations, tests its reality billions of times every hour. It is the same world in which we ourselves life, experiencing it as a process, structures, and meanings, interacting with the same events that the plants and other animals do.[5]

The ideology of Uniqueness is our burden, but it is a burden we can ultimately relieve ourselves of.

Language Makes Us Animals

The presumption of grammar as unique presents another problem. If grammar is uniquely human and all humans have a natural tendency for language, as Chomsky and Steven Pinker argue, then the Pirahã represent a big question.

The Pirahã are hunter-gatherers living in the Amazon Forest in central Brazil. Their language is unique in that it was previously believed that they had almost no grammar, or at least no apparent rules of grammar. As a linguist and former missionary, Daniel Everett took up the challenge of trying to understand their language to translate the Bible. Ultimately it was a failure, but through trying to get inside the language and culture, Everett himself, in a sense, became converted. The Pirahã live without numbers and time, making them a prime example amongst other hunter-gatherers for understanding life without symbolic culture.

Lacking the kind of rigid grammar rules that Chomsky and Pinker established, Everett found that the reason their language functions so well and the Pirahã are as capable as anyone of relaying complex thoughts is because their language is enmeshed in the forest. Their world is not separated. As Everett states:

> *...there is nothing primitive about the Pirahãs cognitive abilities. There is nothing bizarre about them or their language. Rather, their language and grammar perfectly fit their esoteric culture.*[6]

This is an important point, language, in and of itself, can be used to fuse a culture to its place.

Within our wild context, language may be no different for us than the songs of the birds. Unfortunately that is a threshold that Everett himself was unable to cross. Echoing the bias of the uniqueness of humans, he states:

> *This layered organization of human speech is what enables us to communicate so much more than any other species, given our larger, but still finite, brains.*[7]

This notion of correlating brain size and function has received another challenge: the recent find of the *Homo neladi*, a hominid relative of *Homo sapiens*. The discovery of 15 *neladi* bodies deep within a cave had all of the indications of ritualistic burial. This was a move of deliberation, but also a move that had been previously understood as almost uniquely human. That is to say, this is behavior that had been previously linked to the kind of culture only made possible by larger brains.

Their culture, on the face of it, likely resembled the nomadic hunter-gatherer cultures that take us further and further back down the timeline of human evolution. And the kicker: the *neladi* had much smaller brains. As it stands, we have no way to identify the age of these bones, but the finding serves to show the level of ambiguity we have to hold about our own timelines. And our own biases. If our uniqueness is such a thin line and based on something as speculative as when we were able to start using grammar and as underwhelming as our case that other animals don't use it, then that is ambiguity that we should embrace. The wall between human and animal has and should crumble.

The response to the *neladi* finds shows this to be true:

> *The notion of such a small-brained creature exhibiting such complex behavior seems so unlikely that many other researchers have simply refused to credit it.*[8]

As we begin to unwind this fallacy, then perhaps our understanding of human language needs to incorporate its likeliness to the language of other beings rather than set out to defy it. Singing, for example, plays a constant and central role in hunter-gatherer life. Among the Huaorani, hunter-gatherers of Ecuador, Laura Rival observed the central role of chanting. They "usually chant several hours a day when resting in their hammocks or when busy with some home-based activity."[9] The lyrical content is relatively arbitrary: often just narrating the task at hand, particularly the mundane ones. That's something I think many of us can relate to.

Amongst the Mbuti, songs are considered a part of the chorus of the forest. In a place where depth of vision is limited, sound is amplified. The songs of the Mbuti work with Young's "Cacophony of Harmonies." Colin Turnbull noted that their song patterns had more complexity than classical music, but also that their songs were so enmeshed with their forest context, that when those melodies carried into the village, they were considered "empty sound" or, put bluntly, "noise."[10]

Anthropologist Jerome Lewis, also working amongst the BaYaka, elaborated further by arguing that singing shaped language.[11] That through replicating the songs of the forest, we came to form our own communication in unison with our surroundings. That musicality brings to mind Hugh Brody's observation that the Khoisan language of the hunting and gathering San contains 140 separate pieces of sound. Contrast that with English that uses about 40 pieces of sound.[12]

It very well may be that we can continue to further our delineations or that human language is truly unique. But I find that search to be so doused in speculation about when humans changed that I think it's more immediate to show how humans haven't changed. Circumstances, absolutely. Clearly symbolic culture has taken part in furthering the behemoth of civilization. Clearly our lives of isolation and alienation have taken us to dire extremes.

But it is also undeniable that language will remain a part of our path back home. I would argue further that a deeper understanding of language and its correlates through the wild world will help awaken our senses. That a widened sense of language and awareness will help us find our animality again.

Ultimately it is that primal animality that no alienation can endure.

Subjects Object!

Endnotes

1. John Zerzan, *Elements of Refusal*. Columbia, MO: CAL Press, 1999. Pg 35.
2. This is a point I will elaborate through upcoming essays for *Black and Green Review*, but I see an important distinction that a number of anthropologists can be sloppy about: attributing "healer" roles to "shamans." Unlike shamans, healers are not specialized. Noted amongst the Kung of the Kalahari, Richard Katz found that by adulthood, "more than half the men and 10 percent of the women have become healers." *Boiling Energy*, Cambridge: Harvard UP, 1982. Pg 35.
3. For more on this, see my 'Spectacle of the Symbolic' in *For Wildness and Anarchy*. Greensburg, PA: Black and Green Press, 2010. Drawing out this critique of the symbolic was also the focus of *Species Traitor* no 3 (2004).
4. Jon Young, *What the Robin Knows*. Boston: Mariner, 2013. Pg 1.
5. Paul Shepard, *Traces of an Omnivore*. Washington DC: Island Press, 1996. Pg 162.
6. Daniel Everett, *Don't Sleep, There are Snakes*. New York: Pantheon, 2008. Pg 207.
7. Ibid. Pg 198.
8. http://news.nationalgeographic.com/2015/09/150910-human-evolution-change/ Accessed September 23, 2015.
9. Laura Rival, *Trekking Through History*. Columbia: Columbia UP, 2002. Pg 100.
10. Colin Turnbull, *Wayward Servants*. Garden City, NY: Natural History Press, 1965. Pg. 255.
11. Jerome Lewis, 'How Language Evolved From Singing'. https://vimeo.com/114605825
12. Hugh Brody, *The Other Side of Eden*. New York: New Point Press, 2000. Pg 282.

Part Two:
The Ecology of Resistance

Do Humans Deserve to Survive?

The world still sings. But the warnings are wise. We have lost much, and we're risking much more. Some risks, we see coming. But there are also certainties hurtling our way that we fail to notice. The dinosaurs failed to anticipate the meteoroid that extinguished them. But dinosaurs didn't create their own calamity. Many others don't deserve the calamity that we're creating.
   - Carl Safina, *The View From Lazy Point*[1]

Fatigue.

Decades of fighting the wholesale destruction of the wild, witnessing the displacement of wild communities, seeing the war on wild beings continue, failing to stop fragile ecological niches from being crossed and decimated by access roads and channels, and this is how it feels: exhausting.

I'm sure the earth is all too familiar.

We see the studies and reports. They never improve. Previous assessments (already bleak) for the impact of climate instability on wildlife put 7% of mammals and 4% of birds in the "heavily impacted" range. The International Union for the Conservation of Nature (IUCN) just updated that analysis to move nearly half of all mammals and a quarter of all threatened bird species into that category.[2] That doesn't include the quarter of all the world's mammals that currently are threatened with extinction from habitat loss and poaching.[3] That doesn't include the 90% of the Great Barrier Reef suffering from coral bleaching.[4]

This list literally does not end.

"One in five species on Earth now faces extinction, and that will rise to 50% by the end of the century unless urgent action is taken."[5] That is the summation of the threat that a group of ecologists, biologists, and economists (of all people) came to after a meeting this month at the Vatican (of all places). There are models: attempts to quantify what can only be considered a catastrophic turn of events in the timeline of the Earth. There are campaigns: attempts to tap into some deeply buried empathy on the part of the civilized by reminding us that statistics mean rhinos, elephants, gibbons, black-footed ferrets, and polar bears.

They aren't dying: civilization is killing them. *We* are killing them.

As industrialization crossed a new threshold into a world where carbon dioxide has moved above 400 parts-per-million, seemingly "permanently," we are killing ourselves as well.[6] The UK based NGO, Global Challenges Foundation, found that with current scenarios, "the average American is more than five times likelier to die during a human-extinction event than in a car crash."[7] Not to be outdone, professional doomsayer Guy McPherson believes there won't be a human left on earth by mid-2026.[8]

Like everyone else worn out by having to find a morsel of empathy, even just enough to try to leverage sympathy amongst other civilized humans to even want to care about imminent catastrophe, even likely to directly impact our own lives: there's a breaking point. We're left wondering if we deserve to survive the extinction event that we've started and continue amplifying? Didn't we do this to ourselves? Wouldn't the earth be better off without us?

At times, you get so deep in it that for a moment you actually feel just a fraction of this loss. In those moments, you can almost celebrate the notion of human extinction. Or at least hope that an asteroid hits the planet, setting off a chain of reactions faster and greater than anything civilization and its unfortunate human creators would shoulder. Realistically, that's an escape, arguably one we truly don't deserve.

But this is the problem with that question: it's really fucking stupid.

It's a pointless question that turns a real crisis situation into an existential dilemma. This is the kind of philosophical quandary that got us into this mess in the first place. The ability to disengage from reality and deflect the consequences of our actions happens because we aren't grounded. We aren't feeling this loss. We aren't seeing it.

To a great degree, we can't. Our brains evolved for life in nomadic hunter-gatherer camps. We evolved to know relatively local populations in great and intimate detail. Our impact, prior to being scaled irreparably through technology, was largely negligible on a global scale. Our ability and reach outgrew our evolutionary capacity to understand and control it. This is the tragedy of history.

But it is the underlying basis for our reality and the wild communities of this earth are dying as a result.

We are dying. But this is a biological consequence, not a moralistic one. The probability of human extinction isn't payback. The earth isn't vengeful. A destabilized climate creates dozens of potential scenarios where the earth simply becomes uninhabitable for humans.

That is a possibility.

In terms of certainty, we have a little more clarity, as biologist Carl Safina points out:

> *The current concentration [of carbon dioxide] is higher than it's been for several million years; it's rising one hundred times faster than at any time in the past 650,000 years. The* planet *has survived much higher greenhouse gas concentrations; civilization hasn't.*[9]

To treat this as an existential threat, a crisis of faith, is seeking absolution. It's looking for an easy way out.

That is luxury we surely don't deserve. And for two reasons: the first being that humans didn't create this mess, not as a whole at least. Civilization is a historical epoch. Settled societies, built around granaries and agriculture, begin to spot the earth barely more than 12,000 years ago. The cities that served as the foundation for the globalized civilization that we've inherited are roughly half as old. Civilizations start locally and spread by force.

It is clear that civilization is a human issue, but against the backdrop of millions of years where humans lived in egalitarian bands, our shared lineage of primal anarchy, it is also clear that most of us are captives of this beast, not the engineers. Nearly all humans alive don't get to really reap the benefits of an extinction-causing glut of material and economic or spiritual bounty. As many examples as we have of humans actively destroying this earth, there are infinite counter-examples of how humans have lived with and within its wild communities. If we want to say humans deserve extinction, we doom the struggling nomadic foragers and semi-sedentary gardeners for the same mess they are actively resisting. If we're talking about what is deserved and what isn't, I'd definitely say we don't have the right to give up on their behalf.

The second reason is that whatever conclusion we reach doesn't matter. At all.

The problem with such a grandiose question as the fate of an entire species is that it's unable to recognize the delusion of control we believe we have. Granted, we have militarized our ambitions. There are plots to eliminate mosquitoes now that echo the campaigns that wiped bison, wolves, and passenger pigeons out of the United States as surely as many native populations. If we doom ourselves, it will be incidentally: nuclear power, catastrophic shifts in a survivable climate, or a wholesale dependence upon a climate suitable for agriculture (a luxury we surely will lose).

Unless there's a particularly sinister plot to create a gas that will target and finalize humanity, our discussions on the merits of human survival are pointless. Either extinction will take us or it won't. Whichever way that unfolds, it will be our fault, but it won't be our choice (outside of the individual level).

The arrogance of this kind of question is blind hubris: the same thing that got us in our predicament. And it's the same arrogance that will keep us blind to seeing outside of it.

This is what we know: the earth is changing.

The relative ecological stability that made settlements and agriculture possible is fading, quickly. We know that politicians and priests, in every single instance of civilizations collapsing prior, could never reconcile their vision with reality. Borders increasingly become death traps. Nationalism and xenophobia increasingly become distractions. This is exactly what we face now. Our situation absolutely has precedents.

What has changed is the scale.

That is what must be accounted for. Attempts to correct the course are futile. And worse, they're pathetic. More optimistic figures for human extinction tend to range in hundreds of years instead of decades. Are we really this resolved to defend our children's executioner, in the event that we ourselves are spared? If we recognize that we can't look to political, corporate and religious figures to see the wailing within the walls, then it is vital to recognize that their entire political system can't save us. Civilization won't save us. Agriculture won't save us.

We are heading into unchartered territory. But there is a precedent here as well. As a species, we have survived ice ages. We have survived massive shifts in climate. Deserved or not, humans are pretty damn adaptable. Our ancestors survived the last ice age the same way coyotes did: embracing a fission-fissure society, based around mobility, shifted from being largely hunter-scavengers to hunter-gatherers. Mobility, adaptability, resilience; the things that made us egalitarian are the things that saw us through unthinkable periods of flux.

I tend to think this isn't a coincidence.

All of those aspects are still within us. They still shape the way we see, think, feel and interact with the world. History, the time since civilization, is a glaring contradiction to that reality, but, in the end, that matters little. There will be no cosmic justice.

History, all of the supposed achievements of civilization, abandoned skyscrapers and power plants that will stand as tombstones to an era of unnatural and unthinkable cruelty, will become its own dustbin. There is some reassurance in that, but there is no comfort. There are predictions for how our path unfolds, but there is no crystal ball. There is no one pulling strings.

There are certainties, possibilities and probabilities. A certainty is that things will get worse. A probability is that life will be better off because of it. Most likely, that won't be immediately clear. Our survival, like the survival of half of all existing mammals and a quarter of existing birds, is a possibility.

It may not be a choice, but fighting for that possibility is.

It's understandable to give in. It's comforting to think that we might be powerful enough to wish punishment on ourselves. That penance is on our terms. But it's an exercise in futility. A luxury we can no longer afford. If we want to resist the worst-case scenario, then we're better off starting with the right questions. Instead of pontificating the merit of human existence, we should recognize that our own survival is intertwined with the fate of all other life. Our struggle is inseparable from theirs.

Our lives are inseparable from theirs.

The question should be: when will we start acting like it?

Endnotes

1. Carl Safina, *The View From Lazy Point.* New York: Picador, 2011. Pgs 2-3.
2. https://www.theguardian.com/environment/2017/feb/13/act-before-entire-species-lost-global-warming-say-scientists
3. https://www.scientificamerican.com/article/one-quarter-of-worlds-mammals-face-extinction/
4. http://www.cnn.com/2016/04/20/asia/great-barrier-reef-coral-bleaching/
5. https://www.theguardian.com/environment/2017/feb/25/half-all-species-extinct-end-century-vatican-conference
6. http://www.climatecentral.org/news/world-passes-400-ppm-threshold-permanently-20738
7. https://www.theatlantic.com/technology/archive/2016/04/a-human-extinction-isnt-that-unlikely/480444/
8. https://guymcpherson.com/2017/02/faster-than-expected/
9. Safina, 2011. Pg 71.

The Ecology of a Bubble

I have heard the sound of the Earth screaming. I have felt its heat, its burning. And it will forever be etched into my soul.

The sound was terrifying. It sounded like a thousand children screaming as their bodies were consumed by fire, or at least how I imagine that would sound. In a way that is how it looked too: a ball of flame shooting straight up into the sky. It was mesmerizing and terrifying in the way that only fire can lock you in. On this cloudy night, the flame reflected into the clouds, illuminating the sky as though it was an entire city fighting the darkness of night.

But this was no city.

We saw the reflection of the flames from miles away. Tracked it down winding roads. Tracing its path along an otherwise quiet night. We didn't know what it was, but it had to be seen. It drew us in.

And we found it: the eerie sight of a quiet suburban home in a rural landscape with a ray of burning fire screaming and tearing its way through the sky, reflecting off the slowly melting plastic siding of the house. The flames were literally burning the veneer off of the unsustainable and unattainable mythos of a quaint life in complicity.

The police were equal parts mesmerized and distracted while attempting to divert the other voyeurs of catastrophe. But we were all lost in the sight. The sound. The feeling. All of us except the representatives of the natural gas drillers who operated this well, who sought to bury this other worldly spectacle without context.

They said nothing. There was nothing to see here.

But this was just the beginning.

This was my first experience with hydraulic fracturing, fracking as it is now known. At that point, none of us knew what it was nor what was coming. Before everything was recorded and uploaded in real time, this event had neither name nor precedence. This sight, this hydraulic fracturing natural gas well, blown, burning and screaming, was our new present: a glimpse of the future to come.

A vicious and violent end to the era of cheap energy.

Fracking is not the first economic bubble within the span of the Modernity, but it may be one of the quickest. Fracking, like its contemporaries in tar sands mining and mountain top removal, are trailblazers in terms of ecological devastation. The damage being done here is swift and, at times, endemic. But beyond that these methods of extraction, hailed as the second coming of fossil fueled exuberance, work only as long as the price of crude stays impossibly high.

The problem is that crude oil did jump to impossibly high prices during the 2000s.

At the beginning of the millennium, a barrel of crude hovered in the low- to mid-$30 range. But then the entire Middle East erupts again under the force of Western militaries. By late 2004, the price of crude surpasses an average price of $60 per barrel, ending a nearly two decade long glut in oil prices. Three years later and $100 per barrel became the new norm.[1]

Just as attention was turning slightly back towards looking at Peak Oil, opportunism came knocking.

And in 2005, opportunity came in the form of legislation. Former Halliburton CEO and overall dark lord Dick Cheney was sitting Vice President who oversaw exemptions to the Clean Water Act by way of the Energy Policy Act of 2005. This opened what was called the 'Halliburton Loophole,' which meant that the chemical concoction required by natural gas drillers to drill deep oil wells could remain proprietary and exempt from regulation.[2]

How Fracking Works

The response of oil industry mouthpieces has remained steadfast that, much like human-induced climate change, peak energy is not a concern. The reason? Massive swaths of untapped fossil fuels that technology was going to magically open to bolster civilization. The reality is that all of these potential reserves were known of, but they were largely inaccessible.

At least they were inaccessible in a profitable manner.

Fracking is an exceptionally intensive process of energy extraction. Natural gas within shale formations is far from the concentrated pools of crude that conventional oil extractors bore into. It lies far deeper and needs coaxing to be captured. Never having intended on being used to fuel an ecocidal civilization, it was out of reach.

Sadly the history of civilization is driven by sociopaths with infrastructure and technology to feed the needs of growth in any sadistic manner. In 1947, a group of these earth-plundering profiteers decided they could try to work out the disorganized natural gas from rock formations by drilling deeper, setting off an explosion to crack shale formations and flooding the wells with a mixture of chemicals and water until the gas found its way back to their well sites.

Even more sadly, it worked. Halliburton drilled the first commercial wells during the following decade.

From this start, the rest of the millennium is fairly quiet. The larger shale plays were deeper and the technology wasn't there to really maximize this method of extraction for mass production.

And this brings us back to that pivotal moment in 2005.

For fracking to be effective, it needs to drill deeper, blow wells more aggressively, and operations have to be amplified exponentially. As a venture, it is as economically costly as it is ecologically. Wells that are fracked are pumped with a sandy mixture of water and a cocktail of up to 200 chemicals that flood the natural gas out of complex rock formations and strata back towards the well. The fracturing is the explosions and high pressure flooding that cracks through layers and any other natural boundary far beneath the soil to extract the gas.

Because of the depth of the extraction, wells dig through layers upon layers of strata. They blow through underground water reservoirs and, quite often, the fracking blows into them. If you are unfamiliar with the process, it shouldn't be hard to imagine what happens if you decide to set off some fireworks underneath a glass of water. That is essentially what is happening here.

Not an assuring picture.

Ecologically speaking, this is an absolute assault on the earth. It is a rupturing of ecosystems in untold means. And it is absolutely sickening.

But we'll get back to that.

Capitalists have no values other than to make money. The programmers and architects of civilization, particularly in this hyper-technological late era, uphold that single virtue above all else. If fracking didn't make money, they wouldn't do it. That is their sole barrier. Laws and regulations, like politicians, can easily be bought.

And when a barrel of gas broke the $60 mark and then shot up past the $100 mark, everything was back on the table. This is how a bubble works. There is no long term planning or thought, it is a blood thirsty and cannibalistic gorge. Nothing else mattered.

Make moves, make them fast and you will make money.

And some people did just that.

Before ramming his natural gas-powered Chevy Tahoe headfirst into an underpass at 78 miles per hour, former Chesapeake Energy CEO Aubrey McClendon was the poster child of the natural gas bubble. Prior to bursting into flames literally, he was known for his explosively reckless business savvy. He co-founded Chesapeake Energy Corporation in 1989 to focus on unconventional gas extraction during what was otherwise a pretty lengthy lull from that first experimental well in 1947 and what was to come.

And he got his payout.

By the time the fracking bubble really got underway he was dubbed the "Reckless Billionaire." That's a fairly apt title. And for it, he was among the highest paid CEOs of 2008.[3]

The bold extravagance of McClendon's life should have been proof of how much money was to be had from the supposed "Saudi Arabia of natural gas" that the talking heads of the gas industry, such as McClendon and T. Bone Pickens, boasted that the US could be. Those myths have been greatly deflated, so I won't focus on them here.[4]

But if any of that was true, this wouldn't be the story of a bubble.

McClendon made his fortune the same way that the heads of Enron did: elaborate Ponzi schemes. Natural gas rights come from landowners when they're fortunate enough to have secured them. Chesapeake, like every other natural gas venture (and there are plenty of them), largely didn't buy land; they bought the mineral rights and wrote overwhelming contracts granting full access to them. Savvy and wide-smiling salespeople, who were willing to parrot the dreams of wealth and prosperity that sold the bounty of drilling locally, procured those contracts. Even energy independence was used as a sales pitch despite interest in exporting liquefied natural gas.

As hard as it can be to sympathize with landowners willing to sign over their mineral rights, the context is one we're all familiar with: the American Dream. This is the dream of making it and of winning the lottery: the dream of winning the capitalist game. If the person who is willing to write you a check tells you what you want to hear and down plays the risky new technological innovation they are going to be using on your home, then there are grounds for suspending disbelief and indulging. Besides, if you didn't sign, the horizontal well they drill next door can get under your property anyways, might as well join the winning team, right?

The number of companies out there drilling and securing leases has been unprecedented. Each of the companies maintain levels of fragmentation to add to the smoke and mirrors of the Ponzi scheme. No one is really sure of who is doing what. Without state and federal regulation, little pressure was applied to do otherwise.

And without knowing how badly this would play out, more moving parts meant less focus.

The executives knew what they were doing. This was a smash and grab operation. The quantities and qualities of shale plays were greatly overestimated. The production was massively exaggerated, being based off of the best production numbers from the early days of the most strategically placed well heads in a shale formation.

Then landowners were gloriously bathed in what amounted to a fraction of the price tag that lease buyers sold to investors.

On paper, so long as crude prices stayed high, fracking was a numbers game. A numbers game sold to investors so that McClendon and scum like him could fill that third "trophy wine" cellar and buy his sixteenth antique boat.[5] In reality those numbers didn't add up. As Peak Oil analyst Richard Heinberg points out, fracking is impossibly costly:

> *Hiring personnel, renting the drilling rig, paying for the lease, hiring trucks—all of this is expensive. By the time you turn on the tap, you probably will have invested $10 to $20 million in your well pad—which, if you've been drilling for gas, may produce only $6 to $15 million worth of product over its lifetime at today's prices.*[6]

And it caught up to McClendon too.

His risky business practices didn't earn him a lot of support within the company he co-founded, leading him to step down as CEO on April 1, 2013. True to form, he started a new natural gas drilling corporation the very next day, just down the street from Chesapeake's headquarters.

What really did him in was the shady economics he used to falsely prop up the natural gas industry. In June of 2014 crude was still striding high at over $105 per barrel. But the conventional industry shifted back.

The price of crude plummeted.[7]

By January of 2016, a barrel of crude had dropped below $30 per gallon. McClendon's personal fortune was halved in the process. Accelerating his drive towards self-implosion was his indictment on March 1, 2016 by a Federal Grand Jury on charges of rigging the bidding process for oil and natural gas leases which was a violation of antitrust laws. Having destroyed the land was fine, but crossing other capitalists is a federal offense.

Having hit a wall figuratively, he did what any power-hungry narcissist would do and ran into a wall literally the next day.

Having used his rise to power and prestige as the poster child of the fracking bubble and its potential for exploitation he unwittingly became the martyr for this very brief era. Unfortunately, this isn't a cautionary tale. At this point it is quickly becoming history, but the daily reality of it is the one we are left in.

And that's where things get scary.

How Fracking Actually Works

"It just ruined everything."

At 80 years of age, Shirley Eakins of Avella, Pennsylvania is an unlikely figurehead against fracking. And that's because she isn't one. She is a victim of it.

Her story is one that has quickly become common in Pennsylvania, just as it had in North Dakota, Oklahoma, Texas, Wyoming, Arkansas, Colorado and Louisiana. Just as it is becoming common in Ohio, Kentucky, and West Virginia. In 2009, Atlas Energy began fracking up the road from the Eakins. And that is when things went sour. They started getting rashes and moles after showering. The water became slimy and no longer usable.

Between 2007 and 2016, 2,800 complaints had been filed over water violations caused by fracking in Pennsylvania alone. Ever the puppets, the Department of Environmental Protection claimed only 279 were linked directly to fracking.

In 2012, a couple living a hundred miles to the north started getting sand coming through their showerhead with high levels of iron, manganese and chlorides.[8] Elsewhere videos started showing up on the news and online with people lighting the water from their tap on fire.[9] Livestock and pets started getting sick and dying.[10]

The well sites and derricks set up to frack a well are impressive. Towering above the landscape, the derricks are intensive work sites. Crews work around the clock and the lights never shut off until the well is up and running, usually off at least one permanent diesel fueled generator.

The expenses of setting up a well come down to this. The clearing and preparation of a well site is possibly the smallest part of the operation, even when land is graded to leave open the massive clearing necessary to get a well blown.

And a well may be fracked as many as twenty times before the gas begins to flow.

This is no simple equation.

A single well site may require up to 8 million gallons of water. Additionally upwards of 40,000 gallons of chemicals may be used in the fracking process. That's 40,000 gallons of a chemical mixture that has been found to span over 1,000 chemical products and 650 individual chemicals. A group of doctors isolated at least 59 of those chemicals, finding that 67% were harmful to humans.[11]

Transporting those chemicals breaks down to upwards of 2,000 tanker truck trips *per frack*. Where those used chemicals are transported is always a spot of contention. Often the water and chemical mixture is left to air out in open pits at the well sites, but most of it never comes back out. 60-80% of it is never retrieved.[12] Some of it is claimed to be recycled through additional fracking sites, but a lot of it is injected back down into the fractured shale formations through deep well injection sites.[13]

The process of blowing wells is about as precise as you can imagine.

The intended goal is to dig deep into the shale formation, then drill horizontally, setting off a series of explosions to flood the water-chemical concoction into. As terrestrial beings, our knowledge about this depth of the earth is subject to the whims of the same scientists who think setting off explosions down there to flood with toxins is a good idea.

Having been living in Pennsylvania, the first earthquake I experienced stood out fairly prominently. The sound, amplified through the rolling mountains, was enormous. Almost overwhelming anything that was felt. It was such a foreign experience that I was barely able to register what had happened. Not true the second time. Nor the third.

What was as clear as could be was the relationship between blowing wells and earthquakes. But no one was willing to talk about it. At that point, few even really knew what was going on despite the fact that the link between fracking and earthquakes was acknowledged in the UK in 2011.[14]

But this is quantifiable.

Oklahoma, where the fracking boom has picked up steam

only more recently, was forced to issue a government statement about the indisputable creation of a new norm of constant quaking. That doesn't mean they had to be honest about it. In fact, their intentional wording is almost hilariously bad:

> ...we know that the recent rise in earthquakes cannot be entirely attributed to natural causes. Seismologists have documented the relationship between wastewater disposal and triggered seismic activity.

That's laughable because the situation is truly dire. Earlier on in the boom, in 2013, there were 109 earthquakes in the state. That number grew exponentially to 585 in 2014 and a staggering 907 in 2015.[15]

The entire fracking industry is standing on shaking grounds.

The Ecology of Fracking

The consequences of this process don't end at the fracturing.

A well isn't simply fracked and that is it. The entire structure of the industry is built around the overreaching Halliburton Loophole. Get in, get your funds, drill, and bleed it dry. There is no thought here. The company that created the loophole to push aside oversight (not that it would have done anything) is the same company that is selling the equipment, tools and technology to blow the wells and keep them pumping.

No one in the industry seems to have thought it was worth thinking beyond getting their fortunes set. And why would they? To them, the earth is dead. Anything beyond the sacred Self is sacrilegious unless they're giving stump speeches on the virtue of "creating jobs" or maximizing the earth that their created God has given us to plunder.

It's the same story that colonizers, kings and priests have always told to those willing to believe they will get their reward through playing along.

The imprecise blowing of wells leads to a series of unknowns.

There is no long term example or study here on how water is impacted by fracking: just a litany of excuses for how fracking isn't to blame for declining water quality in proximity to new wells.

True to the nature of a bubble, what we do know is that the hastily created wells and infrastructure weren't built to last.

Not only is there little to no thought put into the actual process of fracking, there is no long term thought or action on how to operate the wells. The *Wall Street Journal* found that "industry studies clearly show that five to seven per cent of all new oil and gas wells leak. As wells age, the percentage of leakers can increase to a startling 30 or 50 per cent." Fracking wells are the worst offenders, the fracturing process itself often leading to cross contaminating wells increasing the likely catastrophic spread of fracking compounds even before leaks may occur.[16]

Virtually every stage of the process is prone to failure.

Methane leaks that have resulted in explosive faucets are due to sealant failures on the well lines or eruptions into wells during the fracking process. Sand coming out of showerheads comes from fracking compounds flooding wells and reservoirs. This is easy to say, but it's almost impossible to absorb.

The reality behind these numbers is grim and we can only psychologically cope with it by biting the industry perspective and believe that a contaminated or leaking well is an isolated and containable or solvable issue.

But they aren't.

This is the new norm of life within the shale basins. Even without having property you live on or near being fracked can't isolate you from the devastation that comes with the process. And we only become aware of its span when it is too late.

Not surprisingly, the earth is far more complex than the industry geologists would like to believe it is. Underground water is far more connected than they would like to believe or than they are willing to acknowledge. Such is the fractured and specialized perspective that a scientific mentality is only capable of understanding. But multiple wells and reservoirs (surface level or underground) are often subject to a litany of wells surrounding them.

If we believe the industry numbers, statistically if twenty wells surround one water source, one will leak. If we use our brains or eyes, we acknowledge that means the entire body of water is at risk.

Reality is a bit more depressing than that.

In Pennsylvania alone, of its 9,794 wells, there had been 5,790 violations.[17] Makes that terrifying industry number of "five to seven percent" seem almost palatable.

At this point, there can be absolutely no question about the industry talking points. There can be no question about the motives behind the Reckless Billionaires.

This is a full on assault on the earth. On all of those who live in these areas: those who breathe the air or drink the water. Any being that walks through the clearings, burning their feet on the residual chemicals that settle in lawns and into streams.

This is far larger than any kind of "not in my backyard" issue.

This isn't just about showerheads and faucets, those are just the indicators we become aware of. The ecological consequences here are devastating. I saw this as the Allegheny National Forest turned into a parking lot of well sites. I saw the forest being reduced to the scenery between clearings, as roadless areas suddenly were crossed with crude roads. As the core of the forest turned into a roadside, reducing the areas for deep forest dwellers to exist. Eliminating the breeding grounds for birds. Increasing the disturbed soil where fast growing invasive species would suffocate the existing ecology.

This is an amplification of the omnicide that civilization carries: a technologically assisted ability to push further beyond the bounds of ecocide. Even putting the roads aside, the ecological toll of running a single well site is strong enough to risk *up to thirty acres per well*.[18]

Animals wander or fall into the open wastewater pits, suffocating on its fumes and contents, or withering away from direct exposure if they make it out. A single leaked well into a river in Ohio in 2014 resulted in the death of 70,000 fish and other aquatic life.[19] The water for fracking a well is often pumped directly from creeks, streams and rivers, isolating populations and resulting in die offs. Methane released into streams and rivers suffocates fish. The immediate and constant rise of sound and light pollution in remote areas has proven fatal to the more ecologically sensitive species that sought those spaces out.[20]

While natural gas and the methane released from its drilling may be colorless, odorless and non-toxic, they are also explosive and highly flammable. But for all living beings in proximity to the well-heads, they are exposed to a number of other chemicals: hydrogen sulfide, ethane, propane, butane, pentane, benzene, and other hydrocarbons, among others.[21] For species and places already feeling the pressure of logging and subsequent road construction, all of this just adds to the impact on all wild beings, just as it does humans.

This is the reality for all beings that are stuck with this legacy, this persistent wound.

We are stuck with this mess. They are stuck with this mess.

And then it explodes.

When the Bubble Explodes

When the fracking bubble burst, it carried a toxic stew of exposed lies, outrage, destroyed regions, wrecked lives, and all the maladies of an economic free-for-all.

Like fracking fluid, all of this was inevitably going to come to the surface. The dangers had slowly been more and more apparent. The payoff was quickly revealing itself as an overstatement and after years of having to truck in supplemental water for cooking, cleaning and showering those who were convinced to sign away their mineral rights were getting fed up.

In southwestern PA, the area I considered home, that bubble fully burst into flames on April 29, 2016.

On that day, there was a blowout on Spectre Energy's 36" Texas Eastern pipeline. The resident of the home where the blast occurred suffered extensive internal and external burning, but watched his home burn as flames eclipsed the tree line. And it drew a crowd. The blast was so strong that my own family members had windows rattling over three miles away. They felt the blast up to eight miles away.

This was hardly the first blowout or victim, far from it. But what was particularly telling about this incident is that while the blast happened at 8:30 AM, Spectre had "declared force majeure at midday."[22]

Force majeure. Legally speaking, "an act of God." This means that a company can remove itself from all liability for damages and, often, cleanup, because, well, it couldn't have been *their* fault.

And this is where we are left off.

For anyone opposed to fracking and civilization itself, there should be reason to celebrate when a bubble like this bursts. Every single well site or proposed pipeline that doesn't happen is just that much more of the earth and of wildness that stands a better chance of surviving the collapse of civilization.

In every sense, that is a great thing.

However, it's also a complicated kind of joy. The problem with an energy bubble isn't that it will end quickly—that is the only upside. The downside of it is that the profiteers and architects of these schemes move very quickly. All of those jobs that politicians and corporate heads were talking about came through; often bringing a bolster in crime, alcoholism, drug use, and rape with them. And then they're gone. The micro-economy they created and politicians used, that's gone too.[23]

Everything else is here to stay.

Frantically assembled, horribly executed, and with zero foresight into the future, what they did remains. And it will continue to erode, decay, leak into the water supply, and explode violently.

This is the new reality that we've inherited. One that has come to fruition faster than the fracking boom started.

What happened is that when those high crude prices crashed, they shut down the economic argument for fracking very quickly. The money stopped flowing and all the proposed wells were dropped. That is great news.

As of February 2016, the drilling rig count in the US fell to 571, the lowest count in the last century. During the fracking peak of 2012 there were over 2,000. Over the last year, 35 rigs were shut down in Pennsylvania alone.[24] Cabot Oil and Gas cut its 2016 budget 58% from 2015. A restructuring firm purchased Chesapeake Energy only further fueling rumors of bankruptcy.[25]

North Dakota, home of the Bakken shale play (one of the largest in the US), had its largest production decline in April of 2016 dropping down 70,000 barrels per day. The number of drilling rigs went down to 28 rigs in the state. That is compared to 27 in July of 2005, before the boom, and the all time high of 218 in 2012.[26]

Immediately that translates to pulling proposed rigs off the table, bringing pipeline projects into question and keeping assured long-term damage away from these areas. The light pollution, the deforestation, the increased traffic, the chemicals, spilled intentionally or not, are not going into these areas.

But on the flipside, the brevity of this bubble and seeing how quickly it has accelerated and withdrawn highlights the dangers it leaves behind.

Explosions are nothing new.

In June of 2016, an oil worker was killed and two others injured during an explosion at a well operated by a subsidiary of ExxonMobil.[27] This kind of accident is something that is par for the course. But what stood out more was when a Pennsylvania oil worker died after being engulfed as flames consumed the backhoe he was operating.[28] It's hard to sympathize with oil workers, but what he struck was something that is far more telling about the nature of how fracking companies work: he hit an unmarked, unregistered "gathering line."

Gathering lines are lines that take gas from the wellhead to a larger transmission line or processing facility.[29]

And they are unregulated.[30]

The oil worker who hit a line with a backhoe hit an unmarked, unregulated line. An unregulated line that is totally legal, carrying extremely volatile and explosive gases. The corporations, their subsidies, and anyone who could foster up the money to have a drilling rig set up could run their gathering line and bury it without having to mark it.

So long as natural gas is being extracted in these areas, it remains likely that people, animals, or anything will continue to unknowingly strike them. And then they explode.

These lines could be anywhere within the shale regions.

But the explosion threat hardly ends there. What stands out far more are the explosions like the one in New Alexandria, PA: pipeline explosions. In December 2012 the Sissonville gas pipeline exploded in West Virginia producing a massive and intense flame that destroyed three houses and melted a chunk of Interstate 77.

Pipeline explosions, unlike gathering lines, can happen anywhere gases or crude are transferred through, meaning they can happen hundreds of miles away from shale plays. Most of the pipelines that are currently being used were built for smaller amounts of natural gas for years, but are just one more part of the aging infrastructure that the frack boom sought to use against any and all logic. The Sissonville pipeline was a 20" gas pipe that failed, in the words of the NTSB, because of "severe wall thinning caused by external corrosion."[31]

It is possible to catch a leak before it explodes, but even where high tech methods of detecting leaks are used, they typically fail. When leaks are discovered at all, prior to explosions or blowouts, it's typically by locals.[32] For the most part, the supposed "high tech" detection hardly happens. Detection software typically only goes off when a line drops over 2% in total production.[33] Any size oil spill is an ecological catastrophe, but when lines are pumping around a half-million barrels per day, 2% of that is a nightmare. For the most part, old pipelines are just repurposed without renovation.

Kinder Morgan's Tennessee Gas Pipeline is currently set to transport liquefied natural gas from Ohio and Pennsylvania to Louisiana and Texas. This pipeline seeks to repurpose an older pipeline and its use requires reversing the flow. Flow reversal in pipelines was found to be the reason for 20,000 barrel and 5,000 barrel crude spills in North Dakota and Arkansas, respectively, in 2013. The pipeline that Tennessee Gas seeks to repurpose and re-flow includes 343 miles that were installed in the 1940s and over 1,000 miles installed before 1970.[34]

And this is what we are left with: a quick bubble that has filled and covered the earth in a pit of toxins, cut roads through isolated areas, destroyed the water reservoir, resulted directly in fish kills, threatens sensitive and threatened species, while leaving the landscape scoured, wounded and crossed with pipelines and gathering lines that are ticking time bombs.

Like all of civilization, it is only once it is too late that we even stop to wonder if it was worth it.

Like all of civilization, it wasn't worth it.

It isn't worth it.

Ecology of a Bubble

This is the new landscape that arises and the fragile ecology of a culture that no longer considers itself a part of the ecology while systemically destroying it in new and ferocious ways.

This isn't a cautionary situation. This isn't just the canary in the coalmine of a flaunted new energy revolution.

This is happening. This is going on now and the *only* reason that it was reigned in, en masse, is that the economics of the situation shifted against it. It is the cutthroat nature of the energy monoliths that permitted the price of crude to drop and sink their supposed alternatives.

That move, we can be assured, is temporary.

A result of this is feeling like an ecological exile of the place that I love: the Monongahela Valley into the Appalachian Mountains. I have lost family because of the fracking. Many of them once took the bait on the sales pitches, but when their neighbor's houses start blowing up, their moods shifted. When I went to New Alexandria the week after the Spectre pipeline explosion (entry into the area was under strict control by the company that destroyed it), many of the one-time supporters were out for blood.

That should be reassuring. In some ways it is. When civilization starts taking out your water, your home; just attacks your entire life, you should be angry. And they are. Some have started putting the pieces together, but many are just defeated.

What can I do?

What can anyone do against this?

Those questions feel like defeat. I can't even say them enthusiastically, but I don't ask them rhetorically. The problem is that this isn't just an analogy for what civilization does, for what technology has permitted: this is the problem.

And it remains the problem.

I maintain hope, against all logic, that these regions will heal in time.

The Monongahela River valley hosted over 1,000 smokestacks at the turn of the 20th Century that would have felt equally impossible to recover from. It has made some improvements, but so long as these wounds continue to be inflicted it doesn't stand much of a chance. Having fractured the strata of the earth and then pumped it full of toxins that will surely find their way to the groundwater (where they haven't already) is a problem that will span generations.

Perhaps even longer than that.

The stay of execution that the downturn in fracking has seen over the last year remains a threat, but perhaps the bigger threat is what may come on the next round. What horrid thing are technocrats and programmers working on now? I see the areas that I love after having been fracked, I have seen water that can no longer be touched, wild beings that have been caught in the consequences of all of this and wonder if it can get worse. But when you look to the history of civilization, you quickly realize that is the kind of question that doesn't end well.

It is easy to look at this and to give up.

But I can't. I won't.

There is no safety in submitting to despair, of giving in to the rampant individualism of civilization and just try to make the most of our own lives. That is the hard part about grounding, about getting a sense of place and belonging: you can't just turn your back and pretend that it isn't happening, no matter how grotesque the sight becomes.

The future of our ignored ecology demands that we don't allow it to remain obscured by pathological distancing through economics, philosophy, theorizing or posturing. The distinctions we make between our way of surviving and the ability for wildness to continue existing are arbitrary, but they are constantly reinforced. As participants in our own demise, as those who want to stop the wounds, giving in to the despair simply isn't an option.

I mourn for loss. I will mourn as more family and wildness succumb to the cancer that fracking has created.

But that mourning does nothing for them.

This is our problem. It cannot be ignored. We have to be prepared for both our future of living in wounded places and dealing with the remnants of a decayed and decaying infrastructure: even beyond the final stage of civilization collapsing.

It will mean nothing to wait for that moment to speak honestly about what is happening, why it is happening and to act with foresight instead of sulking into despair in hindsight. Hope alone

isn't enough.
    This earth, our home, is worth fighting for.

Endnotes

1. http://www.macrotrends.net/1369/crude-oil-price-history-chart
2. Richard Heinberg, *Snake Oil: How Fracking's False Promise of Plenty Imperils our Future*. Santa Rosa, CA: Post Carbon Institute, 2013. Pg 39.
3. http://heavy.com/news/2016/03/aubrey-mcclendon-net-worth-home-homes-oklahoma-thunder-salary-income-wife-billionaire-aep-mansion/
4. Heinberg's *Snake Oil* is the shortest and sweetest summation of all of this. I highly recommend it.
5. http://www.reuters.com/article/us-chesapeake-mcclendon-profile-idUSBRE8560IB20120607
6. Heinberg, 2013. Pg 44.
7. For more on this, see the 'Over a Barrel' interview with Richard Heinberg and 'Fieldwork in the End Times' interview in *Black and Green Review* no 3.
8. http://www.huffingtonpost.com/entry/pennsylvania-fracking-water_us_576b7a76e4b0c0252e786d5e
9. See http://www.newsweek.com/fracking-wells-tainting-drinking-water-texas-and-pennsylvania-study-finds-270735 and Josh Fox's documentary *Gas Lands*.
10. http://www.mintpressnews.com/livestock-falling-ill-in-fracking-regions/211720/
11. http://nysaap.org/update-on-hydrofracking/
12. http://oilprice.com/Energy/Energy-General/The-Facts-about-Fracking-Fluid-and-its-Disposal.html
13. https://stateimpact.npr.org/pennsylvania/tag/deep-injection-well/
14. https://www.newscientist.com/article/dn21120-how-fracking-caused-earthquakes-in-the-uk/
15. http://earthquakes.ok.gov/what-we-know/
16. http://www.resilience.org/stories/2013-01-10/shale-gas-how-often-do-fracked-wells-leak
17. https://www.fractracker.org/
18. http://www.biologicaldiversity.org/campaigns/california_fracking/wildlife.html
19. http://www.frackcheckwv.net/2014/07/22/over-70000-fish-aquatic-creatures-killed-by-pollution-from-ohio-frack-well-fire/
20. http://www.onegreenplanet.org/animalsandnature/no-fraccident-how-animals-are-hurt-by-fracking/
21. Heinberg, 2013. Pg 85.
22. http://www.bloomberg.com/news/articles/2016-04-29/spectra-energy-responding-to-pennsylvania-natural-gas-fire
23. http://www.mcall.com/news/nationworld/pennsylvania/mc-pa-gas-business-decline-20151213-story.html
24. http://www.pennlive.com/news/2016/02/pa_rig_count_lower_than_before.html
25. https://stateimpact.npr.org/pennsylvania/2016/02/17/drilling-down-

turn-hits-marcellus-shale-industry-hard/
26. http://peakoilbarrel.com/north-dakota-down-over-70000-bpd-in-april/
27. http://www.rigzone.com/news/oil_gas/a/145183/One_Killed_3_Hurt_in_North_Dakota_Well_Explosion_AP
28. https://stateimpact.npr.org/pennsylvania/2016/02/19/worker-dies-in-pipeline-accident-puc-steps-up-calls-for-reform/
29. http://pstrust.org/wp-content/uploads/2014/06/Pete-Chace-Gathering.pdf
30. https://stateimpact.npr.org/pennsylvania/2015/08/04/unmapped-unregulated-maze-of-rural-pipelines-poses-hidden-risks/
31. http://www.wvgazettemail.com/News/201403100090#sthash.g2MSYHU6.dpuf
32. http://www.wsj.com/news/articles/SB10001424052702303754404579310920956322040
33. http://www.huffingtonpost.com/entry/dakota-access-pipeline-protests-water_us_57d85a51e4b0aa4b722d12b1
34. http://www.courier-journal.com/story/tech/science/environment/2015/04/09/new-pipeline-plan-draws-fire-across-kentucky/25532167/

Means and Ends:
The Coming Nomadism and the Struggle for Community

Resilience.

This is what has permitted humans a place in our world. It may be the defining trait of *Homo sapiens*. We adapt. Ice ages, rising temperatures, changed climates, evolving terrain: for better or for worse, we are exceptionally adaptive beings. And for nearly the entirety of our time on this Earth, there was no reason to believe that it was anything but for the better.

And yet the very thing that allowed us to live through ice ages, to navigate the oceans in boats built with stone tools, to master fire, is the very thing that permits us such leniency in diet as to find a way to continue sustaining on fast food. It allows us to continue the natural and necessary internal functioning the body of a nomadic hunter-gatherer requires while it spends an average of over 10 hours per day staring at screens. It allows us to celebrate the creation of technologies that may prolong our existence long enough to witness the catastrophe that awaits us.

The catastrophe that civilization has initiated.

Against all odds, against all likelihood, in a wave of horrid and vile extinction events, we are still here. We are still killing. Through our active or inactive participation, we remain spectators of a world in the decline of our own making. And we get to enjoy the delusion of pretending that it isn't even happening or that it doesn't even matter.

We have scientists within NASA proclaiming the probability

of human extinction and we don't blink an eye. But why would we? How do you fathom the very real potential for human extinction, the immediate and aggressive alteration and shattering of ecological feedback loops and just erasing the possibility of seeing any kind of stability in weather patterns again?

To put it mildly, our circumstances were unforeseeable on an evolutionary timeline.

Our sea faring nomadic hunter-gatherer ancestors utilizing stone tipped spears and arrows hadn't evolved to dominate the world, to create a circumstance where the actions and choices of the individual could impact all life the world over. Like many other species, our minds could grasp and work around the use of tools.

But that was not true for technology. Technology, driven by its need for complexity, organization, labor and social hierarchies, created and fostered a divorce between action and consequence. Foolishly our adaptive, resilient bodies stuck along for the ride.

The core principle of technology, echoed infinitely through technological society, is that control is possible, that it is in our hands. It is that belief that made civilization possible. That belief carried civilizations across the Earth, maiming, raping, pillaging, decimating, and dismembering every step of the way. That belief blinded the power hungry, the elites, the priests from being able to see that while the consequences of civilization were very real, their belief in control was not.

Our belief in control is not.

Resiliency may be the defining trait of humanity, but uncertainty is the defining trait of our future.

We do not know what will happen. We don't know the consequences of our actions, of our technology, of its social and ecological warpaths: we have ideas, but we don't know how civilization will fall apart. All we know is that it will fall apart.

That it *is* falling apart.

It is this reality that has allowed the more individualistic among us to decry any notions of rewilding as fantastical. It is this reality that has allowed the more optimistic among us to cling to the hopes of permaculture as lifeboats for the coming storm. In an honest assessment of our circumstances, it's hard to not teeter-totter between those two opposing sides. Both reflect some hope for the necessity of control: for our ability to persevere at the helm.

It can be just as easy to look around and fall in line with the nihilistic embrace of hopelessness. But this itself is another type of control: nihilism dissolves into a belief that control is mine to do away with.

All of this is about varying degrees of control. About the maintenance or shifting of power: another reiteration of the mythos of technology. Faced with sheer and unrelenting uncertainty, any and all of these reactions are logical.

The problem is that *logical* is what got us into this mess.

I am a proponent of rewilding. I am a proponent of resisting civilization and domestication. I cannot and will not distinguish those approaches as separate. If we are to fight civilization, we must learn to give up our hopes for control, we must give in to uncertainty, to root our lives and our resistance into the struggle, the pain and the loss felt by all wild beings. To embrace our wildness is to trust in our own resiliency.

It is through building and immersing into the communities of wildness that we find our strength. That we become strategic in learning to target the elements of control that technology requires to perpetuate itself.

This is illogical, but intentionally so. And it takes work.

The domestication process requires constant upkeep.

Civilization is so counter-intuitive to who we are that we have to be trained and retrained constantly to ignore our instincts. Unable to defeat the wild urges within us, domesticators have learned to redirect those needs and wants. We are sustained at barely functioning levels and encouraged to indulge our quest for self-worth. We become workers, consumers, and spectators.

But we also break.

For the most part, medications and other stimulants/supplements keep pulling us back in. For many, that break is violence. Random or misdirected violence underscores the day-to-day reality of Modernity: spoken, thought or enacted, each of us is boiling over in a pit of rage and confusion or subdued by complicity and hopelessness. So much so that when we do wake up to the reality that we face, we struggle to overcome these hurdles in opening our vision of what can be done.

And so we default, we back slide. I'm not here to point fingers, I'm no less guilty of this than anyone, but no one ever said breaking the domestication cycle would be easy. It's ironic how rough it can be learning to listen to our own intuition again.

This brings us back to the unthinkable uncertainty that lies ahead and one particularly difficult part of the pathway ahead: land projects.

I want to be clear that largely speaking I have nothing against land projects. Considering the primary alternatives are renting and living in cities, it's not a hard argument to say that any element of self-sufficiency and, ideally, lesser impact living isn't a better alternative. If you can bolster wildness on that land by creating refuges then all the better.

There are arguments against owning property. As a landowner myself, I'm only more familiar with them. There are compelling arguments against being in situations where you are paying land taxes or buying leases from national agencies, all of which are completely valid. But in practical terms, they can often be the same kind of problems that we're stuck with in all aspects of life until civilization is gone.

Fortunately that time is coming.

Which brings me to my point on the matter: the problem that I see with land projects is that they can become an oasis for logical thought. With homesteading, with off-grid living, with the influx and rise of survivalist projects; land projects can slide back into that realm of control where we want to hold on to the delusion that civilization has given us.

That delusion is the idea that self-sufficiency in off-grid living is resiliency.

What we have seen throughout history is that it most definitely isn't.

Now it is easy to say that my steadfast insistence upon focusing on nomadic immediate-return hunter-gatherer life is simply ideological. Some have even accused me of moralism. I see it as pragmatic.

But that pragmatism comes with benefits.

The reality is that nomadic immediate-return hunter-gatherer life is our most ancestral, primordial and instinctual way of being. This is how we, as humans, have evolved. Our senses, movements, sight, and intuition arise from this mode of subsistence. And it is the community that arises from it that has created and bolstered our resiliency. It has allowed us to move. To switch gears when hunting or foraging while a particular species of fauna or flora was in ebb and flow. It has given us the chance to respond to long-term and short-term ecological change.

And I believe that this is also our best chance for surviving the current and on-coming ecological crisis.

The problem with land projects is that they are, by and large, fixed. Sedentary. Permaculturalists have set out to create *food-forests* (a very civilized projection) that are meant to sustain communities with or without civilization. They can be far more diverse and far more resilient than gardens, certainly far more ecologically sane than farms. They may be more set to withstand the unprecedented cycles of heat and freezing, of drought and flooding that this destabilized climate may bring, but it is far more likely that they won't.

What we are currently seeing in the world is the new era of refugees. *Climate* refugees are now joining the ranks of *political* and *economic* refugees. As Story Teller discussed in *Black and Green Review* no 3, *grid* refugees are likely to arise. While Syrians have become the face of climate refugees, we overlook those who have and will continue to lose their homes to rampant and unchecked wildfires as they blaze through the boreal forests and the parched regions throughout the entirety of western North America. It is likely that the fuel being added to the fire by overwhelmed and hastily repurposed pipelines that are flooded with natural gases and fracking supply lines or as the number of train derailments continues to escalate carrying that thick, heavy crude from tar sands will cause those wildfires to spread into central and eastern North America forcing evacuations.

This is our certainty: instability will feed abrupt and unpredictable change.

Land projects are not fail-safes.

In times of uncertainty, the very sense of self-sufficiency that they have sought to offer is the very thing that could make them targets from dislodged survivalists (current or future) or it could weaken the potential of any community on them to prepare for the coming era of refugees: the new nomadism of a world of shifting climates.

For me, this all comes down to a question of means and ends.

Is the purpose of a land project to create self-sufficient communities through off-grid, smaller-scale living, possibly even emulating horticulture? If so, it may do well. It may thrive. I don't doubt that life there would be infinitely more fulfilling than edging out a living and trying to stay sane through any other civilized "options".

Or is the purpose of the land project a means of fostering community, rebuilding ties, creating a basin for rewilding? Is the land project the ends or the means? This may be a simple question, but it's a framework and perception that can be a threshold for our own resiliency.

On the ground, it may not even look any different.

Seeing a land project as a place to build community capable of nomadism doesn't mean that the land itself shouldn't be respected or that the return of wild beings and fauna shouldn't be a priority. The purpose of rooting is that we should be respecting and partaking with the wild community and helping it heal and regrow regardless of what may lie ahead for us.

That is another part of the uncertainty: we have to realize that having trained and rooted all the resilient, nomadic hunter-gatherer parts of our bodies and minds doesn't give us any more certainty that we are equipped or given a free pass to weather the coming storms. It certainly helps. But we don't know what is coming ahead; we just know that it is coming.

It is easy to see this as a cop-out, as a chance to give in to nihilistic urges and shrug off any effort as idealistic play. But that's the thing about community, the part that gets lost when we allow our understandings to be based in the all-loving trap of a hippie or liberal commune or to maintain that it is a relic of sub/urban neighborhoods: building community isn't easy.

It is not a coincidence that the immediate-return hunter-gatherer communities that were based on nomadism were also the most egalitarian societies to have ever existed. That is the added benefit of embracing the coming nomadism and the direction of building land projects around movement instead of stagnancy. When we break down those antiquated notions of community and start to really understand resiliency through movement, even just the ability to trek, to understand what it can be like to live without civilization or how to build a society without state infrastructure, then we begin to really root ourselves in our own animality. We build self-sufficiency that transcends place and circumstance.

The truth is that we don't always get along.

Nature isn't a passive reality; it's just a bandage term we apply to the wilderness we see around us. *Wildness* is an active reality; we ignore it because the domestication process has taught us to. But wildness is within us and surrounds us. And it impacts us just as we impact and interact with it.

Nothing about this is to imply notions of perfection or angelic life ways where we magically co-exist with everything.

That simply isn't what is going to happen.

Wildness, to borrow a term from Tamarack Song, is a state of *dynamic tension*. It requires awareness, grounding, perception, intuition, and, above all, a readiness to move and react abruptly at any time.

This may sound overwhelming, but that's because we look at it as outsiders. We don't recognize the stimulation overload and complete lack of empathy that Modernity provides. We are deadened to the world by technology, numb to our need to constantly assess and respond to the massive killing machines surrounding us, such as cars. We are deadened to each other as we are drowned in sheer numbers of equally wounded, damaged and breaking people all around us. Even if we hate the State we can get too used to the presence of overarching structures that corral some of the violent among us while bolstering and empowering others.

Rewilding is not surrender to the world: rewilding is embracing it. It's about becoming an active participant rather than a spectator or passive participant. It means undoing the delusions that make domestication possible. The delusions that permit civilizations to exist.

When we open our awareness, when we learn to walk through wild communities and to hear their warnings and communication, we begin to see the cracks in the Empire of civilization more clearly. We see the weak points that an anti-ecological system holds and how delusions serve to bridge the gaps.

And we feel it.

We feel the pain that is inflicted. We feel the loss that comes with feeding civilization, especially a hyper-modern technological one. We see the weakness in its infrastructure and its philosophical underpinning. We awaken our own empathy to that unthinkable, unquantifiable pain and loss in the context of community and we build a platform for resistance in our own resiliency.

And we learn to stop relying on someone or something else to take care of our problems for us.

We learn to act without mediation.

None of this is easy. None of this is simple. None of us have allowed ourselves to really get there.

But if we are willing to make that perceptional change, to learn to embrace the coming age of nomadism, to see beyond ourselves and to empower ourselves through taking part in something much larger and more magnificent than our own lives, then we have the world to gain from it.

And this is where land projects can focus.

I interviewed Andrew Badenoch of *Feralculture* in *Black and Green Review* no 1 to discuss the idea of land projects being built around *nodes*. The idea that he has pushed and now others have been pursuing is to build up networks of smaller properties that embrace the nomadic spirit. Nodes can have a particular draw to them: a better spot for hunting, a better spot for fishing, a better spot for foraging berries, nuts, tubers, or whatever. Embracing the original means of conflict resolution: they give a network for individuals or families to disperse and move.

A large enough network also gives the ability to explore and become accustomed to different bioregions. It allows us to become familiar with different climates and to understand their challenges and promises. It gives us the chance to meet others seeking the same, to build connections with them.

The community we will be building now, if we walk this path, is a disjointed one. It spans large spaces and focuses of ebb and flow, but it is an innately different conception of land projects than that of homesteading, even if homesteads remain a part of the larger network. What it can offer is a slow shift back to our nomadic minds: to become rooted in places so we can think, act and move as will likely be necessary to both prepare for the shifting climate on the horizon and to actively take part in the fracturing of civilization's infrastructure.

We have a lot of work to do in terms of undoing domestication in our own lives, but we can foster circumstances that will help us take larger steps. Ones that bring us further into that dynamic tension without leaving us feeling lost and isolated there. Moves that can undo the survivalist mentality that life within civilization requires.

And it is a process.

We will likely continue to live between two worlds: of wildness and of civilization, until the end. We have to get over notions of puritanism. Of thinking that we will shed all civilization from our lives so long as it continues existing. Saving ourselves from civilization means nothing so long as civilization continues to pull itself along and destroy the potential for all life.

We get no guarantees. We have no certainties here.

But we have no certainties anywhere beyond one: uncertainty is here. Uncertainty is growing more erratic as it gains speed.

Is our end to continue to survive: to hold on to some semblance of civilized normality through turbulence? Or is our end to move beyond domestication entirely? This won't happen quickly. It likely will take generations. We simply don't know.

But that is all the more reason to embrace uncertainty rather than to give in. We are participants in this reality whether we chose to acknowledge that or not. But we can embrace our wildness. We can become resilient again.

We can rebuild communities of sustenance: communities of resistance.

We have seen the world we want to live in and it is struggling. It is resisting and striving to outlast civilization. It exists within us and around us.

And it is worth fighting for.

The End is a Good Start:
Activism in the Context of Collapse

Let's be honest, Earth First! Despite the fact that the green anarchist and Earth First! worlds have always run parallel to each other and typically overlap, we haven't always been on the same page.

The late 1990s and early to mid-2000s were an exciting time. Things were heating up all around. The ELF and ALF were turning up the heat. The riots were kicking off anytime CEOs, politicians, and bankers got together. There was a lot of potential in the air. We started looking beyond traditional activism and the EF! campaigns of holding off the bulldozers, loggers, and the like lost some of their appeal.

It's not that we grew apart; we just saw and did things differently.

But the times have changed. In an era where activism is reduced to posting a picture of you holding some moderate sign on Twitter, your banner hangs, sits, and cuffing gets a bit of that zeal back.

Realistically, we can use each other. Your basis of action without compromise can hold back plows and halt bulldozers. Our hacking at the roots can identify larger targets and give context. We can do well together.

So where do we start? Let's go to where we are now, let's start at the end.

Over the past years, the EF! campaign focus has rightfully moved to incorporate a new threat: post-peak oil production methods. We're talking about fracking for natural gas, tar sands mining, and mountain top removal. From extraction point to transportation and pipelines, we aren't facing a new monster, but we're facing a renewed monster. We are facing a boom.

The Marcellus Shale region is a place that I will always consider home. I saw the Alleghenies get cut and crisscrossed with roads only to let the forest look like a natural gas oilfield. I've seen that wretched fracking platform set up near my home, near the places that I love, and felt earthquakes in places where they should not happen.

I've lived in areas where train after train has derailed spilling tar sands crude. I've seen the waterways that could burn and I've seen the life escape them. I've seen those very derailments become arguments for pipelines which only ready the chainsaws and amplify the drive.

I've seen mountains blown apart. I hope that I never deal with the sludge and slurry of that extraction process, but I've seen what it can do.

And it is fucking heart wrenching.

The speed with which these events are unfolding and the cutthroat intensity is alarming. These aren't just a continuation of what has been going on, they are a desperate grapple, the throes of a dying civilization, an overstretched reach. These are new methods fueled by the promise of quick cash.

These production methods are a clear and logical follow up to the world that cheap oil has created, but they are not an answer.

And therein lies our strength.

As fracking, tar sand and mountain top removal continue to expand the consequences of resource dependency into back yards; the fight against these methods and, hopefully, industry expands. You can only fuck with people's water for so long.

And so we have a crossroads. We have people who are signing on from a traditionally NIMBY perspective to fight against these methods and industries. This is a classic example of building a base for single-issue activism. When your water is threatened, you will react to that impulse.

This is where we can work together.

I have long said that if someone's single issue was nuclear power, I'd be hard pressed to argue with them. I wish them the best of luck and hope they are successful. Nothing is forever, but nuclear waste certainly isn't going to go away anytime soon.

I typically extend that soft spot towards the struggle against resource extraction. Considering the immediate and immense consequences of these even shadier methods, any chance to stop or slow them is welcome.

But there are teeth here.

The current energy snatch and grab doesn't exist in a vacuum. This is what the collapse of civilization looks like. This isn't an event, it's a process. It starts with sedentary hunter-collector societies and turns into plows diverting waterways to feed cities. The ecological crisis is domestication. It's the perpetuation of the myth of Progress: the idea that we are destined for something greater.

And in the wake lie patriarchy, sexism, social hierarchies and stratification, politics and religious indoctrination, property, boundaries and the xenophobic, racist responses that they bring. Civilization, the culture of cities, that agrarian curse, the bastion of social and ecological devastation, is a scourge. We've seen what it does in the (anti)social context and those within EF!'s ranks don't need to be told what it looks like in the forest.

From the time that the first plow cut into the soil to propagate storable grains and proteins, the forest became the trees, the world became a resource. As Paul Shepard said of genetic engineering, "domestication was the first step", the same applies to resources.

Everything else is scale.

The Mayans cut cornfields with the same ferocity that oil prospectors look at forests, mountains and pastures. Innovation is the product of desperation. So as the decades old OPEC numbers for untapped oil reserves deflate, the ghost economy of credit and deficits crashes, we are left standing before the reality of a post-peak oil world. Naked. And completely unprepared.

The same terminology used by OPEC to get rights to oil drilling contracts is now being pushed into Appalachia, throughout the West, and into Northern Canada (not to forget the deep water drilling throughout the oceans).

Being at the center of a modernized, globalized, and technologically infused and dependent civilization isn't a good place to be stranded without the proverbial lifeline.

Yet this is where we stand.

All of the new and "modernized" methods for resource extraction are an absolute last-ditch effort to drag the body of Leviathan on for another decade or two. This is the final frontier.

Hopefully none of this is new. Even when not articulated, the bio-centric reaction that EF! is known for is a response to the world that civilization has implemented. EF! stands on the periphery to stake a claim, to take action, to halt the path of Progress.

And this is where the green anarchist vision and the anarcho-primitivist critique cross paths with EF!. Regardless of how we got here, we stand on the frontlines of the primal war: the resistance to domestication and the complete reconnection with wildness.

We need context. We need perspective. We need to be reminded that we are in the end times of civilization and that our enemy is vulnerable. We have teeth. We have traction.

So here we arrive at the end.

As water contamination becomes the norm, the war comes home. The response will be to draw in the dispossessed and concerned to funnel through a single issue, NIMBY activism that stands in firm opposition of extraction methods, but offers little to no answers. These are people responding to dire circumstances and finding their threshold.

Our weapon is that the single issue they are struggling against is THE issue. What happens when those attempting to domesticate and suppress the world start running out of options? What happens when the plow hits the end of the earth and starts turning through it? What happens when mountains are blown apart and the ground we stand on is shaking?

This isn't bad policy; it's the end result of policy. The fracking well is the logical conclusion of the plow. The single issue is civilization itself. It is this simple: do you want water or do you want

The End is a Good Start

electricity for a couple more years?

Obviously this isn't the discussion that is being had. But we aren't really in the discussion stage. The nature of a boom is that things are happening fast. There is only reaction. And to that end, the tactics of EF! are a perfectly apt response.

But here is the potential: we can draw the lines, we can force the discussion, and we can connect the dotted landscape of wells, derailed trains, and chemical spills.

The lifeblood of this modernized civilization is the energy that flows through your surroundings; by railway, through power lines, shipping canals, substations and conversation stations, damming rivers, and cutting roads. This is the manifestation of domestication. If the discussion that is to be had stems directly from the source of that power and what it looks like to extract, pump and transport it, then we have the chance to be on the offense instead of the defense.

This is the time to stand by no compromise in defense of Mother Earth. The end is in sight. The vulnerabilities lie before us. The failure of activism is in the defeated hopes of holding off the destruction. The promise of resistance lies in bringing on the destruction of the infrastructure that is unfolding before us: in joining with the world of wildness and bleeding out Leviathan, in pulling the plug.

We're on mutual turf here and the Earth is on the line.

The roots of civilization have been exposed and the extent that the domesticators are willing to reach to is becoming clearer. The chance to dig deeper is in our hands.

Let's take the actions. Let's take the discussion. Let's bleed the machine.

Social Media, Revolt, and Civilization:
An Interview with Kevin Tucker

This is an interview I did with the anarchist news site, It's Going Down, which was published on February 17, 2016.

Across North America, cities are hit by wave after wave of crisis. From drought, to poisoned water, to rampant police brutality and violence, to crumbling infrastructure and deepening austerity. At the same time, even mainstream scientists have been heralding the end times; claiming that the 'point of no return' in relation to global warming is fast approaching, if not already here. Plankton levels drop, temperatures continue to rise, massive amounts of species die off, and the effects of climate change become much harder to ignore. In the midst of this unfolding, there is growing interest in "re-wilding" and getting back to the land and to a simpler life as the mainstream culture laments the increase in addiction to technology and the internet as smart phones proliferate in daily life. Kevin Tucker, a long time participant in green anarchist initiatives since the 1990s, sat down to talk with us about this deepening reality, as well as drawing from lessons over the past several decades and point towards where we might go in the face of civilization's increasing stranglehold.

In the first issue of Black and Green Review, *you discussed how the radical ecological, animal liberation, and green anarchist movements and currents never recovered from the Green Scare. Why do you feel this to be so? What was weak about these formations that allowed repression to sweep people away so quickly?*

There's a couple ways to look at this question in terms of what happened then and why it was so effective in suppression.

I think unequivocally the greatest impact in terms of the Green Scare was that the first rule of resistance, the importance of Security Culture, wasn't taken seriously. I don't say this to blame anyone in particular for what happened, but it's obvious: there was a lot of snitching. These cases were built on a combination of informants, infiltration, and loose tongues. The ingenuity of the ELF/ALF cell structure should have been enough protection: keep everything small, autonomous and absolutely need-to-know. Maybe there was too much comfort in that structure and word spread a bit too much. It's hard to say for sure. But someone like Brandon Darby shouldn't have been able to bring down so many people. Yet that's exactly what happened.

That's only a part of the picture. Looking at the mid-2000s, things did change. I think a pinnacle was Rod Coronado getting thrown back in jail for befriending someone on Facebook, something that happened while there was an increasing change on the legal front over what constituted "advocacy" or even what was action. The sentences that the SHAC folks and the AETA arrestees got really emphasized that. Suddenly this buffer that people like myself thought we had in terms of speaking and writing was shifting and that made it harder to say anything at all.

The increase in repressive pressure was tangible. We all felt that. The response for a lot of people, sadly, was to lay low. It's hard to push in that grey area and it became harder to justify the risk.

But in terms of the milieu, we simply failed. We failed to address what was happening. We failed to keep up vigilance in terms of snitches. We failed to catch these trends as they were mounting.

That certainly continues now. Suzanne Savoie, a known Green Scare snitch, is still trying to stay involved in forest defense campaigns. It was particularly disgusting when David Agranoff was outed as snitch: Will Potter (Green is the New Red) broke the story and got death threats! People were arguing that David snitching was less of an "offense" than people breaking veganism. It's just absurd, but I can't see that having happened 10, 15 years ago: that's an internet forum kind of response.

We also historicized the Green Scare in a way that makes it look like it's over. It most certainly isn't. We still have friends behind bars and the repression is still there.

And that brings me to the overarching context: as a culture, technology has really become completely enmeshed with day-to-day life. Through the anti-globalization movement and street riots that take root in the late 90s through the 2000s, you saw this element of involvement form into spectator roles. There was a change in focus on taking part in resistance to documenting everything. Suddenly Indymedia was the focus. There were certainly pros to it, but at the time it felt like it stole the spotlight a bit. In hindsight, it absolutely did.

And it made sense in a way, as repression raised the need to document it was important. But in some ways we made the documenting the story, not the means. The spread of the internet was really the necessary piece of the puzzle to make that happen. I'm not sure if you can say it's coincidental or not, but there's a mirroring of shifts within the milieu and the culture at large towards a more internet savvy approach to radicalism.

In the 90s, there was a kind of rowdy spirit of anarchism that I often felt like Profane Existence kind of typified. Building through the late 90s that started to transition towards this Crimethinc. styled personal revolution. I feel like that kind of paved the way towards blogs and social media: a focus on the individual over the ideas. That flows directly into what praxis looks like and action falls by the wayside.

In hindsight, it almost looks like this master plan: channeling this voracious, rowdy movement into online posturing. Whether that was the goal or not, who knows, but it echoes through civilization at large. There's unquestionable intention in creating the social media world but I don't want to sound convoluted in thinking it was aimed at anarchists, it just turns out that it worked out the same. No doubt something that would be considered an added bonus from the eyes of the State.

So you have the interplay of two things: the rise of repression and the rise of social media. In my eyes, it was the combination of the two that really decimated this milieu. In some regards, it could very well die on Facebook. Everything becomes so absolutely personal in nature and so tied to the individual that we lose the ability to even think about these ideas as existing in their own merit. You don't have arguments: you just have reactions. So you go round and round with the same argument, but it doesn't matter. What is being said matters less than who is saying it.

That opens the door for a ramp up in oppression politics to further those divides. The ideas and the drive are what suffer. Arguments replace discourse. Praxis becomes impossible. So when everyone who laid low in the mid-00s started coming back around and saw what the "anarchist milieu" currently looks like, they just kept moving. Why wouldn't they? We've just opened ourselves up to external influences to the point where repression, by and large, isn't even complicated. A couple Facebook profiles and the State can just undermine anything.

So long as we use social media as the platform for communication, then we have no ground to stand on. No traction, no hope for meaningful dialogue and certainly not any kind of engagement. Having a critique of technology or capitalism doesn't make you exempt from its consequences. Get off of social media is definitely my weakest call to action, but it's sadly a necessary one. If we want to move forward, we have to recognize this.

In the case of counter-information websites such as this one, how do you think that a project like this can avoid falling into the trap of just constantly wanting to produce more and more online material for the sake of just producing more? For us, we see a problem in that generating a lot of content has the effect of generating people that simply consume it. Whereas we want to create a resource that people can use in struggle, in honing their analysis, and also finding comrades. To say it plain, in the current age, how do we use cell phones to, theoretically, take down cell phone towers?

Unless people stop looking to be spoon-fed answers, there's not a lot that can done here. There is plenty of information out there about how to deal with specific problems, information that's been put out for historical or simply educational reasons only, of course.

There are pragmatic issues here as well as idealistic ones. There is a line between advocacy and information. There is a chasm between sharing a historical look at effective strategy and trying to flush out cannon fodder to implement "the plan."

That's part of the Green Scare change, reflected in the way the State has defined "terrorism": there are reasons why you can't just lay out a list of effective targets, but among them is the reality that the more you try to fill in the blanks, the more you set yourself up to just get that pressure. Fortunately, there are historical circumstances we can look at to try to understand more, but the language has to be particular.

But there is no shortage of information on the internet. Or within public reach offline really. How much of it is disinformation, well that's hard to say, but I think there has to be some combination of just putting relevant information out there and wanting to really build up a basis under which the struggle against domestication is no longer an external concept, but a perceptible reality. I think it's important to always link domestication back into our daily lives because that really is the universal thread. The designers of Jericho tore apart our needs as humans and redirected them the same way that the programmers of Modernity do today. This isn't abstract: this is the functional totality of civilization. If there's a barrier to break down, I believe that's the one. Everything else is further context.

To the extent that there's a way to ensure that some of that context is more useful and not just a consumable set of factoids for militant appeal, posturing needs to constantly be challenged. The increase in social media has strangely brought this to the surface: "Well, what are you going to do?" That question has never had a positive outcome. Lacking alternatives or the space for anything else, that's why subsistence and social movements have gained such traction as solutions; particularly things like permaculture, land projects, and the like.

The flip side is this draw towards "anything is good," which is how Deep Green Resistance got its 15 minutes. In the end, it's this sense of a very American kind of individualistic entitlement that leads towards wanting to appear the most radical or radicalizing personal liberation as praxis. Both of those are non-starters in my eyes.

I hold a certain level of pragmatism on the matter. There's an edging here around questions that shouldn't be asked and ones I refuse to answer. Anyone who can't figure it out on their own probably isn't the right person to discuss with, if anyone even is.

Looking back on the period of the mid-1990s to the early 2000s, what lessons do you think could be passed down to the current wave of people?

This is complicated. I tend to think that I probably sound like I romanticize that period from 1999-2008 or whatever. I don't, we didn't have all the answers and obviously we had holes large enough to undo it, but we did have traction that we don't now.

I tend to talk about *BAGR* as habit. This is how we used to do it. An anarcho-primitivist arguing for a print journal sounds kind of funny in context, but it's this simple: we had something before and we don't now. I don't know if this move is the "right" one, but it's something.

For the "new people," I think it's absolutely vital to draw this out. We have generations coming into the fold that have lived their entire lives through devices. We need to shake that up. If you don't have unmediated connections then what can you really feel? Again, it's not the most radical starting point, or at least it shouldn't be, but sadly it is.

Social media takes over-sharing as a given. That's so contrary to the way I came up with Security Culture and even just the perpetuation of ideas in general. If you make yourself the story or the argument, then you are the target. I'm not sure what that can really get you, but we see where it leads.

To me it underlines the importance of rewilding: here is something real, something tangible, something you can experience without interpretation. It's also why I think rewilding is so crucial to resistance. If you fight solely for ideals, then you stand for nothing. If you can feel that connection, it's an entirely different situation.

I see rewilding as a process of observation to integration with wildness. Clearly I'm advocating a similar path in terms of creating discourse: stop talking, open ourselves up to our surroundings, get some grounding in the real world and then taking the obstacles on. Be prepared to get humbled and have your ass handed to you a few times in the process.

Green Anarchy and Species Traitor, two publications you were involved with, fit into a time period of the anti-globalization struggle as well as the growth of anarchist resistance both in the US and around the world. In the late 1990s, places like LA and Eugene, Oregon popped off in a real way. Looking back at this time now, what do you think that people in these moments did well and how did they fail?

I won't rehash the above much, but we left ourselves too open. Issues started to arise and we didn't do enough to respond to them. That's easy to say in hindsight, but the history is there to show it.

I think that the arguments about "activism" are easily removed from context and unfortunately that set the pace for generations of anarchists. I think all of us who came into this at any point prior to, say, 2002 had some grounding in activism or at least it was a given. When we were questioning "activism" in *GA* at the time, it's because of a specific reason: the street protests were just becoming predictable bait, everyone was getting locked up and sentenced before the first brick was thrown. It was a practical consideration that this was increasingly becoming a symbolic notion instead of a gesture. And there were alternatives to that kind of resistance at the time that we didn't even have to point directly towards, they were obvious. We also weren't questioning the Black Bloc tactics as they were happening in Greece, among other places, where they were clearly effective.

Removed of context, it simply became any kind of "activism," be it riots or forest defense, was ineffective. I'm afraid that set the tone later, clearly a misstep when you look at where things are now.

John Zerzan said that the green anarchist current was an attempt to bring the urban anarcho-punks together with the tree sitters in the forest connected to Earth First! Do you feel like this goal was achieved? If so how, and if not, why?

My perspective on it is a bit different. I grew up in the midwest and moved to the northeast, so tree sitters weren't a part of my world outside of reading Earth First! Journal or going out West and seeing how different the milieu was there. In Eugene, that certainly seemed to sum it up. You had a cross over in terms of people, but on the pages it still seemed divided. What John is talking about to me definitely explains an earlier publication like *Live Wild or Die* that came out of the 90s in the Pacific Northwest. No question that it set the table for *Green Anarchy*.

Outside of that area, it came together in different ways. Coming from the anarcho-punk world myself, I can see it, but I grew up in St. Louis where the die-hard anarchists were anywhere from 10 to 30 or so years older than me and pretty removed from the punks. I wouldn't say green anarchism was a draw for that crowd though.

But there's certainly some merit to that argument: the appeal of green anarchism is that it gives an anti-political basis for understanding ecological destruction in a meaningful way. So while a lot of people didn't have tree sitters surrounding them, they certainly had places they loved destroyed for Progress. Same kind of connection: different scenario.

NASA now says many of the things anti-civilization anarchists were saying in the 1990s. How can we push the debate about civilization through word and action in a time when most people agree that the current industrial framework is going to lead to extreme consequences?

That's the big question. I felt kind of crazy when I was trying to take part in these arguments online; people saying that green anarchism and anarcho-primitivism were dead throughout this period of unquestioning decline and extremities in terms of resource extraction, social unrest, and climate instability. I think in the first issue of *BAGR* I mention about how sometimes it just feels wretched to be right. We were literally watching our predictions follow through in some of the worst ways imaginable.

The importance here is to push that bottom line. We simply can't back down. All of these things are happening for a very real reason and they will worsen. If we don't call it as it is: that civilization will destroy the world to feed itself, that technology is the carrot and the stick, then what are we here for? What are we doing?

I've seen people water their message down to get traction in the anti-fracking movement and it baffles me. Here is the reality of the mathematic impossibility of civilization in people's yards and drinking water: why wouldn't we point that out? That's crucial!

The problem is that we need to find ways to connect these dots without just sitting on social media and arguing. If this isn't driven home in a meaningful way, then it's all just adding noise to the nonsense. It doesn't amount to anything. How we do that? I wish I had an answer. Hopefully putting it in print helps, but if anything it's a concrete alternative to point to.

I'm on the persistence hunt approach right now: just keep moving and don't stop. I'd rather risk finding out I was wrong than to wait until I find the "right" answer on how to do this.

You've stated in past interviews that the Native resistance to fracking and pipelines is some of the most inspiring struggles happening in North America currently to which we also agree. What advice would you give to people that want to take part and engage in solidarity with these struggles but are geographically far removed and also don't come from a Native background or community?

Realistically I'm one of those people. I've been trying to get a line into some of these movements without success. I'm always hoping that changes.

What's important is to recognize that none of these things are happening "there" anymore: we are all tied by this hyper-technological civilization. I live just outside the Marcellus Shale region right now, but there are (or were before the oil price dropped) 3 shale pipelines proposed in this area. 'Bomb trains;' trains carrying tar sands crude, have been derailing all across the States. These things are local only so long as they are perceived that way.

What seems vital, at least how I see it, is to remove that distance, to link cause and effect. We have to break down the psychological barriers in a globalized world. That's no easy task: we evolved largely as bioregional beings with looser connections to the larger world. Not that there was a disregard or total lack of knowledge for the world outside of your bioregion, but if you don't have the means to cause global impact from your day-to-day life, then it's a non-starter.

For me, personally, getting immediately involved with the Dineh and Oglala on the genocidal consequences of resource extraction really drove home my "local" issues with deforestation, suburban sprawl, and having Monsanto in my "back yard." Those are necessary connections and these campaigns need support and attention. Literally the least we can give. I hope to be able to offer more.

In recent years as the ecological crisis has gotten more grim, there's been a rising interest in "re-wilding" and "back to the land" living. From the growth of the tiny homes industry to popular shows on National Geographic, the desire for a simpler life back in tune with nature has become prime time TV as well as a growing market. Do you see opportunities to create links between land projects, permaculture endeavors, etc, and on the ground struggles and projects in revolt, or are these alternative ways of living simply more subcultures that are dead weight?

I think this signifies two things: one is that as we've moved further away from wildness, we've left room to expose the gap and the want is still there. The other is that we've lost the drive to seek out an unmediated life on our own terms and the do-it-yourself ethic has fallen to an era of gurus and cottage industries. The latter has grabbed its market stake on the former.

I do see promise here though. It's like society has opened up a place to talk about how hunter-gatherer life shapes who we are as beings. Even if the anarchist world isn't ready to take those steps, it's essentially an anarcho-primitivist argument getting mainstream traction. Ultimately that's a good thing. Everything from Paleo and Primal diets to MovNat and barefoot running, hark back to this primal sense of who we are and how we subsist and interact with the world.

There's a powerful narrative there, but it gets picked up and redirected by marketers in the same way that all domestication works: we have our wants and needs as animals torn apart and sold back to us piecemeal.

It's absurd to see aspects of our innate being commodified, but that's the underlying history of civilization. So it shouldn't be surprising. I think it's important to give context here and that's something we can offer. It's easy to scoff when you see people talking about rewilding on TV or you have a douche bag like Daniel Vitalis attempting to claim "rewilding" and suggesting it as a way to cope with the human zoo rather than attack or subvert it. We just have to keep on pushing through that, to continue making the connections and give it the space to be grounds for resistance instead of a retreat.

The flip side of that is that the culture as a whole has lost all sense of ability to seek things out. There's no way that is separate from having a device on you with Google or whatever on it, just being able to ask a question and get an answer right away. That's a development inhibitor and I can't point to Nicholas Carr's work on the matter enough: we have literally been off-setting brain functions onto technology. Our minds aren't taking in information the same way, we don't develop memories and build up knowledge the same as you do through direct experience. That's a frightening prognosis that applies to every aspect of this world.

But it's a horrible habit that we get used to. Whether we posit this way or not, we turn to the internet for answers about everything. We aren't absorbing reality; we're just regurgitating points. That's a reason why I think rewilding is so vital: it is about experience. Without grounding, what do we have to say or offer? Where can we go?

Rewilding is nothing new to the green anarchist world. It's been a core part of *Green Anarchy* and spreads from there. It was a given that do-it-yourself was a part of that, more importantly, doing it together. In the early 2000s, almost everyone I knew was stealing field guides and trying to memorize them. We all carry on this survivalist mentality that capitalism implants, but it becomes obvious through experience that the knowledge and the skills are context, not goals. Subsistence creates substance.

We went out, we experimented, then came back and bounced ideas that worked and those that didn't against each other. There was no want to profit, at least among the green anarchist scene. We didn't have Youtube, just books and reprinted pictures. My first bow drill fire was with a two-foot spindle and a curved piece of Eastern Hemlock bark as a baseboard. It was hilarious, but with four people and hours of handing off, we eventually got a usable ember. Then we learned from that quickly.

Now everyone wants to make some money off of it. The community element is gone. There's no humility in the process, just a façade of expertise amplified through social media. And the certainty gets dangerous, I've seen plenty of people on "identification" sites get a plant or mushroom pretty dangerously wrong and people just take a response as correct.

But it doesn't end there. We, as green anarchists and anarcho-primitivists, were always very intentional about leaving gaps between theory and praxis. We aren't ideologues with blueprints for the future. The reason is simple: all you can do with ideology is to regurgitate it. People will kill for ideologies, but they will die defending a known. That's the message I got from comparing indigenous resistance struggles and revolutionary movements. One ends in gallows and the other ends with them. Ideologies are a dangerous matter.

Our intent is to give context and open up the fold for forms of resistance. That is what makes grounding so vital. This isn't about having cannon fodder and building a green anarchist army to take on the United States military. That is a futile move, but also unnecessary. If you understand how civilization fuels and perpetuates itself, you quickly realize that it is the ability of power to propagate itself that drives and ultimately undermines civilizations. Machines make far better targets than people.

What that looks like in terms of resistance can be many things, but a coordinated, ideological effort to undermine it will simply be smashed by repression. Gaps are unknowns. If we had answers for how to bring about the end of civilization immediately, then we would have done that. Clearly I don't have answers here and it's problematic to think that anyone should, myself included. What we can do is build that context and foster circumstances where action could arise. That's the goal with *Black and Green Review*, just as it was for *Species Traitor* and *Green Anarchy*.

Yet as social media embeds ideas with individuals, you have this rising need to suddenly be right. You have to account for any hypocrisy or inconsistency rather than focus on ideas. You get this, "well why don't you just go live wild if that's what you want?" kind of questioning, which is disingenuous at best. It buys into narratives of freedom within civilization. I don't go live as a hunter-gatherer for the same reason that struggling hunter-gatherer societies can't: civilization stands in the way. Private property, the expansion of States, the nature of extraction, a shifting climate, and ecocidal rampages are the threats that make life outside of civilization improbable if not impossible.

We aren't anarchists because we live in an anarchist society: we are anarchists because we strive to live in anarchy. Hypocrisy applies only if you believe some liberal shit about "be the change you wish to see in the world". Granted, I'm not standing in the way of anyone who wants to try, but if we want to be honest about the state of the world then we have to be honest with each other and stop getting soaked up in focusing on individuals and look at the big picture again.

So long as civilization exists, everything is on the table and everything is at risk. We can't escape that and we shouldn't try.

The rise of permaculture amongst anarchists and even land projects gets wrapped up in the conflation of means and ends. I hope everyone strives to lessen their impact, to withdraw from domestication at every chance, but my goal isn't about lifestyle choices: it's about bleeding civilization until it crumbles. I have affinity for the drive here, but it arises for the wrong reasons: people wanting to be right, to accept that civilization is here, but that we can lessen our impact.

There's a grain of truth there, but that's not reason to get hung up on it.

And I can sympathize. I'm part of trying to build a land project as a basis to build community. It's a really complicated process, but all-too-often, the land itself becomes the project, not the basis of the community or the connections. Permaculture can become a means of redirecting the controlling elements of domestication:

small-scale agriculture in approach. It doesn't always, but the language of control is pervasive. That it's less impacting than industrial agriculture doesn't change that.

I don't separate this from these greater social changes that I've drawn on throughout this discussion and in my approaches through *BAGR*: they're one in the same. We, as a culture, have to look up and assess the big picture instead of falling into the cracks of the details. Being imperfect is a perfectly fine placeholder compared to inaction caused by trying to simply be "right."

That amplifies into the anarchist world: we spend so much time trying to chase out every boogeyman concept and having the perfectly worded subjective expression of anarchism. Why? What does that do? You see this as prevalent in a magazine like *Black Seed* where subjectivism runs rampant. They see a statement as "civilization is wrong" as moralistic and therefore problematic. I really couldn't care less. If I can't say civilization, the system that is killing the planet and all life on it, is "wrong" then what do I have to say to anyone?

We don't have the time for that nonsense, so I don't want to waste effort on it.

You mention that the goal isn't about lifestyle choices but taking action against civilization. Earlier you discussed about the need to rewild and disconnect from social media. There should be no question that social media exists as a tool of counter-insurgency, but is it a worthwhile endeavor to abstain from it on principle, rather than using it strategically with this in mind? How then does this escape the traps of individualization that you cite as a problem of the so-called 'social media age?' Civilization won't be stopped by people driving Priuses any more than it will be by people deactivating their Facebook accounts or living in the woods. Can you clarify your thoughts on this?

Gladly. It's easy to see that presence feels important in terms of these arguments. I've seen people argue with me that if they aren't on there, then no one will be and the bullshit goes unchecked. On the face of it, that would seem to be truth and I'm sure some people did get genuinely involved with these milieus in a very real sense because they found them on social media.

But it's important to point out that I don't say this from a place of judgment, it's from experience. I did the same thing. I used to spend hours arguing with people over social media and just got this tension all the time from it and just got so absorbed by it. I have reasons why my personal output for years was so minimal and it's because I did exactly this: argued with people on social media, tried clarifying and furthering concepts while taking on challenges.

When I took a minute to breathe, I felt the symptoms of withdrawal. I'd stop and look at my computer and just wonder what I was even doing on there for so long and realized how much time I actually spent on it. That's how this technology works, it's how integrated it is with our own lives and how little we really consciously recognize it that reminds us how our participation really negates critique. That's what the programmers of social media and networks want: no matter what your voice is, if you engage, then you're right there. For them, we're all just data and online habits. That's the market scheme, but it clearly gets much more nefarious than that.

For us, it's techno-addiction. We justify it however we like, but what I came to realize was that I was having these really intense arguments over and over again, often with the same people. I was battling people across threads and some times the context was there, sometimes it isn't. So you're just backtracking with everyone else who jumps in on another thread to explain why you're jumping down someone's throat. It's a vortex in the true sense. The more involved you are, the more entrenched you become.

I don't think shutting down social media accounts is the goal, but I think it's important precisely because we're all addicts and none of us really recognize or want to recognize it. Shut your accounts down for a week, just see what happens: this becomes a sub-conscious habit. Go back in and see the same arguments repeated forever.

My argument isn't about morality, it's not about boycotting Facebook because Zuckerberg is a socio-path: it's that our ideas become real through grounding. They escape philosophical binds when they become mirrored in reality. We need that on all fronts. As much as I think running off into the woods sounds amazing (and I'm certainly not stopping anyone), that doesn't take the problem of civilization on. I found that early on, the more I tried escaping civilization in the forest, the more apparent civilization ultimately became and the need to take it on became more of a necessity.

Socially speaking, deleting social media is complicated, friends and family won't follow suit. I had people think I actually died when I deleted my profiles. I'm sure for some people I did. The real world communication and networks are lost in the vortex. I am sure projects like Black and Green Review could have more traction if I was online promoting them constantly, but I just can't do it. I can't stand seeing those sites. But if we continue to find reasons why we should stay on, then we'll just stay on and nothing changes. There's no easy answer here, but this is a very new problem and it's clear to me that the answer to how we regain what social media has conquered won't come through social media.

I don't think there's a more clear point of entry for rampant individualism than social media.

In every aspect it seeks to supplant reality. As Zuckerberg says it, people on Facebook are "building an image and identity for themselves, which in a sense is their brand. They're connecting with the audience that they want to connect to." Social media decimates true community by subverting it into a place to market the person you want people to think you are. I don't think signing off is about engaging individualism; it's about taking steps to see beyond the lens of the Cult of the Self.

You've come through a lot since the 1990s. How can radical movements and resistance struggles keep a wide range of ages and generations of people involved and engaged? Not only to have a wide range of people involved, but also to keep knowledge from leaving outward?

There are cycles within radical and anarchist milieus. Just kind of comes with the territory really. You get a lot of really enthusiastic younger folks involved and they cycle every couple of years and go back and forth about what gets them hyped. Every two years there was a pretty steady insurrectionalist infatuation. Identity politics are always there, but go in cycles of amplification. Around every election you get some anarchists talking about how voting this time around isn't the same as last time (in case you're wondering, that's never true).

If you stick around long enough, you learn how to avoid or weather the storms and carry on. However, this is one thing that changed with social media and it has to do with the fact that the broader sense of how personal affiliations have taken precedence over the ideas, critiques and praxis. So the posturing upticks and it just becomes a gossipy clique.

There's no draw there unless you just want to be the most radical of your group of friends. Sadly, that retains some appeal. This milieu continues to lose its grounding in the real world just as all of society does. That's a massive social issue that we should be spearheading resistance to, but, largely speaking, we aren't. It's a passé kind of joke to focus on social media and the Interface Revolution, but over half of all living adults have a cell phone.

As of the end of 2015, 23% of the entire global population uses Facebook monthly, that's up from 20.5% at the end of the first quarter of 2015. Short of fire, this is the most widespread and rapidly acquired social change in the history of the human species. That's fucking insane. When you use those platforms content fails in light of participation. The medium truly is the message and it dictates form.

This isn't to say that anything about anarchism is dead. The ideas and realities it bespeaks are very real. There are innate truths that we've struck upon and as the façade of domestication tightens and cracks become more apparent, people will break out. I thought Occupy couldn't have been a weaker campaign, but I've met people, young and old, whom it opened up doors for. The appeal of green anarchist and anarcho-primitivist critique comes from this search to understand how power functions, how civilizations perpetuate, and how domestication binds us on a daily basis. There's no demographic for this: it literally impacts everyone. I've seen this working in campaigns, getting in conversations or arguments with people (I'm not one for keeping my mouth shut), doing speaking tours, and anything really.

I'll never forget stopping in a gas station late at night while travelling years ago. I was wearing a "Better Dead Than Domesticated" shirt that I used to print and this older woman working the cash register, just kind of seething the depression that comes with working a shit job for minimum wage and being stuck on an overnight shift. She just stares at the shirt and looks me in the eyes and says, "Well ain't that the fucking truth." These aren't exclusive ideas and perceptions, it's something we all face and know if we acknowledge it.

Coming back to the actual question here, it's vital that we don't lose sight: we're all in this. If we don't keep our focus on understanding how civilization functions and seeking to undermine and attack it, then we have nothing. Our form should reflect that. Keep focusing on the ideas and less on the gossip and drama, there's a lot more at stake here than any one of us.

Anything you'd like to add?

I appreciate the questions and hope that we can take more time to assess what happened and move forward. I don't know if our steps are the right ones, but it's worth taking a shot. Our goal with *BAGR* started out as wanting to advance green anarchist ideas and push debate, but it's proven quickly that we can't limit ourselves to speaking to anarchists.

So much of the first issue was dedicated to focusing on technological change (the Interface Revolution) because it was the elephant in the room. It was impossible to address anything else until we took that on directly because it's clearly standing in the way and has been for some time.

It may be ironic to argue against online engagement in an interview that is being published online, but we're hitting this wall and it needs to be reiterated until we start listening and responding in kind.

Our goal with *BAGR* is to make these connections, to force the search to understand the domesticating process and how civilization works. We actively want its end. We push on this two pronged method of deepening bonds to build up a foundation for attack. "Wild existence, passionate resistance" sums it up. We want people to read it and respond. We want to build things up again and learn from our mistakes.

about the author

Kevin Tucker is an anarcho-primitivist writer, re-wilding human, and father. He is the author of *For Wildness and Anarchy* (Black and Green Press, 2010), editor of *Species Traitor: an insurrectionary anarcho-primitivist journal* (2000-2005), founder of Black and Green Network, was a regular contributor to *Green Anarchy* (2000-2008), and is the founding co-editor of *Black and Green Review* (2015-). He lives in the Ozarks of central Missouri.

kevintucker.org